The Borzoi

The world of dogs

Dr Desiree Scott

t.f.h.
KINGDOM

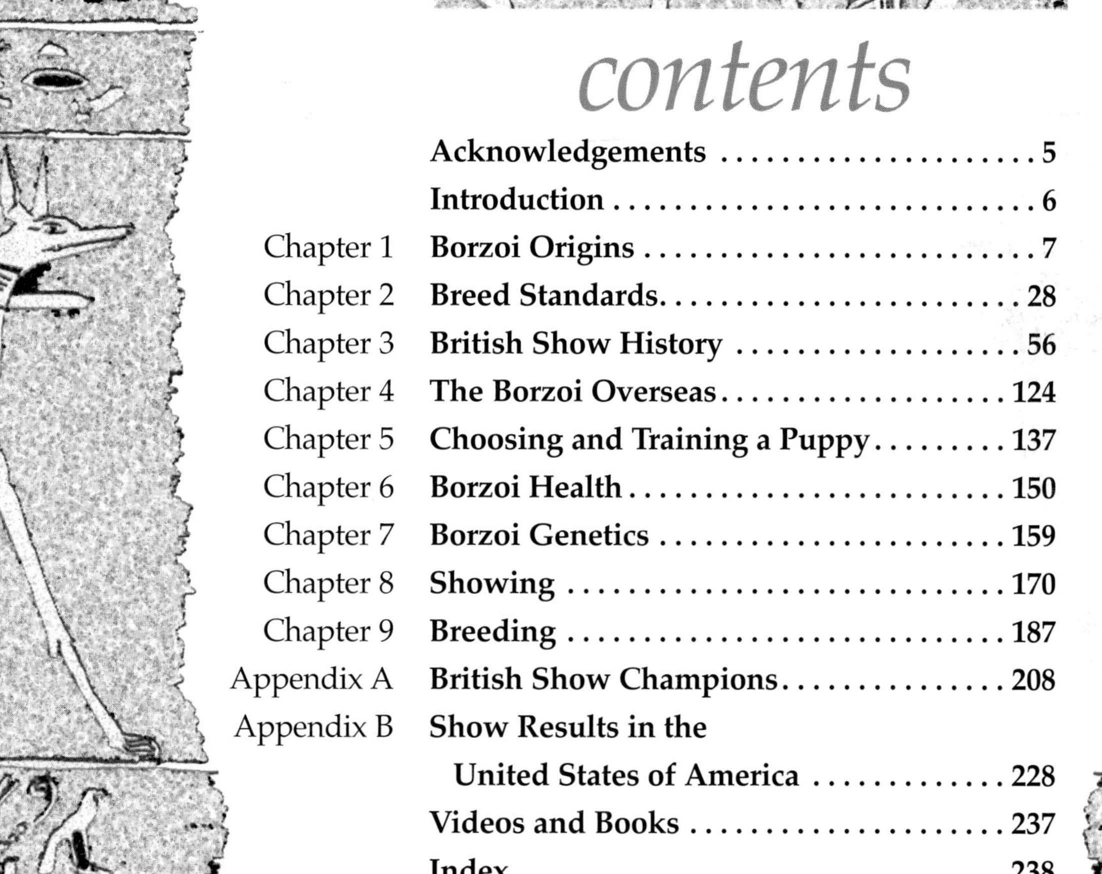

contents

Back cover and title page:
Ch Colhugh Claude of Longuin.
Photo: Barry Greenwood

Cover illustration: Dan Lish

acknowledgements

I would like to thank the following people for their help and encouragement:

Mr Reg Bassett
for help with the Breed Standard chapter, especially the picture of the skeleton.

Mrs Eleanor Bothwell
who nurtured my obsession with shoulder construction.

Mrs Rose Cadman
the first person to let me go over a champion, the grandsire of one of my own 'babies'. When you are studying Borzoi construction you must teach your hands what to feel, and this experience can only be gained with the help of those willing to let you examine their quality dogs.

Mrs Dot Forrest
who when asked 'Isn't that a lovely bitch in the photograph?' said 'No!' She then proceeded to explain why, starting the many hours I have spent considering shoulder construction.

Mrs Rosie Knott
next-door neighbour and student of the cat who has introduced me to some important ideas about mammal behaviour.

Mr Edward McKenzie
British Telecom have made a fortune from the many hours he has spent explaining many things about Borzois, especially about type and puppies.

Miss Nikki Morgan
who suggested the 20th re-drawing of the Borzoi skeleton. ('The toes are too small.')

Miss C Pettitt
who compiled a wonderful pictorial record of Borzoi Challenge and Reserve Challenge Certificate winners.

Mr Jim and Mrs Margaret Shankland
with whom I have had many an animated discussion on the sound construction of a number of breeds.

Mrs Ann Tomlinson
for great help in the areas of breed history and correct construction.

Many Other People
for whom there is insufficient space to mention individually who have helped me collect books and papers about dogs and spent much time discussing dogs with me.

Many thanks to all of them.

introduction

I have written this book because, through a series of circumstances, I was asked to. I am a long-time collector of dog books, and occasionally I accidentally buy two copies of the same book. This happened a couple of years ago, and I ended up with two copies of an excellent book about Dobermanns. I took one copy, which had never been read, to one of the stands that sold books at the Scottish Kennel Club show, explaining that it was an unread duplicate, and asking if I could swap it. When answered in the affirmative, I selected a book about the Cavalier King Charles Spaniel, which caused some surprise. We then entered into a conversation about my interest in all breeds, and I explained that I had had published a history of Crufts Dog Show detailing the history of all show breeds in Britain from 1891. I was told that Kingdom Books were looking for authors, and it all just snowballed from there.

I share my home with Borzois, so this was the breed chosen, and there has not been a British book on the breed for many years. This book, I hope, will have something to interest a wide spectrum of dog people; those whose life has been touched by this special breed, and even those whose interest in dogs is based on other breeds.

I hope that the puppy care is helpful for the novice, and that the development of the unborn puppy is of interest to the more experienced Borzoi breeder. The breed standard analysis should be of interest to all those interested in show dogs, whatever their breed, for this covers features the Borzoi shares with many other breeds. And my final wish is that the point that I have taken as my beginning, the start of the development of sighthound breeds, should be the section with interest for the more general reader.

Borzoi Origins

Almost every serious book about a breed has a section on that breed's origin. This book has such a chapter, not to follow the usual pattern, nor for the sake of completeness, but because I do not believe it is possible to understand the Borzoi unless we study where it came from.

The latest theories on the domestication of the dog are based on behaviour rather than anatomy. One of the leading proponents of these ideas is Professor Raymond Coppinger of Hampshire College in the United States. Comparing the domestic dog with its wild relations, he states that the real difference between them is that dogs are trainable and wild canids are not.

Domestic dogs in a non-sheep-owning community: Australian Aboriginal dogs.

Domestication was not a single event, but the repetition of several similar incidents. The great environmental change that precipitated these events was the grouping together of humans in villages. The data used to claim that the dog was domesticated before this is based on scanty and incomplete teeth and jaw bones.

Domestic dog from an environment where humans are not concerned with dog breeding: Indian pariah dog.

The early village was a place where food supplies were concentrated, in grain stores for humans and at the dump for dogs. The dump was a valuable food source for other species as well, but domestication also depended on flight distance: the distance that an animal allowed a villager to approach before running away. Those individuals that best tolerated humans and therefore had the shortest flight distances got the greatest return from foraging on the dump, as constantly running away wastes the energy gained from eating dump waste.

Another good way to use the energy generated from dump waste was to have your babies near to the dump. Once puppies were being born next to the village there was a secondary taming process. It is much easier to have a social relationship with a puppy than with a wary adult. If a wolf or coyote puppy is well socialised with humans its behaviour is more manageable, though it is still not domesticated.

After a few generations the dogs became dependent on humans and part of their reproductive success depended on them breeding in the village. At this stage the human benefit from the dogs was getting the dump and the streets cleaned, and the waste protein was being turned into a form of more direct benefit: people began to eat dogs. In many parts of the world dog meat is still a popular food source: according to Professor Coppinger, *puppies on Pacific islands were a cherished source of protein, and made a good lunch on long canoe trips.* In the extensive collection of dog skulls in Copenhagen there is evidence that 20% of these came from dogs that had been eaten.

(Above)
The medium Podenco hardly looks like a sighthound...
(Left)
... but its relative, the Ibizan Hound, is much more recognisable as a member of the greyhound family.

At about this time we have human intervention in dog breeding patterns – not to breed the most glamorous coat, but to select behaviour patterns. The most easily tamed dogs produced the most offspring.

If we look at many of the dogs in the world today we see a remarkable likeness to a wolf puppy. In regard to behaviour, different breeds have been 'arrested' at different stages in the growth of a wolf puppy. Professor Coppinger has drawn a chart dividing a number of breeds according to where they stopped in puppy development.

- Livestock-guarding breeds like the Maremma Sheepdog at the *adolescent* wolf stage
- Retrievers and scent hounds at the *object playing* stage
- Collies at the *stalking of prey* stage
- Spitz such as Corgis at the *heeler* stage (that is, the stage just before full adult wolf behaviour)

This Greyhound demonstrates that the northern greyhound can hold its ears erect.

Two sets of breeds are excluded from the above development. At the time of initial dog type differentiation, at least one other species had joined dogs and people in settlements: sheep. Both sighthounds and terriers were and are sheep-intolerant, showing the full wolf prey-killing behaviour, but they were still kept by people because sighthounds were exceptionally good hunting dogs and the essentially British terriers were good vermin killers on an island where the cat had not yet been introduced.

The first sighthounds were not so different in shape from the initial domesticated dogs. In Portugal there is a whole series of sighthounds called the Podenco that retain the shape of their ancestors (see previous page). The medium Podenco hardly looks like a sighthound, but its large relative from the island of Ibiza is more instantly recognisable as a member of the greyhound family. We cannot say that the Portuguese Podenco and the Ibizan Hound are the ancestors of the sighthounds: only that the first sighthounds looked similar to these breeds. In any case, the term *breed* really should not be used to describe dogs before the advent of dog shows and written pedigrees. Prior to this it is only accurate to call groups of dogs with similar behaviour patterns and appearance *types*. Similarly, the term *breed* cannot be used for sheep, cattle and the other domesticated livestock until the 18th century.

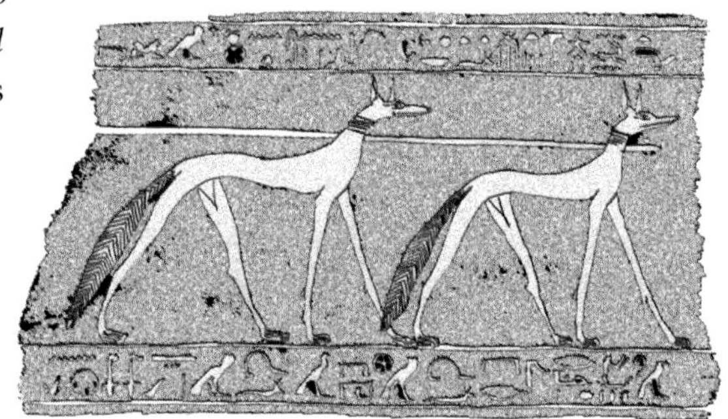

Early sighthounds depicted on the tomb of Rameses VI (1141–1133 BC).

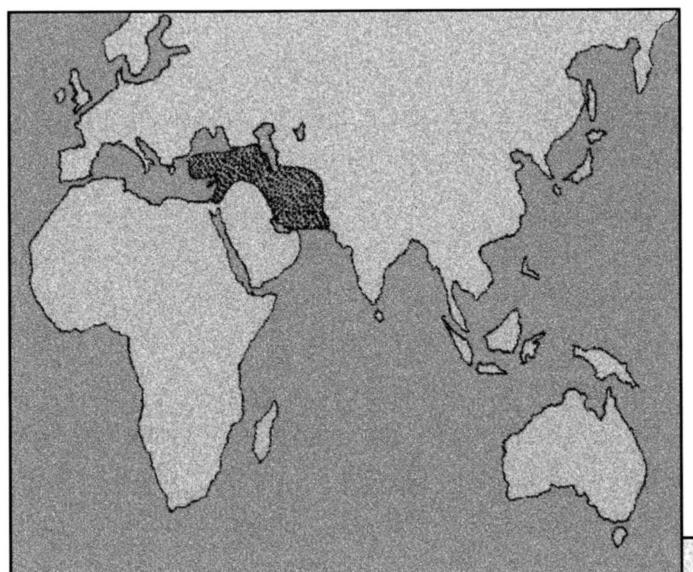

In the brown area above, the original distribution areas of the ancestors of sheep, goats, pigs and cows overlap.

Since the domestication of livestock created the need to develop dogs with differing patterns of behaviour, the area where sheep, goats, cattle and pigs were first domesticated is also where dog breeds originated. This area, the near east, is also where wild grass wheat was first domesticated, encouraging the formation of human settlements.

As wheat and livestock spread into Europe, North Africa and the far east, so did the first differentiated dog types. We have a pictorial record of the first dogs to reach Egypt. Although the selection of dogs had been made purely on a behavioural basis, some physical features were being selected as well. Sighthounds had a finer build with longer legs than the herding breeds, features that we can recognise today.

Sighthounds have altered since the day of the Egyptian pharaohs. Today they fall into two groups, northern and southern greyhounds, with following differences:

A wire-haired coat in a northern greyhound, as demonstrated by this Ibizan Hound, a champion in his native country (Spain).

The Pharaoh Hound is really the rabbit greyhound of Malta.

Northern Greyhounds:

- Small ears that can be held either erect or neatly folded
- Rounded eyes
- Long, straight tail
- Coat options: smooth or wire-haired

Southern Greyhounds:

- Large, low set ears that cannot be held erect
- Almond shaped eyes
- Tail with a ring at the end
- Coat options: smooth or long-haired.

The Egyptian dogs shown in the picture on page 10 predate the split, as they show the ears of the northern and the start of the long coat of the southern greyhound. Among the varieties of northern greyhound are Greyhounds, Pharaoh Hounds (in fact rabbit greyhounds of Malta), Ibizan Hounds and Deerhounds.

The evolution of southern greyhounds

How did the southern greyhound type develop from the original Podenco shape? A current idea is that southern greyhounds were crossed with the livestock-herding breeds, gaining their low-set, drooping ears and long coats from the ancestors of such breeds as the Maremma Sheepdog and Caucasian Sheepdog. Livestock-herding breeds of the near east are typified by the Anatolian Shepherd Dog, which until the late 1960s was bred for work alone. This breed demonstrates both long and smooth coat, and a whole spectrum of colours from pure white to no white at all, though some British breeders are trying to banish all except the smooth-haired, black-masked fawns. However, it was separating sheep-tolerant dogs from sheep-intolerant ones that created sighthounds in the first place, and I find it difficult to imagine hunters being happy to include herder behaviour

This Sloughi from Khurdistan typifies a southern greyhound, with its large drop ears, ring tail and triangular eyes.

patterns into their sighthounds. Livestock guardian puppies are put with sheep from the start, and grow up believing that the sheep are part of their pack. They never develop full adult behaviour, and work by being with the sheep. If a predator approaches they greet it as a fellow adolescent, encouraging the wolf to depart to avoid having its legs broken by a giant-sized puppy at 'play'. Such characteristics would not improve a sighthound.

Livestock guardians: Sarplaniac puppies grow up thinking the sheep are part of their pack.

We do not really know, then, how the southern greyhound developed from the original northern type. The distribution of this hound is over an area in which the Islamic faith predominates, and this leads to some problems in its study. Arab culture considers all dogs unclean, though the sighthound is perhaps less unclean than most.

As it is against Muslim religious rulings to make pictorial representations of people or animals there are no Arab paintings or drawings to tell us about the early southern greyhounds. Fortunately, the Venetians traded with the Arabs, and there are some Renaissance depictions of southern greyhounds. The finest is perhaps the bronze by the Florentine sculptor and goldsmith Benvenuto Cellini (1500–1571). Another illustration from the same era is a miniature of the Moghul Emperor of India Akbar the Great (1542–1605) hunting. This is a southern greyhound, and Akbar came from Sind, an area now at the Afghan border. The appearance of this hound is evidence that a breed called the Afghan Hound did not exist at this time, but that all hounds from Morocco to Afghanistan were simply of the southern greyhound type.

A Cellini bronze showing an example of the southern greyhound.

The southern greyhound in Europe

At the end of the 19th century various southern greyhound types were imported into Europe. Those imported into Holland were given the name *Sloughi* and those imported into Great Britain, *Saluki*. More recently, a southern greyhound breed imported into France was given the name *Azawakh*.

One of the first British Saluki imports was Luman, owned by The Hon Florence Amherst. Miss Amherst was first attracted to the breed while in Egypt with her father, Lord Amherst of Hackney, who was exploring the Egyptian tombs. One of his students was the young Howard Carter, later to win fame as one of the discoverers of Tutankamen's tomb. Miss Amherst's first pair of hounds had been imported from the Saliaha desert in Egypt by Colonel Jennings Bramley.

Ch Taj Mahip of Kaf, winner of the first Afghan Hound CC: a typical Bell Murray hound.

Most Salukis have fringed coats, but there has always been a small minority of smooth Salukis. There have only been three smooth Saluki British champions, with 20 years between the last two. The British dog diet is far richer than that of the near east, so a British smooth Saluki champion has a better covering of muscle and fat than its desert-bred cousin.

In their original homelands, appearance and breed names did not matter to the owners of southern greyhounds. Breed names are a European imposition and, because the hounds varied from area to area, some were chosen to be separate breeds. Unfortunately, the reverse also happened: hounds of different appearance were given the same breed name. This caused problems when proud exhibitors strode into the ring in Europe with hounds they considered typical of the breed, only to meet other exhibitors with very different hounds at the end of their leads.

Luman, one of the first British Saluki imports.

The greatest case of this arose with the importation of the Afghan Hound to Britain in the 1920s. The breed was divided into two acrimonious groups. The winners at Crufts in 1925 were from the kennel of Major Bell Murray: hounds from Baluchistan in the North West Frontier Province of India. These were sparsely-coated, tall and elegant. The other faction was led by Major and Mrs Amps, who returned

A British champion smooth Saluki.

from the east with their Ch Sirdar of Ghanzi, a hound born in Afghanistan. His smaller, squarer shape and heavier coat were very different from the Bell Murray type. For this reason, the Bell Murray camp would not accept that Ch Sirdar of Ghanzi was an Afghan Hound, and the public disagreement was aired in the newspapers. The breed we know today is a mixture of these two types, except in Poland, where two breeds of Afghan Hound are recognised.

The two main bloodlines forming the Saluki were not as different from each other. These were the smaller golden Amherstias and the larger black and tan, or black, white and tan, Sarona dogs imported by Brigadier General Lance after his overseas posting during the First World War. The first Sarona champion was Ch Sarona Kelb, who was bred in Damascus from two desert-born hounds.

Ch Sidar of Ghanzi, owned by Major and Mrs Amps.

The close relationship between the Afghan and the Saluki can be seen by comparing the head studies overleaf. The Saluki head belongs to Ch Tahawi Belinda, a top show winner and brood bitch of the late 1960s and the Afghan head to Ch Mitzou of Acklam, the last of the pure Bell Murray hounds, who was born in the late 1930s.

The gene for smooth coat still exists in the Afghan Hound, though hidden, as they have been bred for more and more coat since the 1920s. In the picture at the bottom of this page, a smooth Afghan of the 1970s is shown with his mother and sister.

Head study of an Afghan: Ch Mitzou of Acklam.

Head study of a Saluki: Ch Tahawi Belinda. These two studies show the close relationship between the Afghan and the Saluki.

The beginnings of the Borzoi

We have now reached the borders of Asian Russia in our survey of the southern greyhound, the area where all sighthounds are known by the generic name of Borzoi. The Borzoi of the western show ring is the *Psowaya Borzoi,* but we have a few other Borzoi breeds to discuss.

Smooth-coated Afghans can still crop up. This 1970s hound is shown with his mother and sister.

We have only an imperfect view of the dogs of Russia today and from the past. This is partly because of the enormous restriction on information during most of the 20th century and partly because of the various inconsistencies in the translation and transliteration of proper names from Russia. The former Soviet Union was a huge country with an extensive Asian border. From the Afghan border area comes the Tazy, the

Russian version of the Afghan hound, pictured on page 18. This is a typical southern greyhound, with large, low-set ears, longish coat and ringed tail. The colours are given as tan, black and tan or grey, and height as 56–63cm (22–28in), but this breed has not yet been recognised by any of the European kennel clubs. It is interesting to note that an old name for Afghan Hound was Tazy.

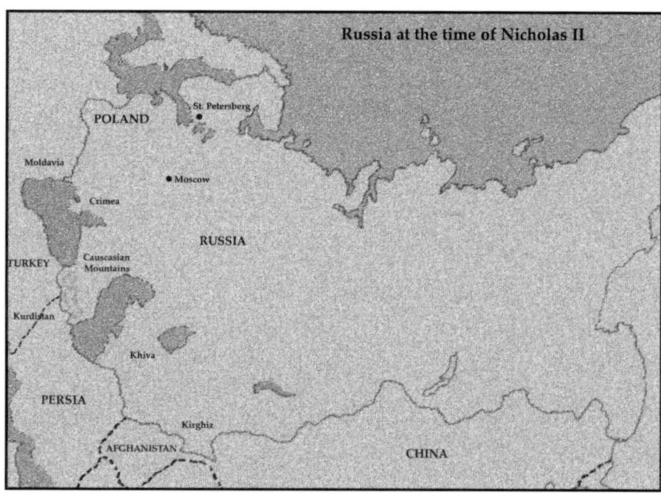

Russia at the time of Tzar Nicholas II.

Much of the information we have about the Borzoi breeds of pre-revolutionary Russia comes from the American Joseph Thomas, who travelled there to buy hounds for his kennel, and spoke to many of the most knowledgeable about all the Borzoi types. He lists several Asian Borzoi types in this book, including the Tazy or Turkomenian Borzoi.

The next Borzoi breed on his list was the Crimean Borzoi. This breed, now considered extinct, was noted for its predominantly black colour and Saluki type.

If we assume that the Persian and Arabian Borzois from Mr Thomas' list, which he took from *The Hunter's Calendar and Reference Book*, Moscow 1892, are Salukis and the Soudan Borzoi is an African southern greyhound type, this leaves us with:

Crimean Borzoi.

- Caucasian or Mountain Borzoi
- Crimean Borzoi
- Khiva Borzoi
- Kirghiz Borzoi
- Moldavian Borzoi

The Kirghiz Borzoi or Taigan still exists today (see overleaf). It is of marked Saluki type and was imported to Great Britain at the end of the 19th century by Mr H C Brooke, who specialised in importing rare breeds, each more exotic than the last. The Kirghiz Hounds, Persian Lighting and his sons, Shatki and Gaffeer, went to Captain J P T Allen. A photograph of them appears in Robert Leighton's *Book of the Dog*, published in the early years of the 20th century. This book also gives a description of the breed as having *the same characteristics as the Tazi of further South, the feathered legs, drooping silky ears, and beautifully feathered tail, which latter, according to the Kirghiz standard, should form a complete little circle at the tip when carried naturally. The legs should have more feathering on the elbow and stifle joints. The weight of these greyhounds varies much – namely, from 60 to 90lb, the average being 70lb. As a rule, the heavier the build the rougher the coat. The larger and bigger-boned dogs are those generally used to hunt wolves, and the smaller ones for hares and foxes etc. These Kirghiz hounds are invariably white or pale cream, and any markings are considered a blemish.*

The Tazy, a Russian version of the Afghan Hound.

However, the only recent illustration of the breed is of a particoloured dog.

The Caucasian Borzoi is now considered extinct, although the younger breed, the Greyhound of the Steppe, is a Saluki-type descendant.

We have only the names of the Khiva and Moldavian Borzois, with no illustrations or descriptions. From a geographical point of view (see map on page 17) I would guess that the Khiva breed was much like a Saluki, but the Moldavian

A particoloured Khirgiz Borzoi.

one may have been smooth-haired. The Borzoi of Poland, a country that was at one time part of the Russian Empire, is the Chart Polski, a smooth-haired breed.

Chart Polski.

Although the Chart was depicted in Polish paintings during the 19th century, especially those by Julusz Kosak the Senior (1824–1898), it was not until 1981 that the Polish Kennel Club opened an introductory stud book for the breed, and at this time most specimens left were to be found in eastern Poland. Kosak's paintings, which I have yet to see, were of the horses and *Korty* of Poland and the Ukraine.

The Chart Breed Standard gives the optimal height as 68.5–76cm (27–30in) for a bitch and 71–81cm (28–32in) for a dog. The head is strong, lean and long with the skull flat on top and the stop (see page 30) barely marked. A small nose hump is desirable. Ears are set level with the eyes and, in excitement, they can be completely raised up, or with tips slightly bent forward. Faults include goggle eyes and a tail completely curled over the back. There is a Russian smooth Borzoi with a very similar name: the Chortaj. The remaining Russian smooth Borzoi is the little-known Greyhound of the Steppe.

Chortaj.

Like the long-haired Psowaya Borzoi (*the* Borzoi breed as we know it today in the show ring), the Chart and the Chortaj have features in common with both southern and northern greyhounds.

- They have small, high set, mobile ears and the long, straight northern tail.
- They have southern eye shape and colouring.
- The Psowaya Borzoi has the long southern coat.

A wise man once said that a breed's origin can be seen in the faults often apparent in the show ring. Faults that often appear in Borzois entered in shows today are:

Southern inheritance:

- large, heavily-feathered, low-set ears
- ringed tails

Northern inheritance:

- large, round eyes

Greyhound of Central Russia.

It seems to me that these three are mixtures of northern and southern greyhound types. Most authorities agree that the southern greyhound is an ancestor and that something has been added to give features such as the small ears. However, they claim that the southern greyhounds were crossed with northern dogs such as spitz. I find it hard to see the behaviour patterns of spitz in the Borzoi. For instance, it is easy to locate Finnish Spitz at a show from the terrible noise they make, and these are the nearest relations of the Russian Spitz to be found in Great Britain or the United States. I am not saying that there are no spitz behind Borzois: only that such matings were not significant in the development of the Psowaya Borzoi, Chortaj and Chart.

Another theory that recurs in many breed histories is that the Borzoi has a Chinese origin. It is true that much of Russia was invaded by the Mongols during the 13th century, the invasion culminating with the sack of Kiev, the principal city of the Ukraine, in 1240. The Princes of Russia paid tribute to the Khanate of the Golden Horde and the invaders, known as Tartars, exercised efficient indirect control over Russia through its Princes for 200 years. The initial invasion disrupted Russian economic life, with settlements destroyed and agricultural land laid waste, but it did not take long to rebuild, and the Tartar occupation actually stimulated trade. There were new opportunities for Russian traders to meet merchants from China, the Mediterranean and other parts.

However, I do not think Russian dog breeds were greatly affected by this traffic with the far east. As has been said, livestock herding breeds and sighthounds were developed in the area that is now Iran and Iraq. There is no clear information on sighthounds in Tibet and, although there is a well-known herding breed called the Tibetan Mastiff, this went *into* Tibet with the sheep and goats. Care was taken with the breeding of sighthounds and horses, and these horses give us another clue to the breeding policies of the people from the Caucasian Mountains and the area from Khiva to Khirghiz.

The Turkmene and Akhal-Teke desert horses from this area are amazingly like the Arab horse. It follows that, not only was the southern greyhound type found from Morocco to Afghanistan and in southern Russia, but the prized horses of this area were of a similar type. They are enduring horses, resistant to intense heart and capable of covering great distances on minimal water rations.

Mongolian Ponies are completely different from these elegant horses. Generally, they have long, rather heavy heads with wide foreheads, fairly long, broad ears and strong teeth. Their heads are usually carried low, in some animals below the level of the withers when they are walking.

These ponies were not used in the breeding of the Arab or Akhal-Teke horses, and I feel that the same is the situation for Mongolian dogs and southern greyhounds.

The Borzoi up to the Russian Revolution

One of the effects of human settlement and agriculture was a division in the diets of the people. The poor had vegetables as their staple food, but the wealthy could afford meat and had to time to devote to hunting as a sporting pastime. The Borzoi was the hunting hound of the Russian aristocracy: people so wealthy that they could devote time to hunting inedible species, such as the wolf.

The appearance of their hounds was not of primary importance to the hunters and, when there was contact with the west during the reign of Peter the Great, sighthounds such as Greyhounds and Deerhounds were imported and used to breed Brudastoy Borzoi (tufted Borzoi). However, the Psowaya Borzoi still continued in its original form. During the 19th century there was widespread crossing with the Crimean Borzoi. An easy way to think of this now extinct breed is as a black and tan Saluki. It introduced the black and tan colour, but was responsible for thinner coats, low set ears and a flat topline. The knowledge of this cross continued well into the 20th century, and there was much discrimination against self black Borzois, although many of them had excellent Borzoi type. The Borzois with the Crimean cross were called *Christopsovoy*, while those without it were *Gustopsovoy*.

An out-of-coat Borzoi of the 1920s. Compare its body shape with that of the Chortaj (page 19).

During the middle ages most European countries emancipated the agricultural workers, freeing them to move away from the village where they were born to pursue occupations other than farm labourer. This was not the case in Russia; not until 19 February 1861 did Alexander II publish an imperial manifesto freeing the peasants. *Serfdom is abolished permanently for peasants settled on landlords' estates and also for house serfs. The landlords, while retaining ownership of all the lands belonging to them, grant to the peasants, for their use in perpetuity, the farmsteads where they are settled.*

There were also provisions for the peasants to buy the land they worked. In each region the state laid down maximum and minimum sizes for the allotments awarded to peasants. The actual size depended on negotiations between the landowner and his former serfs. The state compensated the former landowner for most of the land re-allocated in this way; anything above this had to be paid for in cash or kind by the peasants, who were also obliged to recompense the state over a 49-year period.

Although the emancipation was designed to improve peasant life and encourage the development of a market economy, the heavy redemption payments owed by the peasants and the loss of valuable land to their former lords militated against this. Additionally, this start to the breaking up of the estates encouraged some landowners to sell the rest of their land.

Each estate had its pack of hunting hounds. When the estate was broken up and sold, so was the pack of hounds. Although the breeding of hounds was for function rather than appearance, hounds from one estate often had a uniform appearance. This was not only because they were related but also because some huntsmen believed that certain behaviour patterns were accompanied by certain physical characteristics and bred accordingly.

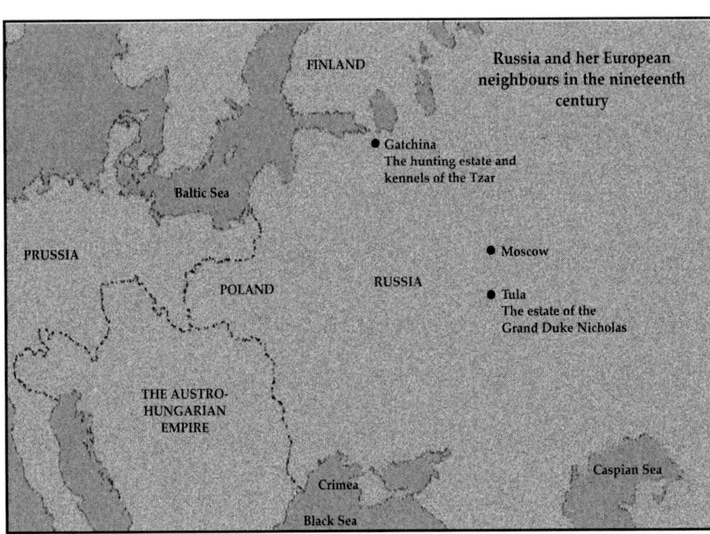

Russia and her European neighbours in the 19th century.

The number of hounds decreased, and the Christopsovoy and Gustopsovoy hounds were mated together, so that once again there was only one Russian Psowaya Borzoi. We do not have much information about these pre-emancipation packs – in fact we do not have

Six Borzois sent over by the Tsar to be exhibited at Crufts in 1892.

much information about the breed in Russia at any time. Some pictures of the 19th-century hounds have been seen in the west, but I find the portraits by Martynow more like caricatures than actual representations of the dogs, the heads in particular being too small for the bodies. As for the famous set of head studies drawn by the German artist Wilhelm Mueller in 1930 of types described by Nikolai Tschelischtscheff – none of them represents a hound I would like to own. However, it seems that it is irrelevant how ugly these hounds are, for the Russian author Peter Semchenkov has written:

Please, have a close look at the heads. Then look at those heads still more intently, and forget it all forever! Since all Tschelischtscheff's writings about the principal pre-revolutionary types are nothing else but a fruit of wild imagination!

In this case, it is hard to say who is to be blamed for this mish mash. Should we blame N Tschelischtscheff, who mixed everything up with the principal pre-revolutionary types; or the artist who dared to draw the portraits relying on just a few clumsy phrases?

It is to be hoped that recent political changes in Russia allow more information to come from that country: photographs of the pre-revolutionary hounds and their pedigrees and discussions (arguments) between the leading breeders, so that it is possible to trace the development of the breed in its homeland.

The best data from Russia come from the visits of the American Joseph Thomas to Russia to find hounds for his Valley Farm kennel. The first American imports were from Britain, and the first British imports did not come from the best Russian kennels. Queen Victoria's granddaughter was married to Tsar Nicholas II and her daughter-in-law was a

Borzoi exhibitor, so there was easy access to dogs from the Imperial Kennel. Unfortunately, these hounds were generally very poor. Look at the picture on page 23 of six Borzois sent over by the Tsar to be exhibited at Crufts 1892. The phrase for the second from the left is that 'you could drive a bus through its front', and as for the others...

'...a beautiful, sound coursing type...'

Mr Thomas first went to Britain in his search for hounds:

In July 1903 I went to England to inspect the several kennels there, of which I had heard so much. After weeks spent in visiting every prominent breeder in England, I was convinced that England was little, if any, better off than the United States. The then principal kennel was most notable for the size and coarseness of its dogs, which characteristic, together with the fact that many of them were unsound, made them anything but coursing types. Coarse heads, with prominent stops to the skull, were here very much in evidence. Hardly any two dogs looked alike. In the minor kennels there were a great many weeds. There was no definite type to be seen, and, as a whole, the English representation lacked character. There was no definite cachet to the breed. There were positively no hounds that had real quality and substance combined.

He had seen photographs taken in Russia of hounds that he called 'ancient type', meaning the breed before the cross with Crimean Hounds. With this picture in his mind he travelled to the Imperial Kennel, just outside St Petersberg, at Gatchina, where there was a hunting estate. The park seems to have been filled with much wildlife for the Zoological Society of London had European Bison from Gatchina as part of its collection.

Unfortunately, Mr Thomas saw *only two out of eighty grown dogs that I should have liked to possess; but what was more discouraging than this was the fact that no distinct type was visible. Some were well coated, others the contrary; some had fairly good heads while others were absolutely poor types – not Borzoi but greyhound. The reason for the lack of type in England and America*

An ancient type Borzoi and huntsman from Woronzova, 1903.

here became immediately patent, as more specimens had gone to those countries from the Imperial Kennels than from any other.

He travelled to Moscow, where the editor of a little sporting paper happened to mention that Mr Artem Bolderoff had an excellent kennel, and that the Tsar's cousin, Grand Duke Nicholas, also had some hounds.

Mr Thomas travelled to Tula, to the south of Moscow, where the Grand Duke had his hunting estate. He was met by Mr Dimitri Walzoff, who was in charge of the kennel. Mr Thomas wrote: *I was not at all prepared for what I saw in those wonderful kennels. The size and evenness of type of the hounds were wonderful for any breed. Originally they were all white and grey; but have now bred white and tan, tan and black, all grey, and even black and pure white.*

When the Grand Duke put the kennels into the hands of Mr Walzoff, who had previously had his own hunt, Mr Walzoff collected together many of the remaining old hounds, from all parts of Russia, which, carefully bred together, created the Perchino hounds. It was possible to build up a pack of top quality hounds because of the lack of financial restrictions.

The next kennel visited was at Woronzova, where Mr Artem Bolderoff had his estate. *No more hospitable welcome or more charming visit could have fallen to the lot of any one in any country, and I shall never forget how nearly impossible it was to tear myself away after a week's stay. Here also I obtained some hounds, but better than all, – in excellent English and French, – a complete explanation concerning Borzoi history and breeding from that keen and extraordinarily well informed fancier, the master of this domain of ten thousand hectares. One's first thought is, why have not English and American breeders secured specimens of these dogs, and why has not more been heard of them? There are three sufficing reasons answering this query. Primarily, these wonderful kennels are very remote from the ordinary travelled route; secondly, owing to the English dog quarantine laws, very few Borzoi have in recent years left Russia [written in 1912]; and, thirdly, years ago when exportations did take place, this type was not fashionable. So far as I could ascertain, no foreign Borzoi fancier, up to the time of my trip, had ever visited either of these kennels.*

The Revolution

The revolution of 1917 almost wiped out the Borzoi breed. As a symbol of Imperial power, many hounds were killed by the communists. The hounds at Perchino were all shot and the Grand Duke's house razed to the ground, for not only was the Duke a member of the Imperial family, but he had been Commander in Chief of the Russian Army. He escaped to spend the rest of his days in exile in France, but several of the hunt servants were shot for the crime of caring for the Borzois.

In 1992 a party from the Borzoi Club visited Perchino with some Russian Borzoi owners and their dogs. The photographs they brought back show a village only changed from the photographs in Mr Thomas' book by years of neglect. The oldest inhabitant of the village was the son of one of the huntsmen. His father had been shot with all the hounds left on the estate. He had believed that every Borzoi in the world had been murdered that day, and wept tears of delight at seeing the breed once again.

Not all the hounds were shot by the revolutionaries. In the 1950's magazine *Riders of the Wind* some letters from an unnamed member of the Imperial Family to an American Borzoi breeder were published.

Dear Madame: I have been ill, but have received your letter. I am feeling better now and will attempt to answer you. I enjoyed very much your amusing accounts of your experiences in, as you call it, The Dog Game. You seem so enthused about Borzoi it is a pleasure to read your letters. You asked what happened to our Borzoi. We destroyed them by our own hand; they were shot and killed and buried on our grounds. I, myself, gave the order for this to be done. This will shock you, dear lady, but it was a kindness to them. You will understand, our day was running out, we were running for our lives, although we did not realise then the full scope of the tragedy about to be played. I came this day to the villa in all haste to destroy or salvage all that I could. It was utmost confusion, most had fled before me, my friend asked me about the dogs who were howling in their places. I said 'Nothing shall be left for the Bolshevicks to burn and kill.' Our horses were all gone, to the army or for food, so after a while we go to the dogs' place, and when they see us they are quiet. I look at them, they look at me, and I know that they are afraid. Borzoi are different from other dogs, I think, they know the peril before it comes. The Borzoi were very dirty and hungry as the cowards of servants had not thought of them for many days, it made me very sad. I tell the man to lead them out to the woods and shoot them.

I and my friend stood beside our horses and watch the men take them from their place, with rope on their necks and lead them away. It gave me courage, dear lady, as I watched the Borzoi walk so proudly to their death in the ruins of their world. When all was done, I and my friend went to see that all were dead and then they were buried where they fell. For 200 years my family took pride in their pack of Hunters. I have not seen a Borzoi since this time but I still feel affection for them; they are a proud race, dear lady, a proud race. The Borzoi of others did not fare so well as mine, as some could not liberate them and they were left to the will of the mob.

Asmodey Perchino.

Some Borzoi did manage to escape to the west, however: to France, Holland and Germany in particular. I have been told stories of a Russian lady who became a British governess, who escaped from Russia by putting on all the clothes she could, finishing with a large coat, and pretending that she was just taking her Borzoi out for some exercise. Dr Wegener, a German breeder, visited Perchino after the Grand Duke had left but before the Bolshevicks arrived and liberated some of the Borzois. One of these was Asmodey Perchino, a dog of vast importance to the revival of the breed in Europe after the First World War.

Breed Standards

What is a breed standard? It is a written description of the ideal specimen of a breed, whether it be cat, guinea pig or dog. Nearly all species of domestic animal have breed standards. Why is this chapter titled in the plural? Because you only need two interested parties together to get two different descriptions of the ideal specimen of a breed. Fortunately, at the end of the 20th century there is only one breed standard for the Borzoi in each country that has dog shows. Before the Second World War breed, clubs were in

An outstanding female Borzoi head.

charge of breed standards, so the popular breeds with six breed clubs had six breed standards. Hence the origin of the name of the Pekingese Reform Association, which was originally formed to breed to a different standard from that of the Pekinese Club.

An outstanding male Borzoi head from Southern British bloodlines.

At the present time it is the national kennel club of each country that is in charge of all the breed standards for the breeds it recognises. The breed standards I shall consider in this chapter are those of The Kennel Club (the British kennel club that predates all the others and is therefore called **The** Kennel Club), the American Kennel Club and the proposed international standard of the International Borzoi Council.

The first breed standards were written during the last quarter of the 19th century, before the era of the motor car, when the horse still ruled supreme. Instead of second-hand-car salesmen there were second-hand-horse salesmen and, if a person wished for a comfortable journey on horseback or by carriage, they or an employee needed to know horse structure so that they would not be sold a dud.

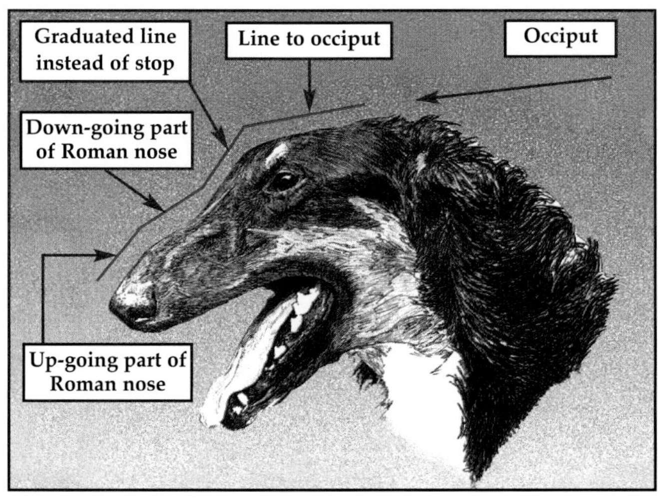

The structure of the head, demonstrated by a male of outstanding type from the Northern British bloodlines (see page 30).

The earliest standards, such as that written for the Fox Terrier, were drawn up by horsemen, using the same terms as those for the points of a horse. As the Australian judge Ken Rowles wrote: *Dog judging inherited much of its custom from the horse world. Dogs are gaited just as are horses in led-in classes, and the serious-*

ness with which movement is considered is also an inheritance from the horseman. Not only should the gait of most dogs be free, easy and with good length of stride, but also, viewed from front or rear, should be straight, in most breeds.

Good movement was really important in a horse. Any faults would lead to an uncomfortable ride, as the strange movements of the legs of a horse with a structural fault would waste energy and tire the horse, and the horse would be *very inclined to strike himself when he tired. And the cut of an iron shod hoof on a leg of a horse going at a good clip can make him go down, a thought not too pleasing to most riders.*

The breed standards, then, were written by people with a practical knowledge of horse structure who assumed that those reading them would also possess this knowledge. This is not the case in our motorised age and leads to problems in interpretation.

General appearance of the Borzoi

Each of the breed standards emphasises the elegance of the breed, the best description coming from the pre-war British standard: *Very graceful, aristocratic and elegant, combining courage, muscular power and great speed.* Within the graceful curves of the breed is a hound with good muscle development, most especially at the hindquarters. The back end of a Borzoi should be very large indeed, because of the big, bulky muscles there which are responsible for the great running power of the breed.

It should be easy to tell a male Borzoi from a female. He should be bigger, with more muscle development and a stronger head, although the head must not be so developed as to be coarse. The tendency is for males to look too much like females – the reverse of the situation in the Bulldog, where it is rare to get a bitch with a sufficiently feminine head.

Head

The Borzoi is a head breed: no head, no Borzoi. I suggest that the reader should spend some time just looking at the drawings of good Borzoi heads on pages 28–29. Once the images of good heads are in the mind's eye we can move on to the written descriptions.

The head is long and lean, viewed both from the side and from above. The eye is halfway between the nose and the occiput. The occiput is the hindmost part of the skull, labelled on the beautiful head shown on page 29, but more clearly seen in fig 3c on page 34. The dogs on page 29 also show the veins of their heads, as is highly desirable. In 'normal dogs' with less specialised structure than the Borzoi there is an indentation in the skull between the eyes, called the *stop*. The Borzoi has no stop.

The line from the nose to the occiput is formed from four distinct parts. The line from the nose forms the up-going part of the Roman nose. The next line forms the down-going portion of the Roman nose. Next comes a gradual inclination in the part of the skull that would include the stop of a 'normal' dog. The final line runs to the pronounced occiput.

The nose is large and black, slightly over-reaching the strong lower jaw.

In contrast, let us look at some poor heads, as shown in fig 1. The one in fig 1a clearly belongs to a Borzoi, but the top line of the head is formed from two lines, not four. There is no Roman nose and there is a well-defined stop. The veining is good, but does not look as if the upper and lower jaw would not close to give a correct bite.

What can I say about the head shown in fig 1b? The kindest is that this is nearly always an unflattering angle. However, this dog would not look good from any angle; its head is very coarse, with giant ears as a finishing touch.

Fig 1: Borzoi head faults.

The head depicted at fig 1c is also very coarse, with no pretensions to veining. The huge, bulbous eye is very different from the correct, obliquely-set almond ones seen in good heads. The only point that I would dispute in the International Borzoi Council standard is their requirement for a *relatively large eye*. Toy dogs have a large or relatively

A plain Borzoi head, showing good mobility of ears.

large eye; the Borzoi has a relatively small, southern greyhound eye.

The head at fig 1d is another coarse one, with bone that is much too heavy. The ear is too large and set too low. It looks as if it is formed from tough old leather and bears little resemblance to the desired small, pointed, delicate ears. Borzoi ears are very mobile and are usually carried tucked back, folded over the rear part of the skull, although the dog is quite capable of carrying them erect. This dog also has bulbous, staring eyes and it looks as if their colour is rather light.

The two dogs depicted at fig 1e–f have the same fault: they have Roman heads rather than Roman noses. The skull line and the stop line are correct, but the rising portion of the Roman nose is missing. This in turn means that the line to the nose itself causes the muzzle to drop, as in the Roman head of a Bull Terrier.

Ears

The very plain Borzoi depicted above nevertheless gives an idea of the mobility of the ears. The Whippet shows what the neatly-folded rose ear required by the Borzoi breed standards looks like beneath the coat.

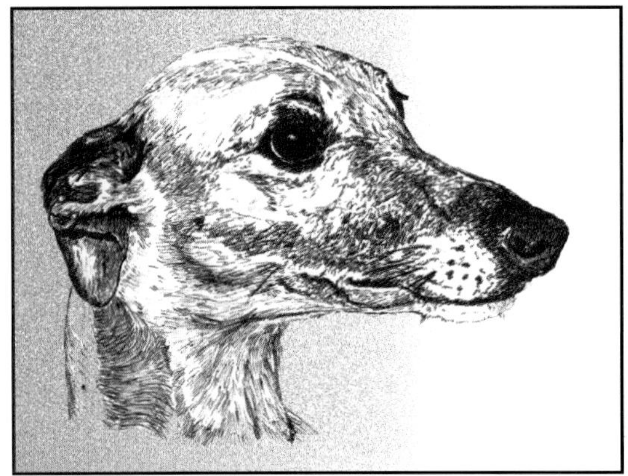

A Whippet head, showing what the Borzoi's ears should look like under the coat.

Dentition

The Borzoi has 42 teeth, as every dog should. Looking at the upper teeth in fig 2a, we see two molars, four premolars, one canine and three incisors, which is repeated by the upper teeth on the left. However, the teeth of the lower jaw are different. Referring to fig 2b, there are still four premolars, but an extra molar tooth makes three molars in total.

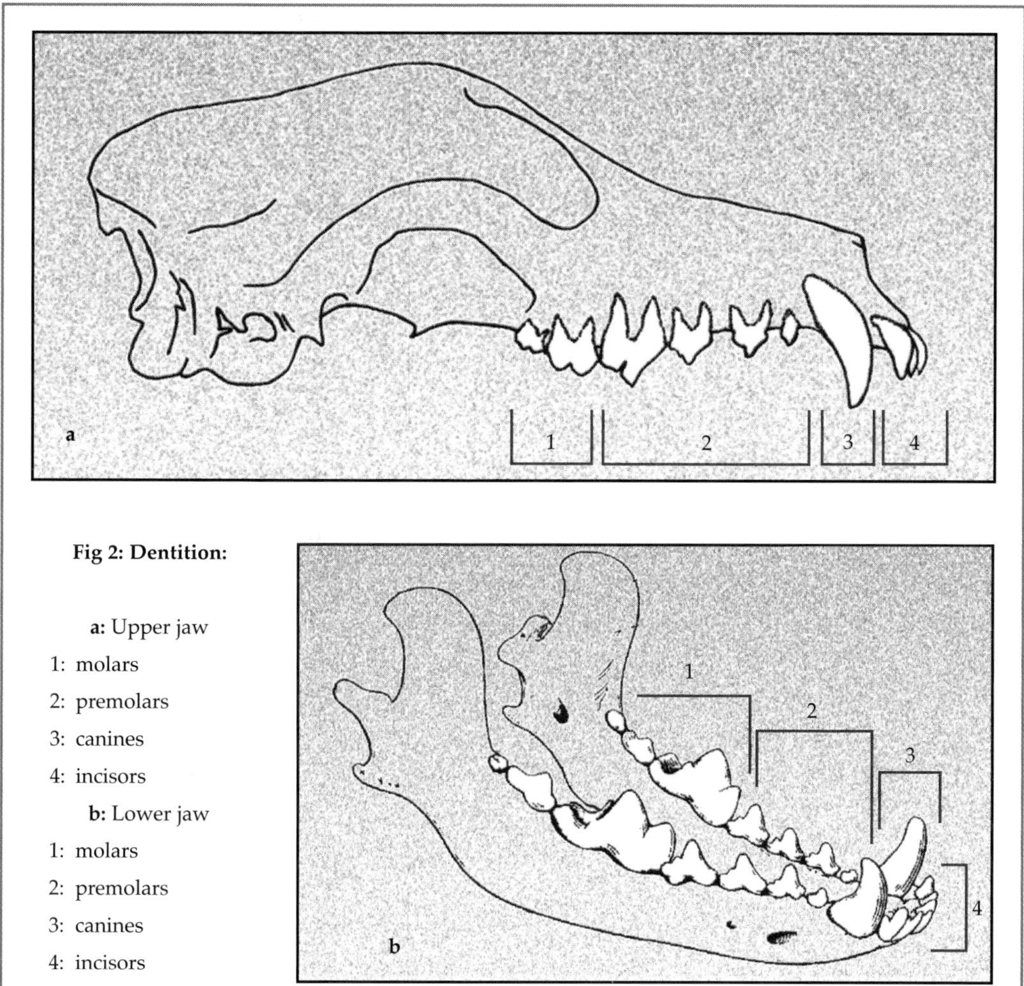

Fig 2: Dentition:

a: Upper jaw
1: molars
2: premolars
3: canines
4: incisors

b: Lower jaw
1: molars
2: premolars
3: canines
4: incisors

Bite

Correct: The upper and lower jaw have to be correctly aligned for the mouth to function properly. Fig 3 on page 34 shows the scissor bite, where the upper incisors overlap the lower ones but still touch, like a pair of scissors. This is the correct bite for the Borzoi and for the vast majority of dog breeds. In Fig 3c, the arrow demonstrates where the lower incisors would meet the upper ones, closely tucked in behind. This view also shows the prominent occiput at the back.

Incorrect: If we look at the books written about dogs at the end of the 19th century, only three types of bite were discussed:

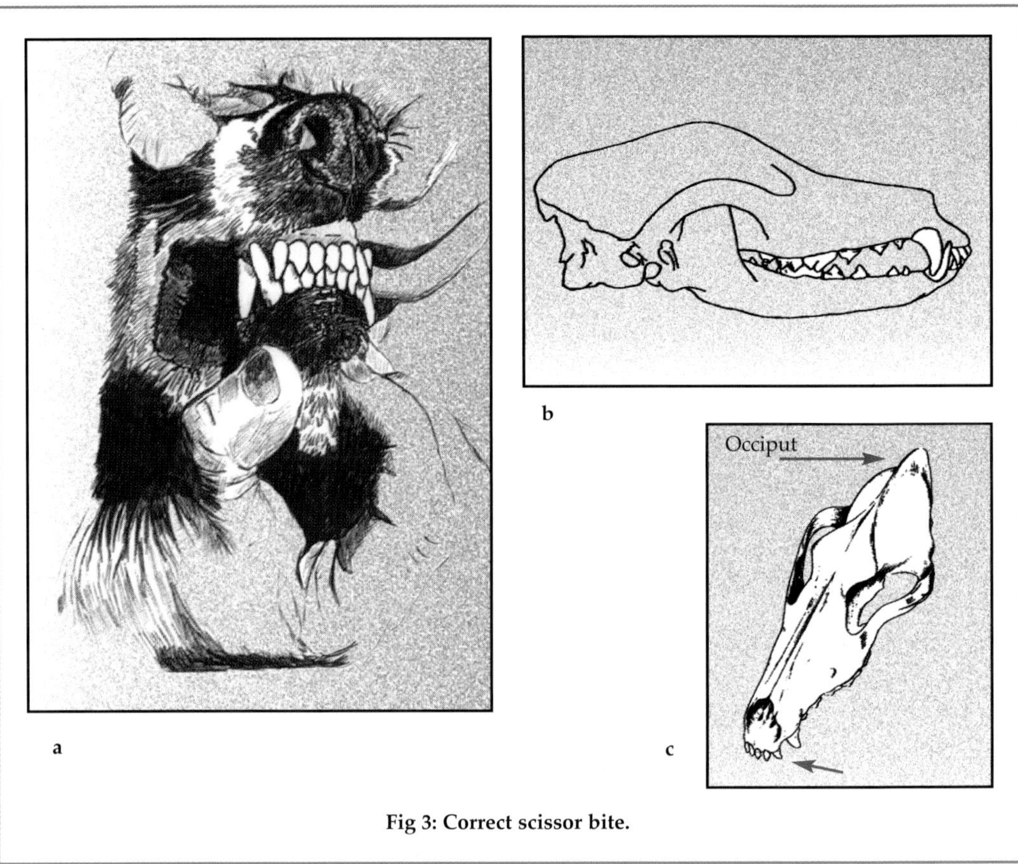

Fig 3: Correct scissor bite.

- undershot (fig 4a), where the lower jaw projects further forward than the upper
- overshot (fig 4b), where the upper jaw projects further forward than the lower
- level bite

The term level bite was used to indicate that the jaws were even. Today we use the term scissor bite for the most commonly correct type of jaw structure. We still use level bite, but it now means a bite in which the upper incisors rest on top of the lower incisors instead of sliding just in front of them. This means that a level bite is just a fraction undershot.

Because so many breed standards were written before the use of the term scissor bite several ask specifically for a level bite when the author really means scissor bite.

In general there are less bite faults in the Borzoi than in other breeds. The Borzoi's jaw is long enough for all the teeth to fit in without crushing. However, faults can occur.

The lower jaw of the dog develops in two parts that join together in the middle to form the mandible. The skull forms from many bones, also fusing in the middle under the line that can be seen as the split in the upper lip and nose of the dog. Human beings go

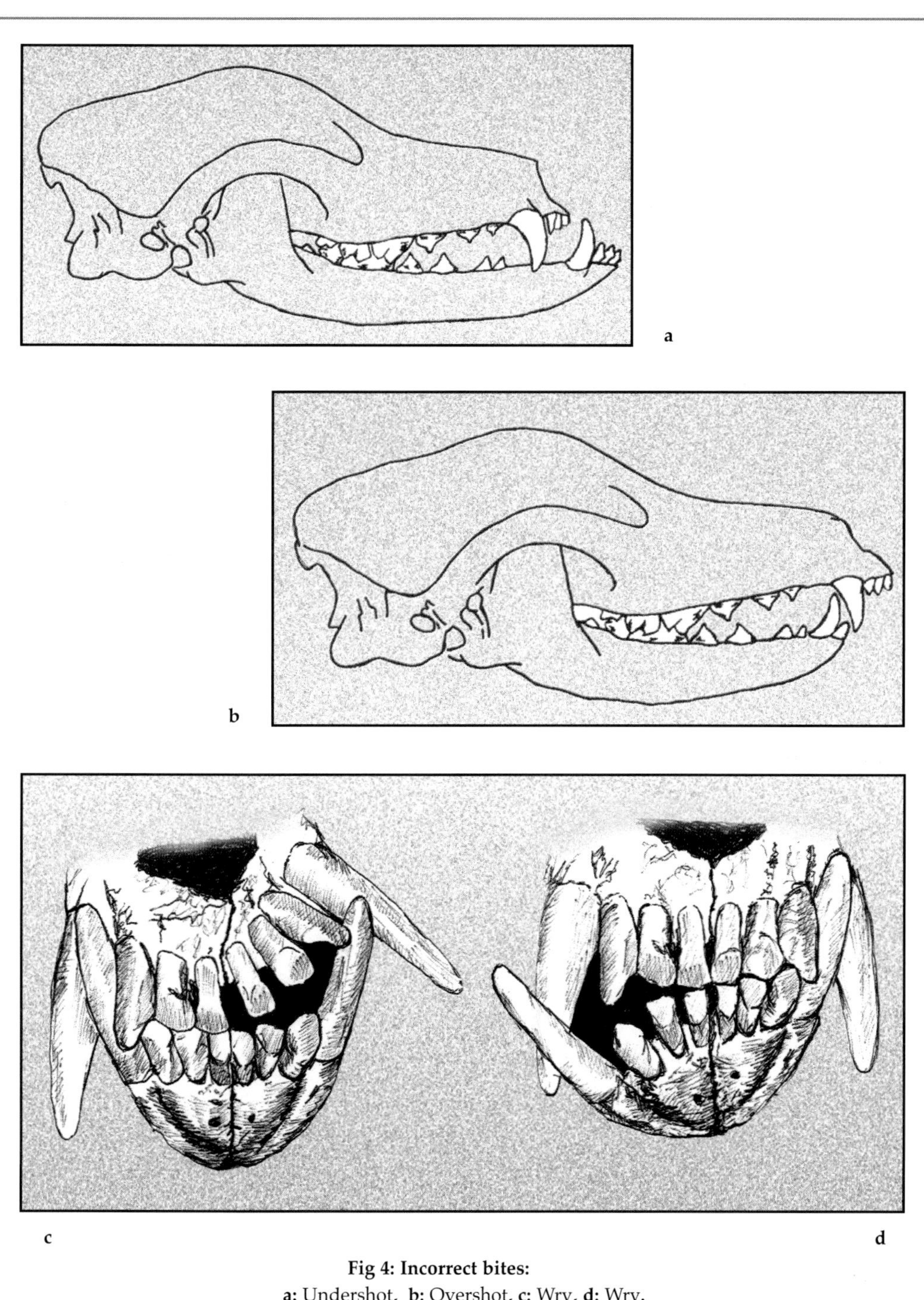

Fig 4: Incorrect bites:
a: Undershot, **b:** Overshot, **c:** Wry, **d:** Wry.

through a similar process of fusion, but this is more complete than in dogs. The condition of cleft palate, found in both dog and man, is due to the lack of fusion in the region that forms the roof of the mouth.

Other problems due to this pattern of facial development include wry mouth. This occurs when the four halves (two in the upper jaw, two in the lower) forming the bony opening of the mouth grow at an uneven rate. Instead of four equal pieces growing and fitting together, one of them may not develop enough.

Fig 4c shows a jaw that is wry because of lack of development on the left half of the upper jaw. The one in fig 4d is wry because of lack of development of the right half of the lower jaw.

An Old English Sheepdog with perfect lower incisors.

Missing and incorrectly placed teeth

These pictures contrast an Old English Sheepdog with good incisors with a Dandie Dinmont with faulty teeth. All six of the Dandie Dinmont's incisors are present, but they are not correctly placed. At first they look like a jumble of teeth but, if you look again, only two are out of alignment: the second lower incisor each side of the lower jaw.

A Dandie Dinmont with wrongly-placed incisors.

Any type of tooth can be missing. In breeds like Pekingese the teeth are crushed into a very small mouth, and it is common for them to have missing incisors. The Borzoi has plenty of room for all its teeth, and the ones most commonly missing are premolars.

Different countries have different emphases on missing teeth. The Germans in particular are very strict about correct dentition, and will not award prizes to dogs with faults in this area.

If one missing tooth is ignored in a

breeding programme the next generation may have less teeth, and this can carry on into subsequent generations. We then end up with a situation similar to that with hairless breeds of dogs, who, along with their missing coats, have missing teeth. What teeth they do have are rudimentary, peg-like structures, unlike the big, strong teeth of a meat-eating animal for which we are aiming.

A Fox Terrier with a good set of premolars.

A Borzoi whose fourth premolar is missing.

Missing teeth are important, but must be taken in context. The dog that can hardly move because of a structural fault but has a perfect mouth should not be placed above the well-constructed dog with a missing tooth.

There is not time in the ring to count the number of teeth in a dog's mouth, but missing teeth can be assessed by looking at teeth patterns and looking for gaps. The top picture shows a Wire Fox Terrier with a full set of four premolars on the left of the lower jaw. We can also see from this angle the lower canine of that side, and at the back the first molar. Below we see a Borzoi whose fourth premolar is missing. The first molar is the largest and strongest tooth, designed for cracking open bones. It is the one that causes acute pain when you are playing with puppies and they are mouthing your fingers while you are concentrating on something else. The puppy manoeuvres your finger to the back of its mouth and then, gently rotating its head sideways, crunches.

Looking for missing teeth patterns needs to be practised, and it is easy to get this practice in the comfort of your home by subscribing to a dog newspaper or magazine. Unfortunately, many people who publish photographs of their prize-winning dogs are actually advertising that you should not make enquiries to use the dog at stud, as his dentition is incomplete.

Skeleton and musculature

To study the skeleton of the Borzoi (see fig 5a on page 39) we need first to determine some anatomical terms. I found relating the multitude of different 'show' terms for parts of the body to those I had been taught as a medical student a very confusing process. Take the term *back*: almost every glossary of canine terms gives a different definition for this. For this reason, I find it easier to use the correct anatomical nomenclature, as this is precise and recognised internationally.

Bones of the front limb

- The *scapula* (shoulder blade) is the uppermost bone of the front limb, and articulates with the humerus to form the shoulder joint.
- The *humerus* (upper arm) articulates with two bones, the *radius* and the *ulna*, to form the *elbow joint*.
- The radius and ulna articulate with a number of little bones at the *wrist joint*.
- These little *carpal bones* are attached to four longer bones called the *metacarpals*. The bony structure formed by the carpals and metacarpals together is called the *pastern*.
- To finish the front limb we have the bones of the *toes*.

All this is exactly comparable to the bony structure of the human front limb. The human thumb corresponds to the 'extra toe' or dew claw sometimes found in dogs. I find it helps me to understand the dog's front limb if I analyse the human arm positioned as if it belonged to a dog. Rest the fingers on a table, holding them as the front toes, and pull the arm up to give the pastern and above. Almost all of the joints are more mobile in a person than a dog: the front limb is for support and movement in a dog, but for intricate manoeuvring in a person.

Bones of the hind limb

- The *pelvis* is attached to the *vertebral column*, a column made up of individual bones, which starts at the skull and passes back to the tail, by which time the individual 'building blocks' have become small and simple in shape.
- The pelvis articulates with the *femur* (thigh bone) to form the *hip joint*.
- The femur articulates with two bones that are firmly attached to each other, the *tibia* and *fibula* (second thigh), to form the *stifle joint*.
- The tibia and fibula articulate with a number of small bones to form the *hock joint*.
- These little *tarsal bones* are attached to four longer bones called *metatarsals*. The bony structure formed by the tarsals and metatarsals is sometimes called the *rear pastern*. It is not the *hock*, as it is so often labelled: that is the joint above. To be exact, this is *the complex formed by the tarsal and metatarsal bones*: long-winded, perhaps, but anatomically precise. Using this phrase we have *the complex formed by the tarsals and metatarsals short* rather than *hocks close to the ground* – a phrase that confuses many people.

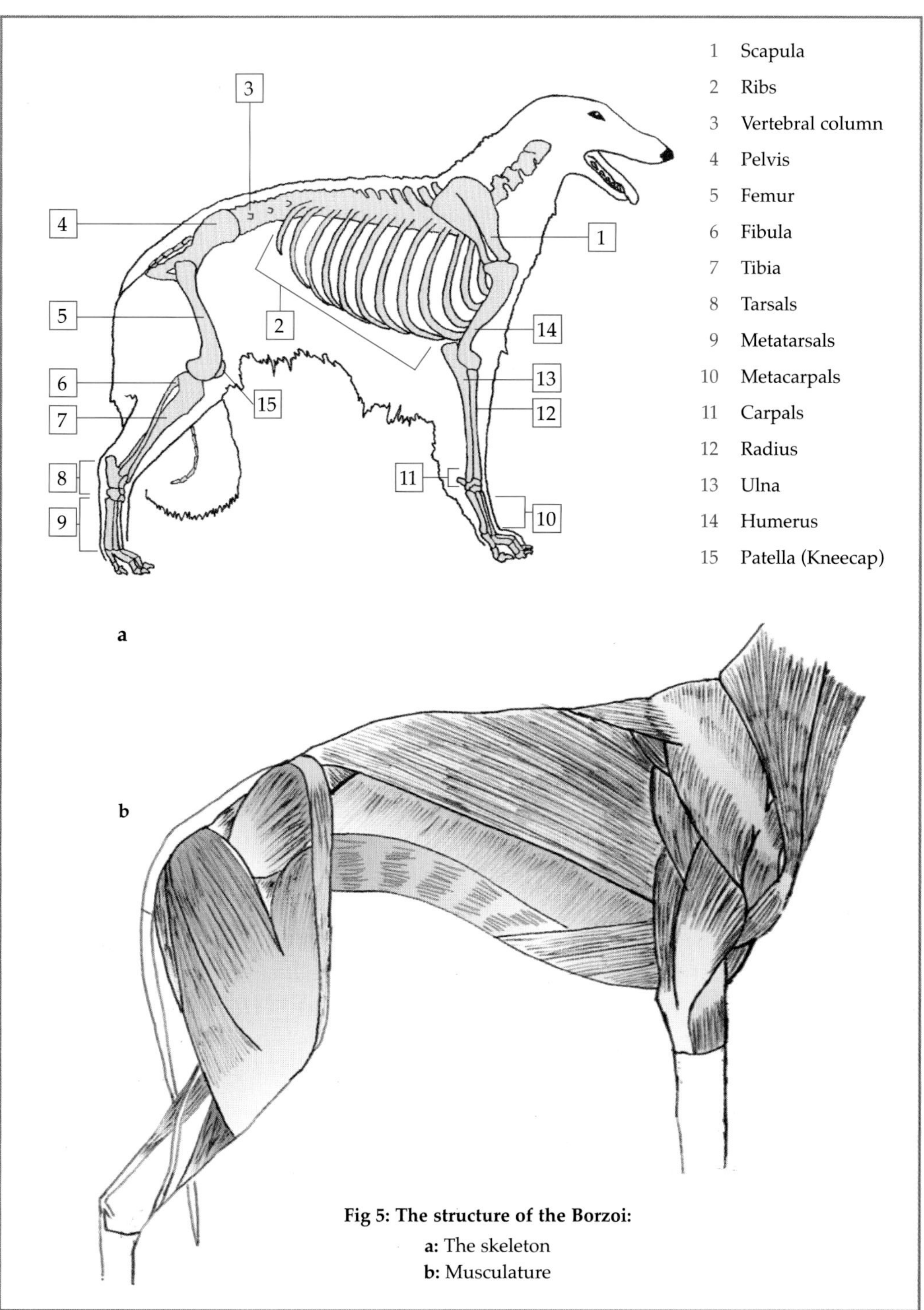

Fig 5: The structure of the Borzoi:
a: The skeleton
b: Musculature

Using the human analogy for the hind limb is a little more complicated than for the front. Starting with the pelvis, the hip joint is the same, and the stifle joint is the same as the knee. The hock joint is the same as the human ankle joint and, if we stand on tiptoe, we can see that the human foot is formed by the complex formed by the tarsal bones and the metatarsals. The toes are equivalent in both species, with the human having a dew claw there as well!

Musculature

Fig 5b on page 39 shows the muscles attached to the skeleton. Note the well-developed muscles to operate the shoulder and elbow joints, and the huge muscles to flex the hip and stifle joints.

Fronts

The front of a dog comprises the two front legs, the *sternum* (breast bone) and the ribs. A dog with a good front will have the correct front limb articulation plus well-developed ribs and good chest muscles.

Good fronts are three-dimensional; the ribcage should be correctly rounded, giving plenty of space underneath, so that the front legs are well spaced apart. A great problem in a fine-boned breed like the Borzoi is bone that is too fine and hounds that look as if their front legs are coming out of the same hole because the legs are so close to each other. However, we must not go to the other extreme, with huge, barrel-like ribs and legs spaced too widely apart.

Fig 6a gives a more three-dimensional view. The scapula is angulated backwards from the shoulder joint, and also inwards towards the spines that arise from each vertebra.

The bones of the front limb are attached to the ribcage and the neck by muscles only; there is no bony connection. This makes all the bones very mobile.

Muscle development is governed by inherited factors and by feeding and exercise. Exercise is not as important in bone development. The 'Mr Universes' of this world have to work hard to develop their musculature, but this exercise does not make their bones get larger. The muscles are very important in giving shape to the front, so the development of a puppy's front is more dependent on exercise and nutrition than the development of its hindquarters. The hindquarters have a more rigid, bony structure as a base for their muscles, so inherited bone structure is more important in this area.

When the dog lowers its head the two *scapulae* (shoulder bones) slide upwards and backwards towards each other. If they are set too close they will move backward slightly, touch and be unable to move any more, so that the dog cannot lower its head. There should be about two fingers' width between the topmost part of the two scapulae when the dog is standing with its head raised, to give enough space for the head to be lowered

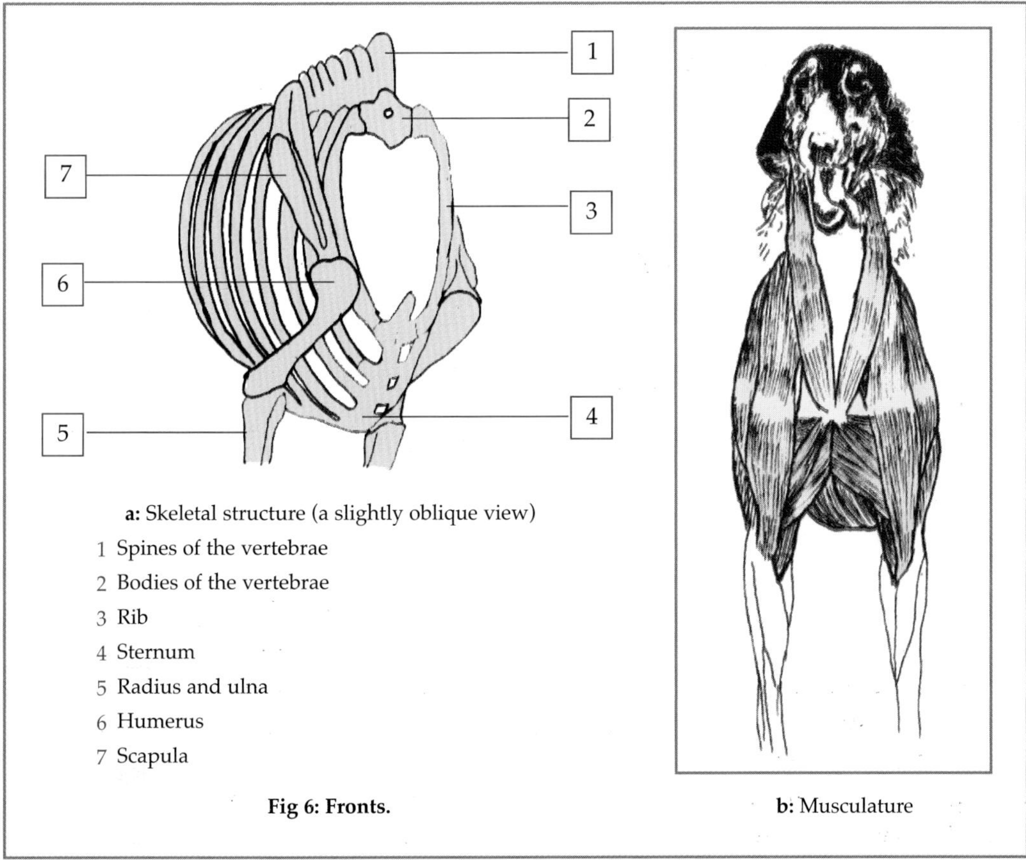

Fig 6: Fronts.

b: Musculature

to the ground.

Fig 6b shows a front view of the musculature of a good front. Note the good space between the legs: there would be no problem slipping your hand between these limbs when going over the dog. Also worthy of note are the long, smooth muscles, which also go up into the neck. Good fronts have good necks.

Shoulder angulation

I have been told that shoulder angulation is the hardest concept to understand in dog construction. I know that many different things have been said about shoulders, and most breed standards completely omit to mention the humerus, the bone I consider the most important in front angulation.

Since the front limb is attached solely by muscles, it is very mobile, and the shoulder and elbow joints change their angles according to how the dog is standing. Fixed angles only belong to fixed objects, and dogs are not fixed objects.

One of the best explanations of shoulders can be found in Robert Cole's *The Basenji*

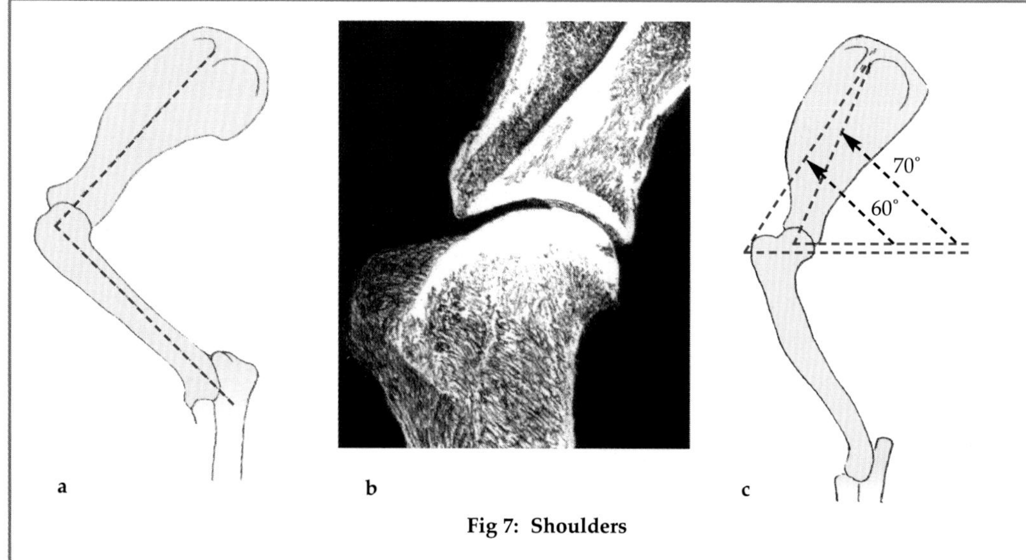

Fig 7: Shoulders

Stacked and Moving. I would call this a 'must have' book for, although it is not about Borzois, much in it is applicable to them. In it, Robert Cole discusses the problem of incorrect diagrams of the shoulder in older books (fig 7a). In these, there is a 90° angle between the scapula and humerus, giving 45° between the scapula and a horizontal line. That humerus, however, has been drawn from a horse.

Fig 7b is a drawing from an X-ray of the shoulder joint of a dog. With the real structure of the humerus in mind, that is, with the bony protruberance to the front of the joint, we have two ways in which to measure the angle between the scapula and a horizontal line, with two quite different results (see fig 7c). This angle is what is described in breed standards as the *layback of shoulder*.

The other 'must have' book for understanding dog structure is Rachel Page Elliott's *The New Dogsteps.* She has done a great deal of work with moving X-rays to see what actually happens inside a dog, demonstrating how the old 45° angle between the scapula and horizontal would make the shoulder joint occur well in front of the sternum – something that does not happen in reality.

I do not think it is valid simply to look at the layback of shoulder. It is the angulation of both the shoulder and elbow joints that gives a correctly articulated front. When the dog stands correctly the radius and ulna are held perfectly vertical and fixed by the dog's weight going down into the front foot. This means that it is the position of the scapula *and* the humerus that governs front angulation.

As a medical student I was taught points called *surface markers,* which can be used to find our anatomical way about the body. In going over a dog in a show ring the judge

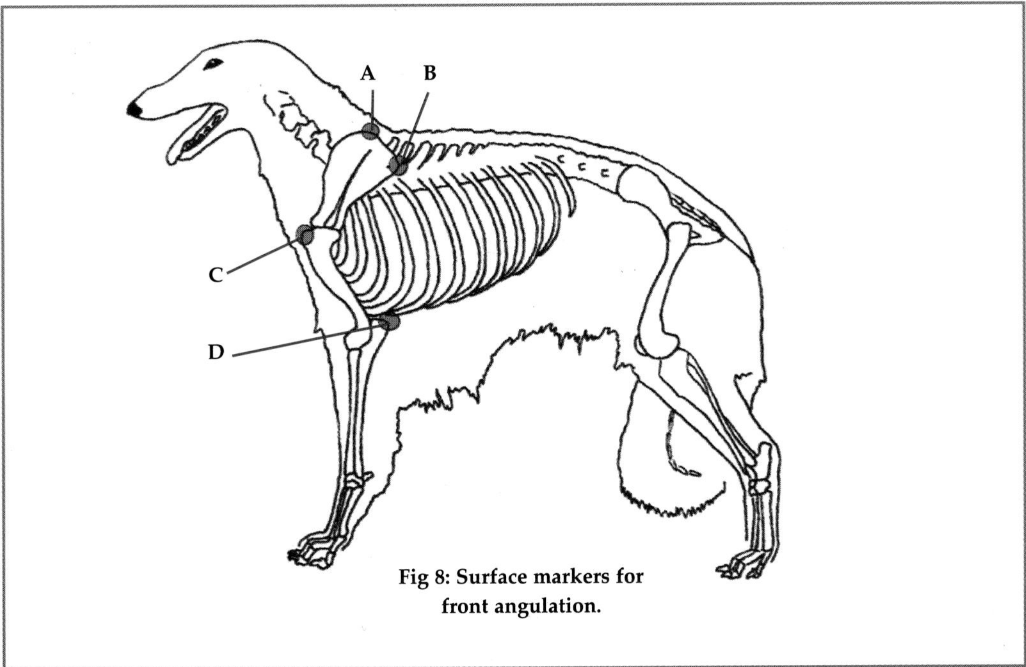

Fig 8: Surface markers for front angulation.

should be looking for these surface markers. If we look at the diagram of the correctly articulated skeleton at fig 8, the surface markers of the correct front assembly are visible:

- A: the uppermost part of the scapula
- B: the rearmost part of the scapula
- C: the most forward part of the shoulder joint
- D: the rearmost part of the elbow joint

In the correct front:

- The rearmost part of the scapula is directly above the most posterior part of the elbow joint.
- The angle between the scapula and horizontal should be roughly equal to the angle between the humerus and the horizontal. Absolute angle measurements do not matter; it is the symmetry and balance of the angulation that counts.

Assess correct angulation by locating these four points. Start with the rearmost part of the scapula and gently run your hand to the uppermost part of the scapula. From there, running a hand down the front edge of the scapula gives a working idea of the angle of the scapula. Once at the shoulder joint it is important to continue back, down the length of the humerus. One of the problems with shoulder angulation is the abundance of muscle hiding bones. The front edge humerus is easily felt; the muscles are at the other side. From the humerus, slip back to the posterior edge of the elbow joint. You should be immediately below where you started, and this part of the elbow joint should be right next to the lower edge of ribcage. I find this much easier than swivelling my fingers to measure absolute angles that are of dubious accuracy in a moving animal, and this method gives the humerus the importance it merits.

Different breeds have different front structures. The front of the Borzoi is 'normal dog' rather than the racing front of the Whippet. In the racing front the humerus is longer than the scapula, so to fit in the triangle between the surface markers the angle between the humerus and scapula is greater. This type of front is for a sprinting dog designed for quick bursts of speed, not for the sustained running of a Borzoi.

Other types of front are those of terriers, where the humerus is shorter than the scapula, giving a completely different construction, and breeds like the Dachshund. In the latter case the growth of the limb bones is stunted, while the head and the spinal column are normal in size.

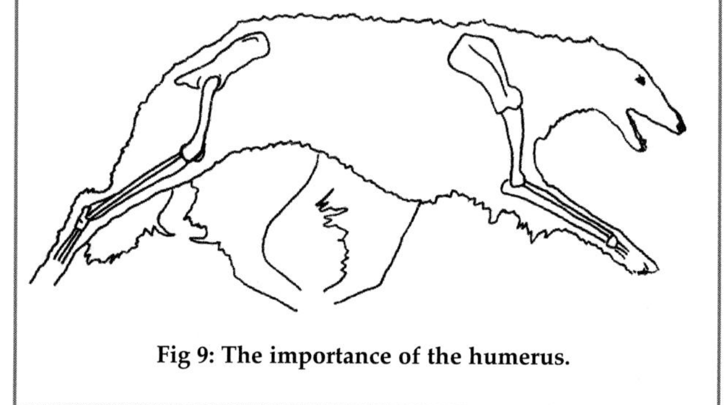

Fig 9: The importance of the humerus.

The importance of the humerus

The humerus must be correctly angulated to give correct front movement. We have already discussed its position in the stationary dog but, if we look at the dog moving at the trot, we can see why its position is fundamental to good movement.

Fig 9 shows the position of the humerus when the dog has its front leg fully extended at the trot. The humerus is roughly vertical. If the dog has an almost vertical humerus when it is standing there is no scope for this swing. If the humerus cannot move very far, neither can the radius, the ulna and the leg. This is why a dog with an upright humerus cannot take long strides: it lacks front extension. The better the angle of the humerus, the greater its swing to the vertical and the amount of reach of the front leg.

Bad fronts

Bad fronts are more easily seen in smooth-coated breeds. In trimmed breeds like the Wire Fox Terrier a skillful trimmer can try to disguise a bad front by leaving hair where muscle is missing and by cutting the coat very close where too much is present.

The Italian Greyhound puppies at the bottom of page 45 have terrible fronts. In the one to the left there is hardly any space between the front legs, and none has sufficient depth of chest. The elbows are nowhere near the ribcage; indeed, they are rotated outwards, a condition known as *out at elbow*.

Another front fault is the opposite: the elbows are rotated inwards towards the chest. This is *tied in at the elbow*.

The worst features of these puppies are their pasterns. The angulation of the pastern should only happen in one plane, being gently angled when viewed from the side only (as in the correct Borzoi skeleton in fig 8). In these puppies the pasterns are angled in more than one plane; they are rotated to the side as well, making the feet point outwards.

In the top picture we see exactly the same faults in a Borzoi.

Neck and ribs

As I have said before, good fronts have good necks because the neck muscles continue down on to the chest. The neck muscles should merge smoothly with those of the shoulder, giving a graceful, slightly arched structure. The head in the Borzoi is held less high than in many breeds, though it must not be too low; look again at the correct skeleton on page 39.

The neck is approximately equal to the length of the head and is not a cylinder; it is gently flattened each side.

There are several muscles set beneath the scapula. If these become overdeveloped, due to too much exercise, they will push the scapulae (shoulder blades) outwards and spoil the muscle line from the neck into the shoulders. This is referred to as *loaded shoulders* and the remedy is less exercise.

The spines of the vertebrae between the two scapulae (shoulder blades) form the withers, the point from which height is

(Above) Italian Greyhounds with terrible fronts. (Top) Borzoi with the same faults. This is the poor quality puppy shown on page 148.

measured. The muscle development on these spines should not be excessive; no muscle development at the front of the Borzoi should be exaggerated. The bone of the radius and ulna is not cylindrical. It too is compressed laterally, its widest part being at the elbow. This is called *bladed bone* (flattened like the blade of a knife).

The pasterns are at an angle to the vertical with a flexible joint with the radius and ulna. This flexibility allows the dog to run hard, the pasterns acting as springs to take the strain resulting from galloping as it speeds along in pursuit of its quarry. When a dog is really motoring along, the pasterns can end up almost parallel with the ground. Inflexible, vertical pasterns, like those in the Fox Terrier, render such sustained, economical galloping impossible. The whole front assembly is jarred by each foot-fall, because there is no 'give' to take the strain. Vertical pasterns would stop a Borzoi from fulfilling its main purpose as a running hound.

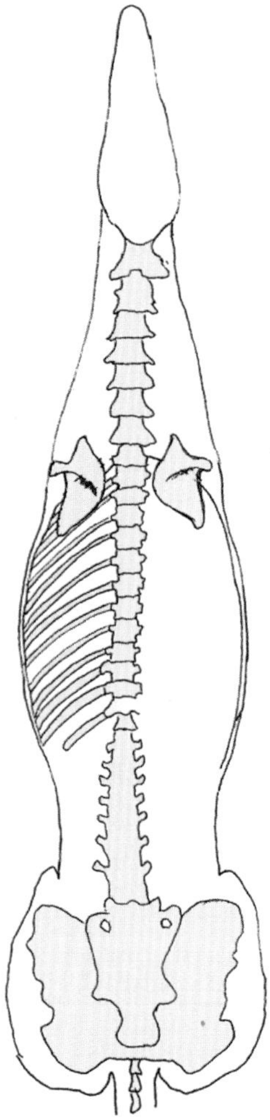

Fig 10: The skeleton of a Borzoi seen from above.

Note the huge development of the hindquarters.

Most of the length of the body should be taken up by ribs. The spring of the rib is less than in other breeds. The space inside the ribcage for the heart and lungs is due to the great depth of this ribcage. However, the ribs should give a rounded curve, not be flat and almost vertical like the sides of a box. A dog with these flattened ribs is called *slab sided*.

The muscles between the last rib and the pelvis are called the *coupling*. These muscles should be shorter rather than longer to give strength, but not so short that the hind legs are too near the front ones so that they collide with each other when moving.

The hindquarters

Earlier I said, no head, no Borzoi. The same goes for the hindquarters. No other breed has such enormous back end development, nor quite the graceful set of curves that gives the unique shape at this end. Underneath there is a graceful curve upwards from the ribcage. On top there is an equally elegant curve from the shoulders, its peak over the last rib, and this curve is prolonged into the fall-away.

Fig 10 indicates the huge development of the hindquarters, especially when compared with the moderate to fine forequarters. The whole shape of a Borzoi from above is the aerodynamic 'Coca Cola bottle' shape. This gives the least air resistance, helping the dog to move fast. The bones of the pelvis are large, giving a large surface area for the large hindquarter muscles.

The International Borzoi Council (IBC) standard describes a back end of this type, as do the pre-war and current British standards and the Russian one. However, there is a problem with the American standard. Here the topline desired is *rising a little at the loins in a graceful curve.* This has meant breeding for a topline that is basically flat with a little rounding at the loins, not the sweeping fall-away that to me means Borzoi. I was delighted to read the IBC standard and this, together with the acceptance of the Russian Kennel Club in international circles, I hope will lead to the American standard coming into line with the rest of the world. There are more Borzois in the United States than anywhere, and it is vital that we are all breeding for the same points. Field trials for Borzois are popular in the United States, and the few photographs I have seen of the American Borzoi that runs for a living show a hound with an IBC topline, not an American show topline.

The croup is formed by the muscles over the pelvis, including those running into the tail. These should add to the graceful curve of the fall-away.

Fig 11a shows the bones of the hindquarters without the vertebral column or the tail. We see the pelvis, formed by two halves, and the two *femora* (plural of femur: the thigh bone). The uppermost crests of the pelvis are important, as they should be easy to feel through the skin and more than 8cm apart. These prominences are anatomically the *iliac crests,* but are referred to as 'hip bones' in The Kennel Club standard. In 11b an idea is given of the large muscle bulk attached to the pelvis of the Borzoi. Only a few of the muscles are drawn.

The two Borzois pictured overleaf demonstrate the fall-away and correct rear construction as seen from the back. The view from the back shows the tarsal/metatarsal complex (rear pastern) to be short and quite vertical to the ground. To be critical, the dog

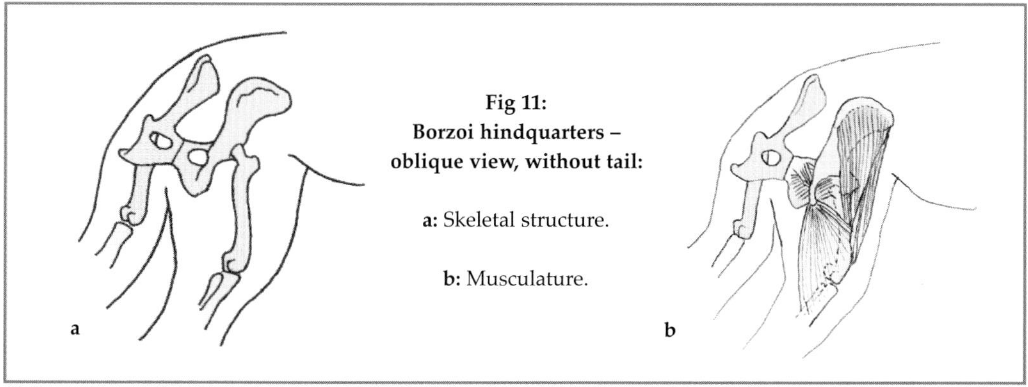

Fig 11: Borzoi hindquarters – oblique view, without tail:

a: Skeletal structure.

b: Musculature.

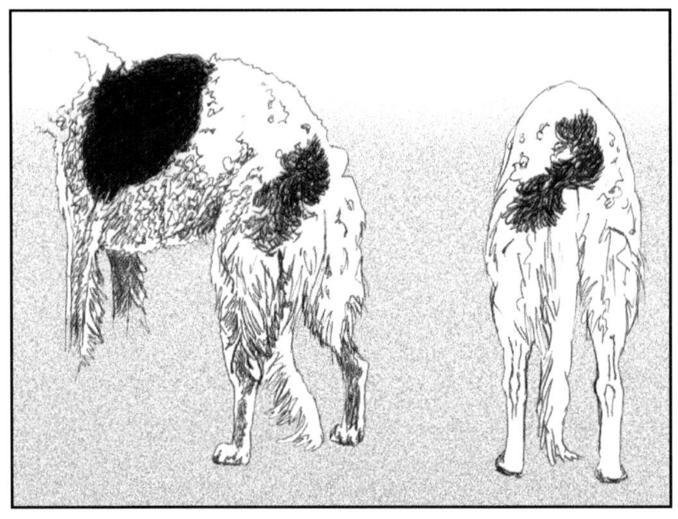

These two Borzois show relatively good hindquarter construction, although the one on the left is a little straight at the stifle joint.

on the left is a little straight at the stifle joint; it lacks angulation here and could do with a slightly longer tibia and fibula.

The Borzoi on the left in the picture below shows a bowed out tarsal/metatarsal construction, which is referred to as *bow hocks*. The dog on the right has a tarsal/metatarsal construction that is bowed in. This is referred to as *cow hocks*.

The dog at the top of the picture on the opposite page has elegantly curved hindquarters, but the whole body length is too great, and the tibia and fibula are too long, positioning the feet too far behind the pelvis. This dog is over-angulated at both hip and stifle joints, giving an exaggerated hind movement, and the hind legs will probably interfere with the more modestly angulated and correct forequarters.

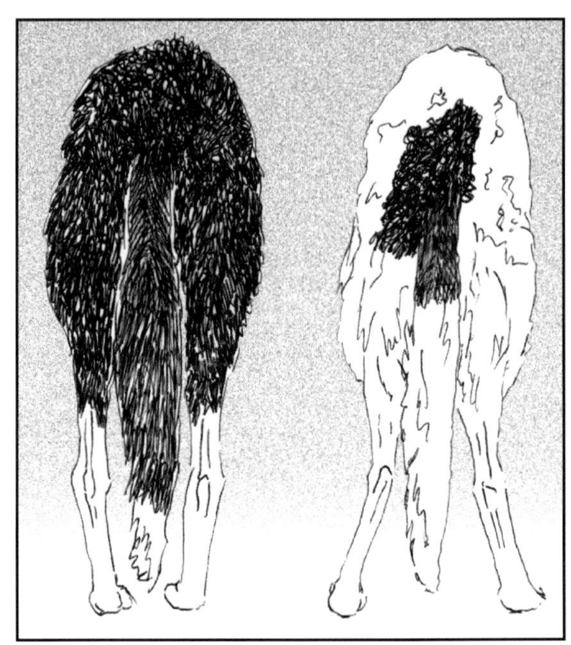

Two Borzois with faulty construction: (left) bow hocks, (right) cow hocks.

Tail set

The tail set and length on the top Borzoi on page 49 is correct. In the ring, the tail is measured by being brought up gently to the iliac crest (crest of the hip bone). The tail should be at least as long as this. The tail on the dog below on the opposite page is set too high and horribly ringed. The only curving allowed in the tail is a gentle sickle.

Balance

A balanced dog is one with the same

amount of angulation in the front limb assembly as in the rear limb assembly. In the case of the dog in the lower picture on page 51 there is balance – there is an equal lack of angulation in both the rear and front assemblies.

There is a paradox about balance. This balanced dog with poor angulation will put less strain on its joints than the dog with a correct front and a poor rear end, or the dog with a correct rear and poor front. This means that the incorrectly angulated but balanced dog should be placed above the unbalanced but partially correctly constructed dog.

Nevertheless, the dog has very poor angulation front and back. The steep hind assembly has given a high set tail that will spring up to be held curled over the back when the dog moves. This dog also has a very long complex formed by the tarsal and metatarsal bones, which will give it an even more inefficient movement. The hock joint is very far away from the ground.

(Above) This Borzoi has elegant curves, but its body is too long. The tail set is correct. (Below) The tail is set on too high and horribly ringed.

Feet

The feet of the Borzoi are called *hare feet* because, like the feet of the fast-running hare, they are longer than they are high. This is achieved by the first toe bone, the *proximal phalanx,* being longer than the second toe bone, the *middle phalanx*. These toe bones, known in the plural as *phalanges,* are exactly comparable to the bones of the human hand. The thumb, which represents the canine dew claw, only has two phalanges. The actual canine dew claw is even more rudimentary than this, often only comprising the nail and a rudimentary portion of the distal phalange. Fig 12a overleaf shows the bone structure of a hare foot.

Dogs that do not have to run for their living have a more compact foot called the *cat foot*. This is illustrated in fig 12b, and is typified by shorter proximal phalanges than those found in the hare foot. This type of foot is a fault in the Borzoi.

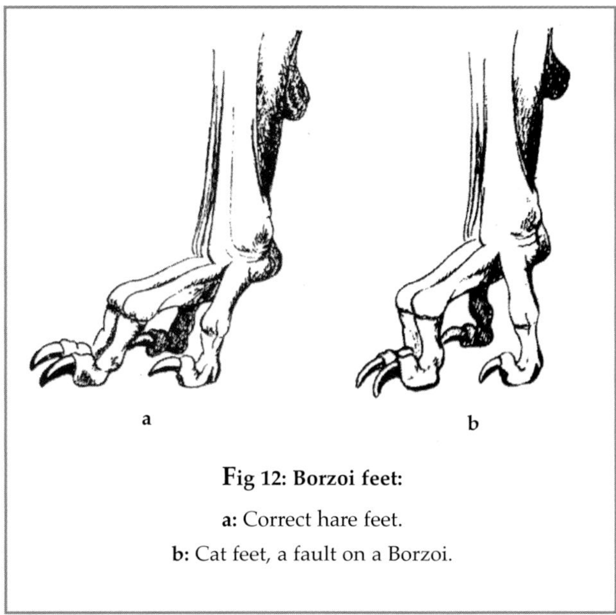

Fig 12: Borzoi feet:

a: Correct hare feet.

b: Cat feet, a fault on a Borzoi.

The Bloodhound pictured below has terrible feet. Completely flat feet like this are a fault for almost every breed. This bitch was actually a working trials champion, which shows that her determination to work must have overcome the problems that her feet must have caused for her.

To finish this section on a positive note, the Borzoi in the top picture on page 51 has very good hare feet. The hind feet are just a fraction shorter in length than the front feet, which is the correct construction.

An example of terrible feet on a Bloodhound.

Movement

It is not possible to analyse movement using the static pictures in a book. The best way to do this is to watch Rachel Page Elliott's video *Dogsteps* many times. The slow motion photography and the moving X-ray photography tell a story that would take volumes of diagrams to explain, and then the explanation would not be as clear as the video.

If a dog is constructed as in my ideal skeleton it will probably move correctly. Bad habits and unequal muscle development may make the dog move less well than its skeletal structure should allow.

On pages 52–54 you will see three Borzois depicted, together with their skeletal structure, each faulty in a different way.

The Borzoi shown on page 52 is a self-coloured bitch with a slightly light eye. She has good shoulder angulation, the scapula and humerus are well angled, and with that humerus angulation she will have good front extension. However, things begin to go wrong behind her shoulders.

The long, elegant neck is associated with the long whole body length. It is nearly impossible to breed for long neck vertebrae and short ones throughout the rest of the spinal column. In this bitch the distance between the point of the shoulder to the hindmost part of the pelvis is far greater than the height from the withers to the ground. The loin area from the last rib to the pelvis is far too long as well. This

A good Borzoi with excellent feet.

This dog's conformation is very poor but, nevertheless, it is balanced (see page 48–49).

area of muscle is short in a dog with a strongly constructed back.

Her topline has the correct curve, but it has been lengthened too much.

Her hind limbs are very faulty. This means that, with her correct shoulders, she is unbalanced and, when she moves, her good front will have to do funny things to compensate for the poor hind movement. She may throw her elbows outwards to stop the over-angulated hind feet from kicking her front legs.

There is a very poor muscle development of the femur and tibia. She is not of an aerodynamic shape from above. Her shoulders are wider than her hind legs: in fact, her build is more like a Bulldog than a Borzoi.

She is standing with all the joints of her hind limb over-extended, her tarsal and metatarsal bones are not even at 90° to the ground. The over-long femur and tibia make her hind leg too long, which is why she has to resort to this distorted shape of hind limb. Just imagine the amount of ground those hind legs could cover. Her greatest problem will be trying not to kick her

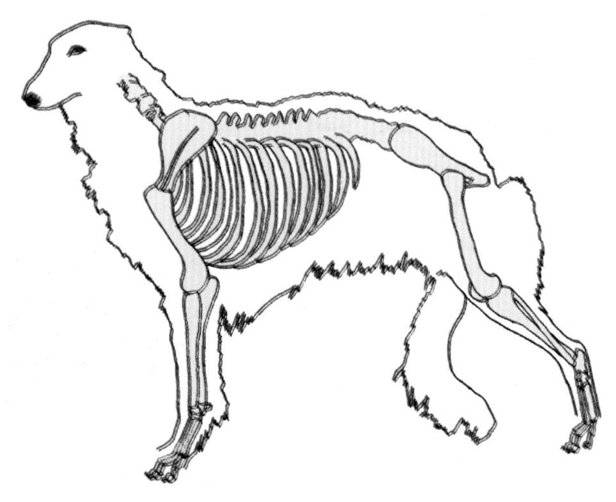

This young bitch has good shoulder construction, but things begin to go wrong behind, putting her out of balance (see page 50–52).

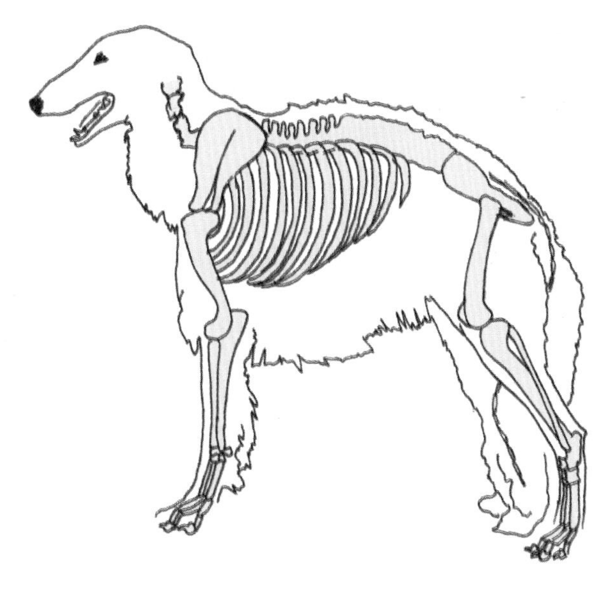

Although this dog has many faults fore and aft, it is in balance.

front legs. This unbalanced structure will probably lead to lameness in later life.

The Borzoi shown on this page is tortoiseshell and white, a form of sable, in colour. This dog has faulty shoulders with a faulty neck. The upper line of the neck is shorter than the lower line of the neck. Indeed, the neck dips as it joins the shoulders. This is called a *ewe neck* but, as most people are more familiar with the neck of a camel than of a sheep, the term *camel neck* would probably be more readily understood.

The neck, as part of the incorrect shoulder assembly, is also faulty. Both the scapula and the humerus are too vertical. With an almost vertical humerus there can be little movement of the humerus to the vertical, as happens when the dog takes a step forward. If the front leg cannot move forward, the dog will have very limited front extension. A vertical humerus is associated with other faults of front movement. The elbows move all over the place, and with them the radius and ulna. Sometimes a dog with this construction has such a loose front that its front legs cross over, looking as if the dog wants to knit a jumper rather than move forward.

The one point in this dog's favour is that it is balanced, since the hind angulation is just as faulty as the front. All the angles of the hind assembly are too small, in contrast with the previous bitch. The fall-away is far too steep as well. Lack of flexion in the knee joint in particular will cause the hind legs to take small steps to balance the small steps taken in front. Try walking without bending at the knee – this dog will move in a similar way.

The Borzoi to the right has good 'normal dog' construction. It will have good movement because it has good shoulder, elbow, hip and knee angulation. However, its construction is 'normal dog' so it will move more like a Labrador than a Borzoi. Borzoi construction is completely missing: the topline is flat and there is no fall-away. Finally, the head is very ugly and quite alien to the Borzoi breed.

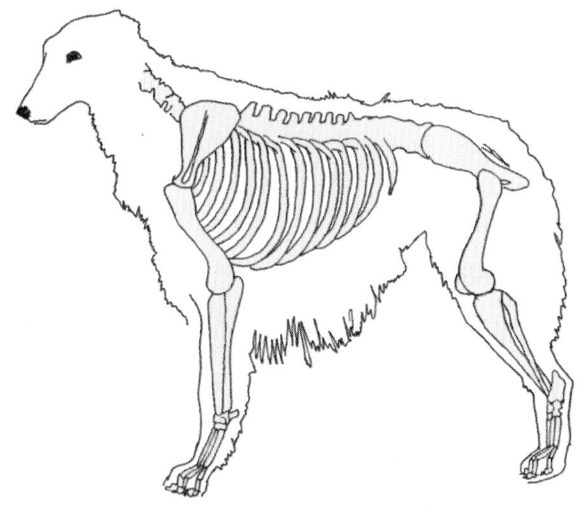

Although this Borzoi has good 'normal dog' construction and would move well, the typical Borzoi construction is completely missing.

Colour

Perhaps it is a good idea to say a little about colour. The Kennel Club Breed Standard states *any colour acceptable,* but Borzoi colours are not always described in the same way as for other breeds.

Kennel Club forms are filled in when the puppies are very small, and strange changes in colour can occur as they grow up. This can lead to some misleading descriptions.

Red and white

The colour most usually found in a Borzoi is white with red markings.

Black and white

In Borzoi parlance, this means mainly white with black patches, plus tan shading on eyebrows, chest and legs; this is not a tri-colour.

Self

If the colour is by far greater than the white the dog is recorded as a 'self'.

A dog that is self black is nearly all black, with a small amount of white, and tan eyebrows, chest and leg shading in the colour scheme of a Dobermann. Again, the Borzoi purist objects very strongly when a dog of this colour is described as *tri-colour*.

Brindle

Brindle is described in The Kennel Club's *Glossary of Canine Terms* as *a fine even mixture of black hairs with hairs of a lighter colour, usually gold, brown or grey, usually in stripes.* Up until the 1950s it was very popular to register dogs as brindle when they were not. Ch Eglon of Rydens and many of his children were registered as brindle when it is clear from their photographs they were white with red markings and a black mask. Probably they had some sable shading of the type that can be seen in the colour photograph of Ch Stonebar Sebastian (chapter 3 page 121). Many of the Addlestone and Bransgore dogs were registered as brindle when in fact they were sable with extensive white spotting. This colour is now called *tortoiseshell and white.*

The brindle gene was imported in the 1960s through Miss Murray's Sunbarr Invader of Fortrouge, and then again through Ch Stillwater Virginia Reel. The only true brindle champions descend from Virginia Reel, most often from her son Sholwood Stars'n'Stripes.

British Show History

Dog illustrated

I have decided to approach British show history in reverse, going from the dogs of today back to the original importations. In this way I can concentrate on those dogs in today's pedigrees. Breed history is important, not just because it is interesting to hear the stories of chance, luck and careful planning that left us with the breed as it stands today; it is important to know as much as possible about the dogs in a pedigree. A pedigree is a very important piece of paper. Unfortunately, when most pet owners collect their puppy, they say, 'Very nice, thank you!' as they shove the pedigree certificate into a back pocket. It should not be just a list of names; it should be a list of key words to jog your memory as to the structure, character and idiosyncrasies of the dogs mentioned.

Looking at the pedigree, it should be possible to see how certain characteristics have been inherited: the splodge of white on one side of the muzzle or that missing tooth. A good idea of how characteristics are being passed on helps to plan the next generation of puppies.

I have chosen a number of dogs and followed their pedigrees back through certain lines to the foundation stock from Russia. It would have been lovely to follow back all lines, but that was technically impossible in book form. Even with the lines chosen, you will see the same names repeated again and again, for the Borzoi gene pool is very small.

Ch Yadasar Huckleberry Horace

I shall start with Ch Yadasar Huckleberry Horace, who descends in male line from Ch Colhugh Clangers, the male breed record holder for Challenge Certificates (CCs) and a dog in almost every British pedigree. Clangers is on both sides of the pedigree. This mating had been planned well in advance, for he had been introduced into Mrs Ann Tomlinson's Yadasar line as grandsire of Yadasar Black Angel before being reintroduced through Ch Olias Oberon.

Horace won his first CC in 1992 at Paignton Show, when the judge, Mrs Sheila Ridge-Reeves, commented: *Self black, this dog put everything he had into showing, never once did he put a foot wrong. Super quality masculine hound, extremely well balanced, beautifully balanced head, good reach of neck, excellent front and body, well let down hind quarters, his movement was*

Ancestors of Ch Yadasar Huckleberry Horace

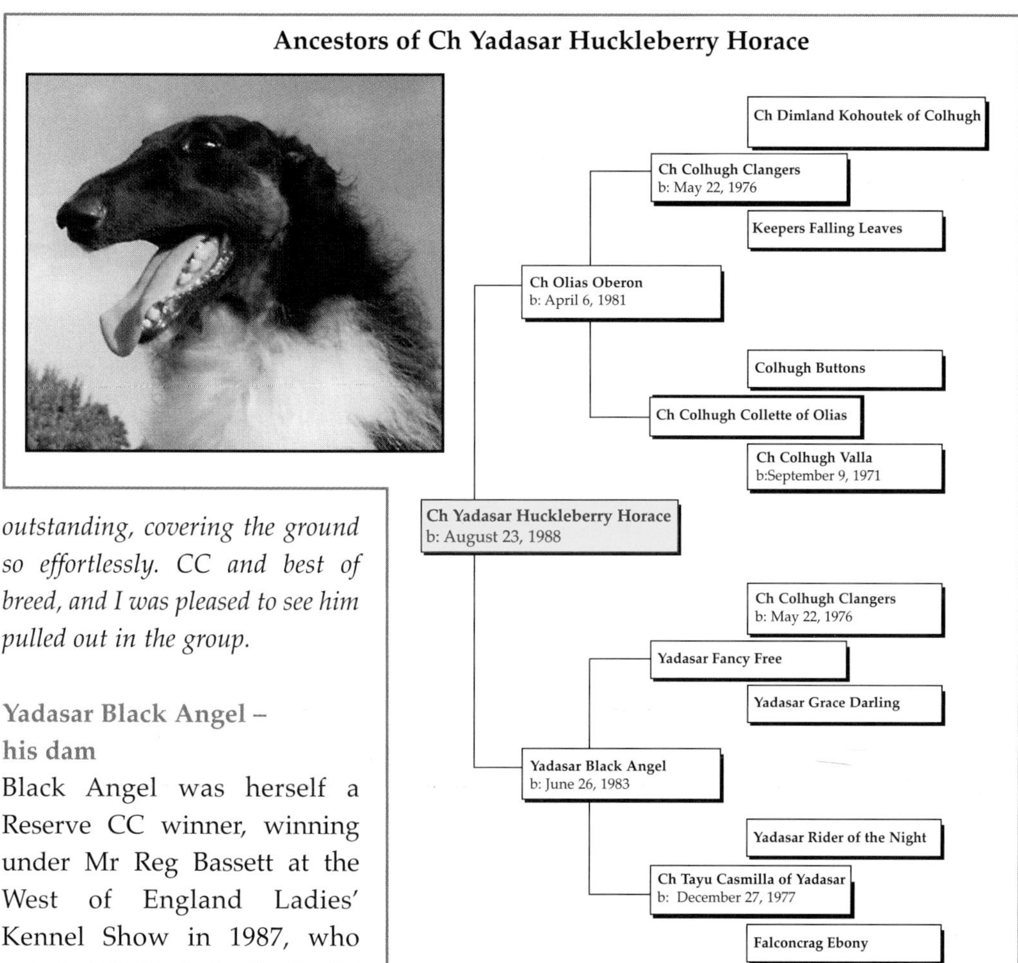

outstanding, covering the ground so effortlessly. CC and best of breed, and I was pleased to see him pulled out in the group.

Yadasar Black Angel – his dam

Black Angel was herself a Reserve CC winner, winning under Mr Reg Bassett at the West of England Ladies' Kennel Show in 1987, who noted: *Self black, lovely headed bitch, nice neck and shoulder, very good depth of body, superb back end, beautifully presented, moved nicely.*

The mating of Black Angel to Oberon produced two champions, Horace himself and Miss Pat Harris' Ch Yadasar Huckleberry Friend, as well as Yadasar Bizzie Lizzie of Olias, winner of two CCs.

Ch Olias Oberon – his sire

Owned and bred by Mr and Mrs Mabey, Oberon won 15 CCs, three of them at Crufts. In 1984 and 1985 he was Best of Breed (BOB) at Crufts. Mrs Betty Hargraves, the judge in 1984, wrote: *Gained his crown today, and well deserved it, very well constructed with great depth of brisket, gentle topline and strong wide quarters, which he used well, never put a foot wrong, well handled and beautifully presented.*

Oberon's dam, Ch Colhugh Collette of Olias, was the foundation bitch of the Olias kennel, and will be discussed further under her mother, Ch Colhugh Valla (see page 95).

Ch Olias Oberon.

Ch Colhugh Clangers – his grandsire

Mr Reg Bassett's home-bred Ch Colhugh Clangers won 32 CCs from 1977 to 1983. The three CCs for his title came from the junior class, a rare event in this slow-growing breed, and the first was gained at Blackpool under Mr G Harrison. The judge's report ran: *Handsome red boy, lovely head and body shape, moved well. I think that this is about the best this owner has bred.*

Ch Colhugh Clangers.

The next show was Windsor, with Mr Fred Curnow judging. He gave Clangers Best of Breed, saying: *Beautiful matured, upstanding youngster, lovely head surmounting a very good reach of neck flowing into well placed shoulders, excellent outline, deep in brisket, correct bladed bone, very good feet, was shown in hard muscular condition, moved freely.*

Clangers' dam was the self red bitch Keepers Falling Leaves, from Mrs Bennett-Heard's Keepers kennel, which bred dogs of a finer mould than the imposing red and whites that had previously typified the Colhugh line of Mr Bassett.

Ch Dimland Kohoutek of Colhugh

Kohoutek was bred by Mr Graham Hill and owned by Mr Bassett. He was a mahogany and white like his son Clangers, and also like his own sire, Ch Wellthornes Tilosky.

The three CCs that Kohoutek won for his title came in 1975 and 1976. Breed specialist Mrs Julia Curnow gave him his first, saying: *Red and white, really beautiful dog, superb body, good strong hindquarters, turn of stifle, good head and eye. When he gets his full coat he should really go places.*

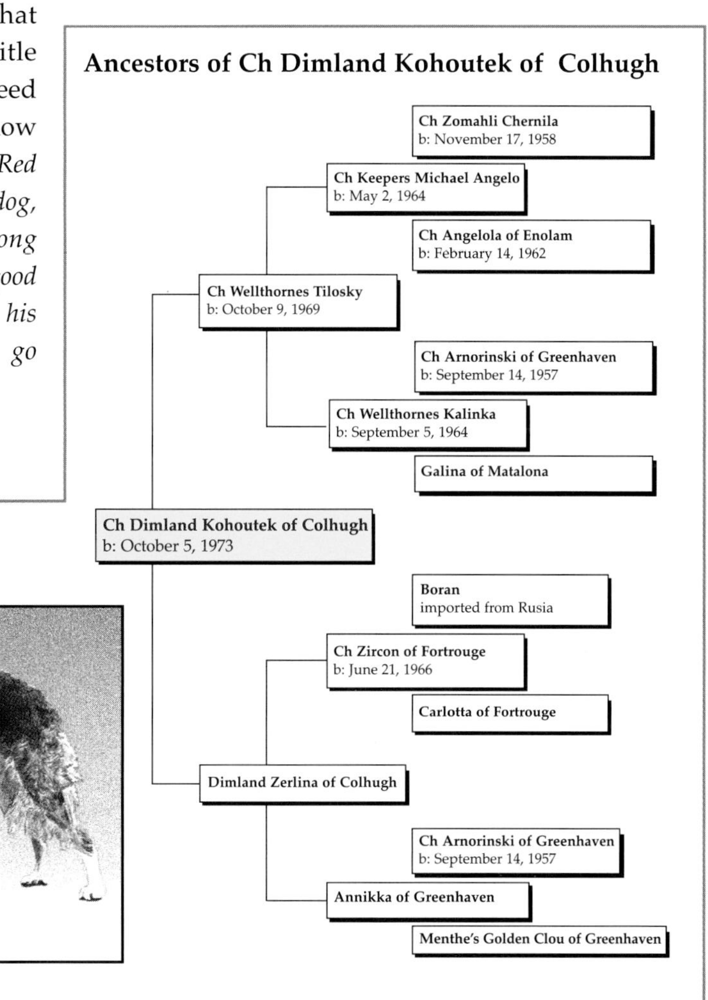

Dimland Zerlina of Colhugh – his dam

Dimland Zerlina of Colhugh had a very interesting pedigree. She was a daughter of Mr Bassett's Colhugh foundation bitch, Annikka of Greenhaven (discussed further under Ch Colhugh Valla), but her sire was the champion son of a Soviet import.

In 1964, at the British Agricultural exhibition in Moscow, Sir Rudi Sternberg presented a Border Collie to the Soviet Premier, Mr Nikita Kruchev, after an exhibition of the dogs at work. Mr Kruchev was so delighted that he gave Sir Rudi a dog described as 'the best in Russia', and this was the Borzoi Boran (see page 76), a prize-winning dog, holding a gold medal and being assessed as 'excellent'. Boran was very important as a dog of Russian bloodlines coming into Great Britain at the height of the Cold War, when normal channels would have allowed neither his importation nor his registration at The Kennel Club. He was a dog of such quality that it would have been impossible to have obtained him without the leader of the country deciding that he was to be exported.

The first person to realise the potential of this new arrival was Miss Betty Murray of the Fortrouge kennel. It was a gamble that could have gone wrong, for nothing was known in Great Britain of Boran's pedigree. Miss Murray took her dual-CC-winning Carlotta of Fortrouge to Boran and bred a litter of 10 in 1965. This litter included Ch Matalona Sudorka of Fortrouge. The mating was repeated in 1966, giving two champions this time: Ch Zest of Fortrouge and Ch Zircon of Fortrouge. Ch Zircon subsequently became the sire of Dimland Zerlina of Colhugh. Boran was also used by Mrs Bennett-Heard, producing Ch Reyas Keepers Kwango and Ch Keepers The Baron when mated to Ch Angelola of Enolam.

Ch Angelola of Enolam.

Ch Angelola of Enolam – his great-granddam

Ch Angelola of Enolam also appears in the pedigree of Kohoutek. Like Annikka of Greenhaven, this beautiful bitch, bred by Mrs Peggy Malone, could be called the Queen Victoria of the Borzoi breed because of the number of champions she produced and, more importantly, the champions they produced.

Angelola, a self black owned by Mrs Bennett-Heard, was the granddam of Kohoutek's sire Ch Wellthornes Tilosky. In 1964 she won the bitch CC at Crufts under Mrs Grace Beresford, who was Secretary of the Borzoi Club for many years and founder of the Yadasar kennel that has been continued by her daughter, Ann Tomlinson. Mrs Beresford wrote: *Ch Angelola of Enolam, a real picture, beautiful, refined head, almond eye, neat ears, lovely compact and balanced body, true front and hindquarters, in spot on coat and condition, free action, I had no hesitation in awarding her the CC and Best of Breed.*

Ch Keepers Michael Angelo – his grandsire

Angelola was the dam of five champions, of whom perhaps the best was Ch Keepers Michael Angelo. All his CCs came in 1969, the second from Mr Robin Searle at Blackpool, who commented: *Lovely self black dog who has now come into his own. I do like this dog's hind action, excels in thrust and soundness, lovely depth of brisket, in beautiful coat and condition. CC and Best of Breed.*

Mrs Malone gave him his title at the Hound Association Show, saying: *Great size and substance, in magnificent coat and condition, beautifully handled. I was pleased to award him his third CC.*

Ch Wellthornes Tilosky – his sire

When mated to the 1969 Crufts Best of Breed winner, Mrs Thornewell's home-bred Ch Wellthornes Kalinka, Michael Angelo sired Ch Wellthornes Tilosky, who was piloted to his 12 CC wins by Mr Bassett, and became the sire of Kohoutek.

Mrs Curnow started Tilosky on the trail for his title, as she later did for Kohoutek. The first CC was awarded at the Birmingham National Show in 1972, when she noted: *Self red, in profuse coat and excellent condition, good head with dark eyes, stands, moves and covers ground on correct legs and feet. CC and Best of Breed.*

Ch Wellthornes Tilosky.

His second came from Mrs Betty Hargrave at Paignton that year, where she wrote: *Self red masculine hound in lovely bloom. Grand head, good front and shoulder, well sprung rib cage giving plenty of heart and lung room, correct bladed bone. Looks as though he would enjoy hunting wolves. CC and Best of Breed.*

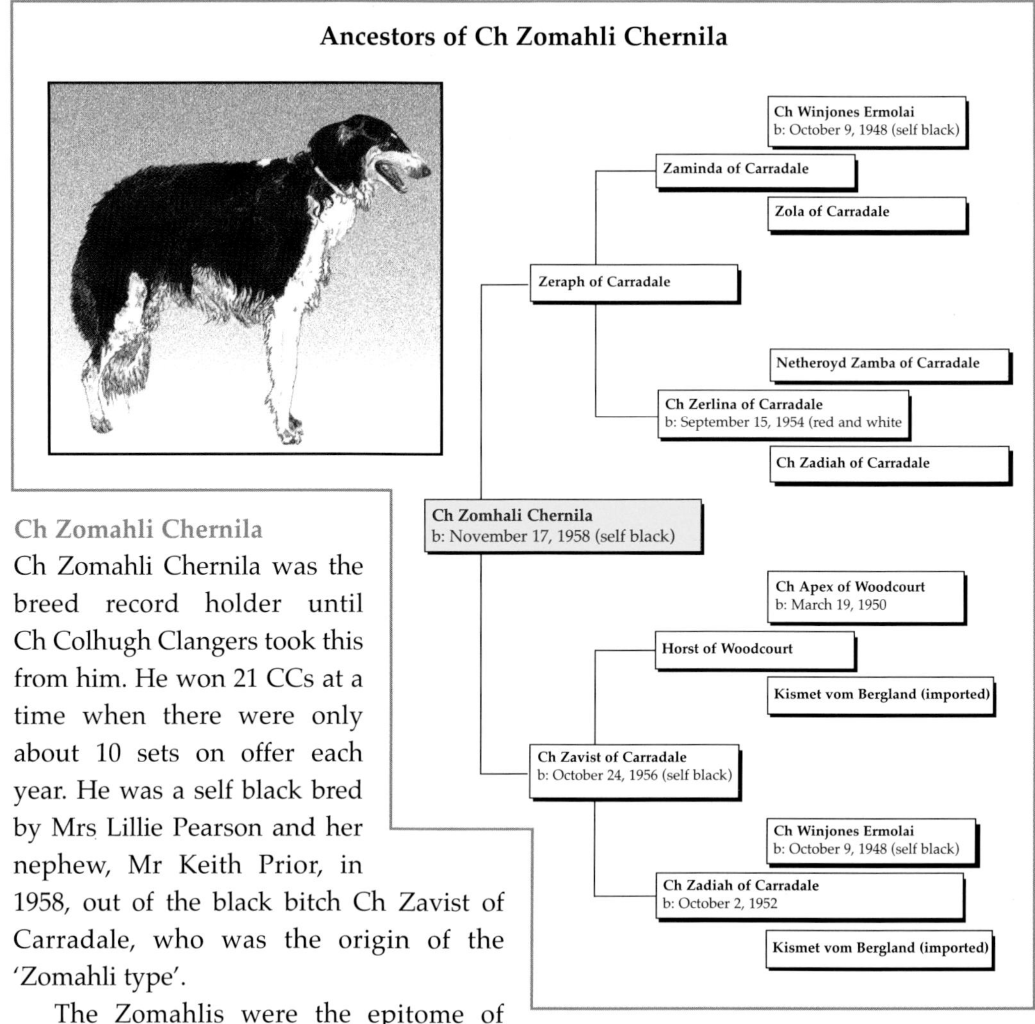

Ch Zomahli Chernila

Ch Zomahli Chernila was the breed record holder until Ch Colhugh Clangers took this from him. He won 21 CCs at a time when there were only about 10 sets on offer each year. He was a self black bred by Mrs Lillie Pearson and her nephew, Mr Keith Prior, in 1958, out of the black bitch Ch Zavist of Carradale, who was the origin of the 'Zomahli type'.

The Zomahlis were the epitome of Northern British Borzoi type, typified by their outstanding movement, correct bladed bone and exquisite shape. Most were self black, and their tan was often a pale, peachy colour rather than the tan of a Dobermann. Having hind legs with white right up to the stifle joint was another Zomahli colour feature.

The first litter was bred by Mrs Pearson alone in 1948, and this included a champion, Ch Netheroyd Zomahli Alexey, who was owned by Mrs Ida Abson (later Mrs Morton). Netheroyd was famous in Afghan circles too, the Afghan Ch Netheroyd Alibaba winning Reserve Best in Show at Crufts in 1953. Even today there are several championship show judges based in the north of England who, having bred very successful Afghans, judge the Borzoi. Mrs Van Schaick has the honour of breeding both Borzoi and Afghan Hound champions. The first Borzoi champion she bred, Ch Call Me Madam of Enolam, had a Netheroyd champion great-granddam.

Alexey won two Hound Groups in 1949, at the Southern Counties Show and then again at the Altringsham Championship Show, where he came through although there were no CCs on offer for Borzoi.

All the Zomahli litters were named in alphabetical order, so it was just in the third Zomahli litter that the breed record holder was bred. The first of Chernila's 21 CCs was won at Birmingham National Show at the end of 1960, with the breed specialist Mr Edgar Sayer adjudicating. He wrote of Chernila: *Really good hound all through, has size and a grand body, well ribbed up of great girth, good coat and condition, moved well particularly in front, we want more dogs with the power and substance of this one, I could find no real fault anywhere, outstanding today and a real pleasure to handle.*

Mr Fred Curnow, husband of Julia Curnow who liked Tilosky and Kohoutek, judged at Crufts 1961, where Chernila gained his title. He noted: *Tremendous improvements in this dog since I last saw him, has matured, completely masculine, solid deep body, glorious coat, very good head and neck flowing into correct shoulders and topline, well developed and nicely angulated quarters, bladed bone, very good feet, easy yet definite gait.*

In 1962 there were only 11 sets of CCs on offer for Borzoi and Chernila won eight of the dog ones.

Ch Zavist of Carradale.

Ch Zavist of Carradale – his dam

Ch Zavist of Carradale was a very important brood bitch for the Zomahlis. She was bred by Mr Hawkin and Miss Sylvia Hawkin and, when mated to Zeraph of Carradale, she produced Chernila, the first home-bred, home-owned champion.

The Carradale kennel was started in the 1930s, going back to a self blue Dutch import of racy style called Ivan Ivanovitch. Mrs Winifred Chadwick of the Winjones kennel, wrote of Ivan: *Ivan was only shown once or twice before he died, people had a feeling that he had Deerhound in him, I should say quite untrue. He was a dark blue coloured self, wonderful hindquarters and I think that he only sired one or two litters owing to his early death after coming out of quarantine.*

Ivan appears in pedigrees through his son, Arncliffe Alexis, a self red born in 1924. Alexis was from a litter of eight, and he was built like his sire. He had a lovely head, dark eyes and the Borzoi expression that is so much desired but not often seen. His contour from his occiput to hindquarters was beautiful, and all who saw him at his first show when he was not one year old felt he was a real flyer. The first show was Birmingham, and he won three firsts and was only beaten by the CC winner.

The line is through Alexis' son Petroff of Beechwood, a dual-CC-winner, described as *a brilliant self red with white feet and a white tipped tail. A good big one with lovely balance.*

He was the reason the Miss Diana Atkinson came into the Borzoi breed to start the Tangmere kennel. She did not fall for his beauty or elegance because the first time she saw him he was in a very sorry state. At this time (he was born in 1925) self colours were not very highly thought of, and he was soaked to the skin and very dirty. He had been the victim of a bad 'beating up', having been set upon by a pack of dogs and mauled very badly.

He came to the door of the house where she was staying and asked for admittance during a terrific thunderstorm but it was denied him. She spent a sleepless night and the next day he became ill from his bites. She bought the dog and took him home and nursed him through blood poisoning. Through all this he never lost his gentleness, his dignity and above all his 'gentlemanliness'. He was in great pain and gave no trouble and never whimpered. He won the hearts of her family and the veterinary surgeon.

She was just eighteen and since then has bred, owned and handled very many Borzoi, nearly all of them descendants of her first orphan of the storm.

In the 1930s Miss Atkinson went into partnership with Mr F W George, whom she subsequently married. The Tangmeres were characterised by self white coats that had what was described as *an ethereal luminous aura,* though the very first self black champion, made up in 1934, was a Tangmere: Ch Achilles of Tangmere.

The first self black champion bitch was Mr Richardson's Ch Nigerette, born in 1937, a daughter of Achilles. Self-coloured dogs were actively discriminated against at this time. The Kennel Club did not take on responsibility for breed standards until after the war, and the Borzoi Breed Standard was produced by the Borzoi Club. This Standard stated that, if two hounds were of equal merit, the white and colour hound should be placed above the self-coloured hound. In continental Europe, self colour was a disqualification, as it had been in the United States.

Miss Atkinson first awarded CCs at Harrogate in 1938. She wrote: *I am very grateful to those who supported me so very sportingly with entries on my first effort at a Championship show. Though not exactly a newcomer to the ring as judge I always find it a thrilling and interesting experience to go over the exhibits, and this time the occasion was of greater interest than usual on account of the presence of Challenge Certificates for the breed. I looked forward to Harrogate greatly. That it is a responsibility to give Challenge Certificates, and so state that you consider an exhibit is worthy of the title of champion, cannot be denied, and it is a task that one can't enter into lightly or without any sense of obligation due to the breed as well as to exhibitors. One has to consider so many factors when signing a declaration on a Challenge Certificate. I think some do not fully appreciate the importance of this. The competition was very hot in all classes except puppy. Nine kennels exhibited, represented by 15 hounds, making a total of 30 entries.*

One of Miss Atkinson's entries was Nigerette, of whom she wrote: *A self black with cream points, she is aged about two years, and this is her first show. Bought for a pet she developed so well that her owner decided to try her luck in the ring. She won this class and the next with a good deal in hand. She is one of the best bitches I have seen for a long time, and quite the best self bitch, as I had never seen her before I found her very interesting, she is wonderfully shapely and short coupled, and is of very excellent type; very good head, long lean and balanced; dark eyes that are well set and of correct shape; very small ears that she carries well; reachy neck and excellent shoulders; her arch starts in the correct place and is good, no exaggeration about it and very good fall-away to the quarters; she had good depth of brisket and well sprung ribs; nice loins and very broad quarters; she has a nice bend of stifle and appears sound all through; she moves well; I eventually put her back because I considered her not so well let down in hock as she might be, or rather there seemed a slight stiffness in movement of them; also she is not quite up enough on her pasterns; it was not weakness in either case, and I felt it was something that time will correct; she gave me the impression that she had not been out much of late and was not 'up on her toes', in a temporary sense only; afterwards I was told that she had been laid up till quite recently with a poisoned leg; she carries a superb coat of glossy and silky texture; I am sure she will go a very long way and win very well indeed.*

The third post-war champion was the veteran Ch Zavan of Carradale, who gained his title in 1948 having been born in 1938, the only Borzoi born pre-war to win a post-war title. The Carradale kennel was responsible for nine champions, from Zavan's sire Ch Zakar of Carradale in 1938 to Ch Zarah of Carradale who was made up in 1962.

Zavist won her first CC in 1958 from Mrs B Ellis, who felt that she was an *outstanding bitch, natural outline, very compact body, deep brisket, well balanced head, dark oblique eyes, good legs, feet, moved very freely, I hope that she will still grow on, I was glad to have the chance of picking this winner.*

Horst of Woodcourt - his grandsire

Horst of Woodcourt was bred by Mr and Mrs Curnow from their champion dog Ch Apex of Woodcourt out of Kismet von Bergland, a German import. The Curnows also exported and, during the 1950s, Woodcourt dogs formed the foundation of the boost to the breed in Sweden.

In 1952, Apex's sister, Ch Aureola of Woodcourt, was the first Borzoi to be in the last few considered for Best In Show at Crufts. Until 1957 the Group system was not in operation at this show, and the show was held over two days. All the Best of Breed winners from the first day competed together for Best in Show winner for that day and a Reserve Best In Show. The Best In Show winner on the first day then competed with the Best In Show on the second day for the ultimate top award. In 1952 Aureola was Reserve Best In Show on the first day.

The Woodcourt Borzois were Mrs Curnow's love; her husband had the Tavey Dobermanns, the most successful kennel of the era. The first Dobermann champion was a Tavey, and she went on to be the breed's first Group winner. The first Best In Show winner at championship level was also a Tavey – in fact nine Tavey Dobermanns won Groups or above.

Frau Hanne Muller first registered her von Bergland affix in 1936. Her home was on a great lake by the Alps in a mountainous area – *bergland* or mountainland. She began with a dog called Granat Ural, and her foundation bitch was the granddaughter of a Russian-bred bitch. Another leading European kennel was Rasswet, brought to a tragic end by a kennel fire, and Kismet von Bergland was a daughter of Rasswet's Fanal.

Ch Winjones Ermolai

The Winjones kennel was owned by Mrs Winifred Chadwick, the author of one of the few books on the breed, published in 1952. Her husband was a keen photographer and they exhibited at most of the championship shows, taking many photographs of the hounds in the ring. Mr Chadwick made up albums of each year's photographs, annotated with the names and placings of the dogs, making these very valuable documents indeed. Some cynics said that he took pictures of his wife's dogs in perfect show stance and of the dogs in 'opposition' from unfortunate angles!

One of Mrs Chadwick's early favourites was a bitch from the 1920s, a daughter of Ivan Ivanovitch, whom she described as *a self bitch with only a spot of white toes, tail tip and spot on chest. She was never much good from a show standard being rather long and not enough depth, a lovely head and wonderful hindquarters and she jumped in the most graceful way; any height, going like a swan and quite beautiful. She went everywhere with me and I never had her on a leash (not much traffic in those far off days). She was Winjones Ladybird and her call name was Meg. I have never loved another Borzoi like her.*

Ermolai won his second CC from Mrs Vlasto, whose Addlestone kennel was the top producer of champions until overtaken by the Colhughs in the 1990s. Judging at the Ladies Kennel Association (LKA) Show in 1950, Mrs Vlasto wrote of Ermolai: *A black with light points, lovely head with very dark eye, sound and beautiful. If only he had more substance and better spring of ribs he would be a flyer, I certainly think that he is improving, seemed less listless than when I saw him last, he went on to win the CC.*

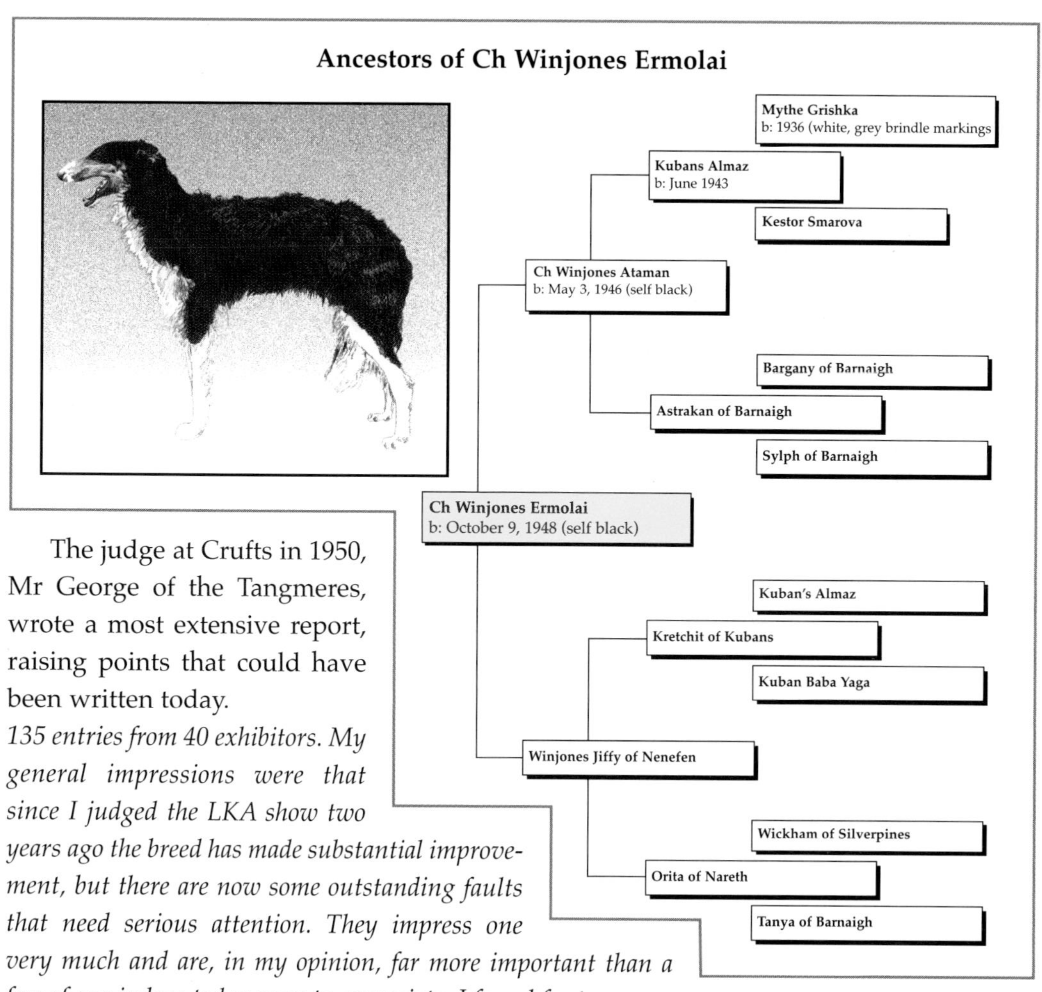

The judge at Crufts in 1950, Mr George of the Tangmeres, wrote a most extensive report, raising points that could have been written today.

135 entries from 40 exhibitors. My general impressions were that since I judged the LKA show two years ago the breed has made substantial improvement, but there are now some outstanding faults that need serious attention. They impress one very much and are, in my opinion, far more important than a few of our judges today seem to appreciate. I found far too many exhibits with bad shoulders, too straight and set too far forward. This is not only structurally wrong but it makes the dog's front and movement bad. Short necks are too frequent.

Eyes need careful attention. A Borzoi must have a dark eye; it should be almond or oblique in shape. I have heard light coloured eyes excused by the colouring of the dogs. Pre-war we had the same colourings, on the whole, as today, but light eyes were not so frequent, nor do I remember anyone suggesting that a dog should be forgiven this fault because of its particular pigmentation elsewhere. Those who minimise the importance of a dark eye or try to pass lightness off as in keeping with the rest of a dog's colouring, do the breed a great disservice. Unfortunately, there are so many dogs today with light eyes that one has to place some which pre-war would have been left right out on account of this. Students of the breed will no doubt appreciate this more than those who have but recently taken up the Borzoi.

Another bad fault I found in exhibits was movement. Unfortunately we had a pitifully small ring, so that it was hard to get the hounds extended in action, but bad movement was so prevalent that I was at a loss to find the true cause. I am of the opinion that it is in many cases due to the fact that present day exhibitors do not seem to take their dogs off the bench and run them round to loosen them up as we did in the old days. They get their hounds clean on arrival, and leave them on the bench, then take them straight to the class with no chance to limber up. These days there is often no bedding (before the war the shows provided straw on the benches for the dogs to lie on) and I see hounds lying on hard boards, and I do not wonder that they are stiff when they get into the ring. Apart from this, the over-straight shoulders spoil the action of any dog, and some are not sound at all behind. This in some cases is due, no doubt, to the illness that so many have suffered since the coming of hard pad. But an unsound dog or one that is bad in movement must pay the penalty. Too many folk these days do not see their own hounds move; if they did they might appreciate this point better. A dog that runs free will move better than when it is on the leash, so it is no good to judge one's hounds by their movement when free at home. Watch them on a leash with someone else.

Arches starting too far back were another fault I consider needs attention, and do not poke your dogs up in the middle like camels. A Borzoi should not have a hump back. A gentle rise that is scarcely noticeable, then a strong, firm fall-away down to strong quarters is what is needed. A humped back dog cannot gallop nor can it extend itself to get the necessary freedom of movement to cover the ground as these dogs should.

Mid limit dog *(12 entries) First Winjones Ermolai, a self black and tan with light points, 16 months, outstanding type and quality, at a difficult age, being all legs and wings as it were, but his undoubted excellence cannot be denied. Beautiful head and expression, I have heard much criticism against him but I could find no cause for it, sound but like many of the shy types, will not extend himself in the ring, and when one goes to handle him he 'tucks up' and flinches, moves nicely, though one could wish he covered more ground in the process, but we had a poor ring and he behaved as do many highly strung hounds; I consider that on maturity he should be an outstanding specimen.*

Open dog *(14 entries) This was a particularly stiff class and any one of the first five dogs' places could very well be reversed in order upon another occasion, as so little can alter one's opinion.*

First; CC also best of breed, Ch Winjones Ataman, self black and tan, light points, one of the outstanding dogs of the breed, he is now nearly four years old and I gave him his first certificate in 1947, but I consider him a better dog today, a long, fleeting gait, so much a part of the true Borzoi, and combines grace with substance and the correct bladed bone. I have seen him go down several times in the past year, but on those occasions he was undoubtedly not at his best and this may have been caused by his having started his career as a stud dog which so often seems to upset big breeds for a time, both in condition and movement; now he is looking superb, perfect eyes both for colour and shape, the true oblique or almond shaped eye of dark hue (the Borzoi with a light eye is bad, and today many have round eyes as well, which is even worse); this dog has great depth of brisket and excellent heart room, a good arch and grand fall-away to good strong quarters; to be hyper-critical he could be tighter in pasterns. He should do the breed good, a hound to be proud of.

Second Winjones Ermolai, son of the winner and should soon equal him.

Astrakan of Barnaigh – his granddam

After the Second World War Mrs Chadwick obtained the bitch Astrakan of Barnaigh from the Scottish breeder Mrs Kathleen McNeil, because she was a self black.

Never were such doubtful motives more generously rewarded, for I not only gained another most devoted companion but on 3 May 1946, at the tail end of a litter by Kubans Almaz arrived a large black pup who was to become Ch Winjones Ataman after being sold to Mrs McNeil at five months of age.

On 9 October 1946 I had bred from Ataman and Winjones Jiffy of Nenfen two self black pups of whom one died, leaving Winjones Ermolai whose path to championship, after acquiring a Junior Warrant, seemed equally inevitable. However, it proved to be strewn with a surprising number of obstacles as this dog was so often a runner-up behind champions, including Crufts, in February 1950, when he was runner-up to his own sire. But the last certificate was safely gathered in at Gloucester, on 13 June 1951, under that most popular authority on Borzois, Mrs B M Ellis.

The purchase of Astrakan was the third time Mrs Chadwick had started to breed Borzois: on the previous two occasions the kennel had been wiped out by distemper. It was not until an effective vaccine against this disease had been developed that she once again began to show, although there was always a pet Borzoi except during the war years when she was unable to keep large dogs.

The very first Winjones were Smooth Fox Terriers, but these had to move over for the Borzois. Mrs Chadwick sent some successful hounds abroad. The first British-bred Borzoi to win Best of Breed at the premier American dog show, the Westminster Kennel Club, was Am Ch Winjones Janda, a win all the more amazing because he was a self black, a colour that was very unfashionable in the United States at that time (1954).

Winjones Jiffy of Nenefen – his dam

Winjones Jiffy of Nenefen (picture page 70) was herself the winner of two Reserve CCs, including one at Southern Counties Show in 1949 under Mr Hawkin (Carradale), who noted: *Bitch of the old type, a good body and quarters, nice neck, good spring of rib, but movement in front did not please me.*

Winjones Jiffy of Nenefen.

Ch Denes Zarina

Few Borzois were born during the war, mainly because of the lack of food. Some of the best stories of dogs during the war are in Buster Lloyd-Jones' book *The Animals Came In One By One.* Mr Lloyd-Jones was the vet who started the Denes pet food company after the war to promote healthy eating for pets. However, he was much less fussy about what his animals ate during food shortages. He was not called up because he had had polio as a child, and he gradually filled his home with large numbers of homeless animals whose previous owners had been bombed out or gone into the forces. Many people had their pets put to sleep because they anticipated the worst. The poor Dachshund, in particular, became a symbol of Nazi Germany and many were put to sleep because it was considered unpatriotic to own one. Mr Lloyd-Jones could not bring himself to destroy healthy young dogs and ended up taking them home. Before long he had 60 Dachshunds, not to mention an assortment of other animals.

Many show dogs were sent abroad, especially to the United States, but others had a much harder time. Mr Lloyd-Jones went to Club Row, an East End market which included dogs, to see if a friend's stolen dog was there. He saw a very bedraggled Smooth Dachshund and, feeling sorry for her, bought her. Once her skin, coat and condition improved he realised what a good-looking bitch she was. A Dachshund breeder dropped in for a chat and recognised her as Tormaid of Loxwood, the CC winner at the LKA in March 1939.

Mr Lloyd-Jones made enquiries to see if she had been stolen, but that was not what had happened. Her owner had dispersed her kennel at the beginning of the war and had given her to her chauffeur. He had been called up and had given her away, and she had been passed on again and again until she ended up on Club Row. Fortunately, she had found a good home for the rest of her life.

A Borzoi champion was bred at Denes: the 1950 Crufts CC winner, Ch Denes Zarina.

Born in 1945, she was a daughter of Ch Winjones Ataman's sire, Kubans Almaz. Her dam was a bitch called Tasha, who made Mr Lloyd-Jones' life difficult:

She was the dumbest of dumb blondes. She would race at a breathtaking speed round and round the paddock, then fly up to you and, where any other would have slowed down and stopped, she would go right on, bowling you over and racing on without any reduction in speed. She was a born hit-and-run driver.

Tasha was a compulsive eater and she was a prodigious jumper and these combined to make constant trouble for me. You would think she was safely shut in but she would gracefully vault a seven foot gate and be away, scouring every rubbish bin between Clymping Dene and Bedfont. You could follow her progress by going from one overturned bin to the next.

Borzois are Russian greyhounds and have barrel chests and tiny waists. This always gives them a hungry look. Again and again I would get a telephone call from a distant house-hold. 'I have a half-starved dog here with your name on its collar,' an angry dog-loving English voice would say, and it would be Tasha who, after being well fed at home, had been gorging herself silly on other people's meagre wartime scraps.

When her time came she chose to whelp in the most alarming place. She had a perfectly good, warm, dry, secluded kennel, but she preferred to have her puppies in the lake. Not on the banks, you understand. In the lake itself.

She waded in, lay down and, her long blonde hair floating like Ophelia's, began to give birth.

One of the kennel maids gave the alarm and we rushed to the water's edge in time to rescue the first, then the second, then the third of the puppies. She had produced five before we got her to the bank and she went on to produce another eight. They were beautiful puppies too, but those first five must be the only Borzois ever to be born underwater.

Tasha appears in the pedigrees through her granddaughter Ch Rydens Destiny of Astonoff, who does not come from the underwater litter but from Tasha's mating to Rodky of Mantavani. Mrs Iona Harris' Mantavani hounds were very important to the post-war revival of the breed. They were a mixture of Tangmere and Mythe bloodlines.

Ch Rydens Destiny of Astonoff was the granddam of Galina of Matalona, who appears in almost every pedigree through her famous daughter Ch Wellthornes Kalinca.

Mythe Grishka

The most important stud dogs of the 1940s were probably Kubans Almaz and his sire Mythe Grishka. The Kubans kennel was active before, during and after the war. It was owned by Mrs Ursula Reed and located in Billericay, Essex, and Almaz and Grishka were its two famous studs. Grishka was a white with grey markings, standing 91.5cm (36in) to the shoulder.

At the Big Breeds Championship Show 1939, Mr C A Jenkins judged, saying of Grishka: *I liked him very much. Beautiful head and expression, in really lovely coat and condition,*

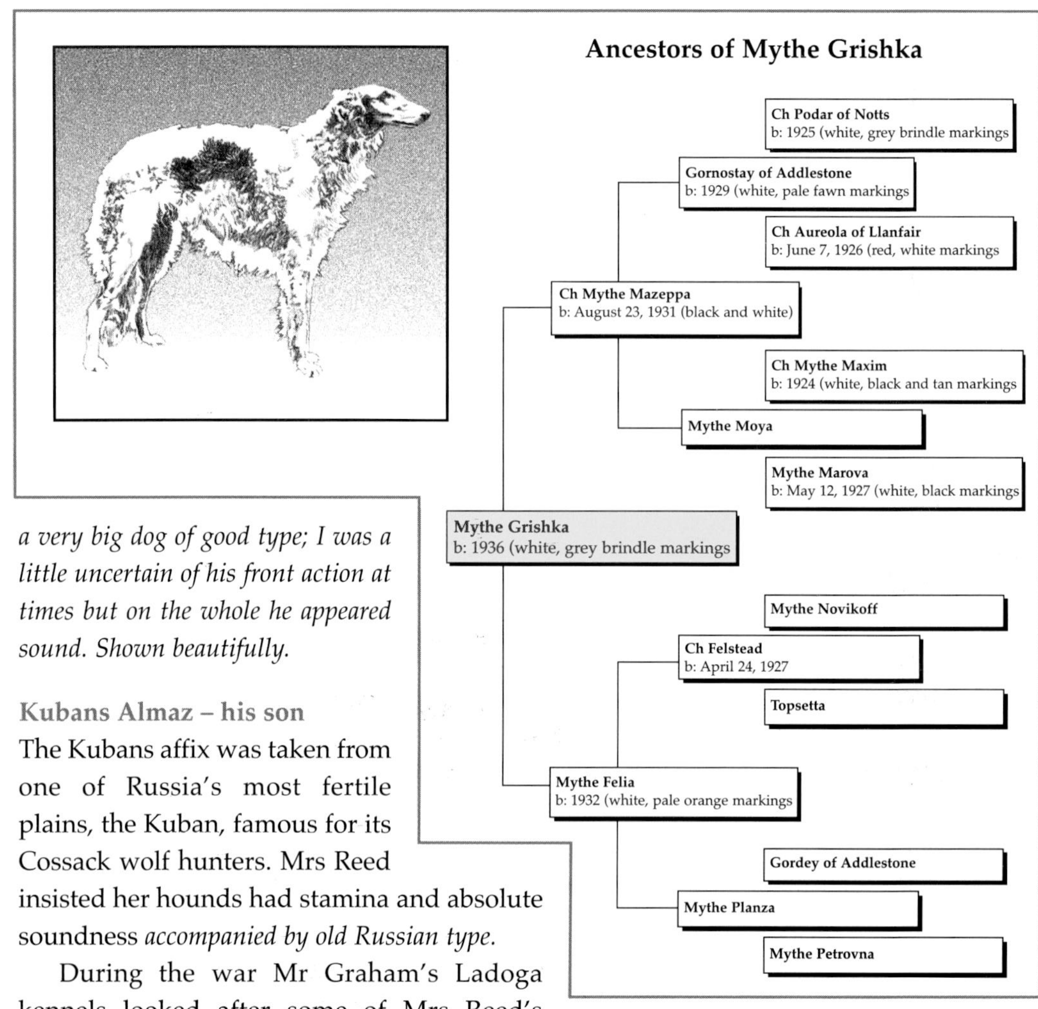

a very big dog of good type; I was a little uncertain of his front action at times but on the whole he appeared sound. Shown beautifully.

Kubans Almaz – his son

The Kubans affix was taken from one of Russia's most fertile plains, the Kuban, famous for its Cossack wolf hunters. Mrs Reed insisted her hounds had stamina and absolute soundness *accompanied by old Russian type.*

During the war Mr Graham's Ladoga kennels looked after some of Mrs Reed's hounds until she could have them again. Mr Graham had German Shepherd Dogs, then called Alsatians, but his wife's housedog was a Borzoi, said to be the first obedience-trained Borzoi in Great Britain! Almaz stood at stud at the Ladoga kennels, siring Ch Ladoga Nalivka, the first post-war bitch champion, out of the bitch Kubans Nadeja.

During the war there was a great shortage of petrol. However, the sale of pedigree puppies abroad had brought a lot of money into the British economy, so the government wanted to keep dog breeding and showing ticking over until peace time. For this reason, some shows were held during the war. These were called *radius shows,* as all the entries had to live within 25 miles of the venue. Nadeja was very successful at radius shows in the London area, *unbeaten in her breed during 1943 and won many best bitch all breeds awards.*

It is hard for us to understand the difficulties war time owners had in feeding one little

Kubans Almaz

dog like a Cocker Spaniel, let alone a kennel full of Borzois. Miss Collett of the Barwick Chow Chows writes: *We occasionally met in one another's homes and entertained on synthetic coffee, dried milk and spam, discussing the war bulletins, our respective kennel activities and food problems.*

Always food!!! It is questionable which had priority – the household or the dogs! And if it was a toss up as to the happy recipient of a cherished rice pudding or a bowl of chicken broth the puppies invariably won.

Later on, when rationing was even more severe, black market transactions were rampant. We had no official allocation of food for our dogs. No definite meat or biscuit rations, and it meant getting hold of a Little Man who knew another Little Man, who perhaps by bribery and corruption would condescend to put one 'on his list' to supplement our erratic deliveries of meat and meal from the original source.

Living in the London area, I found it wiser to have my bulk supplies of these commodities from other ends of the country. Meat from the west of England sent directly by rail. Biscuit meal from the north, and precious, precious oatmeal, on which there was no restriction at all, from Scotland. Milk mercifully presented no problems. I kept a couple of goats at a nearby farm and fetched it daily. Deliveries were uncertain and sometimes long delayed, but the goods always turned up eventually.

I am still teased about my spontaneous answer to a married cousin who was visiting us, complete with a brand new husband and a self satisfied air, during one of the kennel's meatless spells.

'I cannot understand why you don't get married,' she complacently remarked.

'I'd marry a couple of butchers this very minute if I thought it would ensure regular meat for my dogs,' I vehemently answered, spooning a concoction of fish soup, vegetables and meat extract over biscuit meal for suppers, and secretly wondering if I could summon the nerve to wring the necks of our half dozen chickens if need be.

Almaz was the fashionable sire of 1944 and proved his excellence as a sire in a very few years. He was white, very lightly marked with gold-glint red, and was whelped in 1943. He died in 1949, just before the Kuban kennel celebrated 20 years in the breed. His dam was Kestor Smarovna, a half-sister of Kuban Nadeja, both being by Zmarcos of Bransgore.

Ch Mythe Mazeppa – his sire

Ch Mythe Mazeppa was one of the many champions from the Mythe kennel. The three great kennels of the 1930s were the Addlestones, the Bransgores and the Mythes. The Mythe kennel of Miss Edith Robinson was one of the most important in the history of the breed, and her hounds were known for their outstanding heads. The Mythes were started before the turn of the 20th century and were based in Tewkesbury in the west of England.

Miss Murray, whose Fortrouge kennel was founded in the 1930s, wrote of the Mythes: *By the time that I knew Miss Robinson she had moved to Taunton. She was probably the best handler I have ever seen. Her hounds were obviously well trained at home. She would stand quietly beside her exhibit with a loose lead in one hand. Occasionally she would glance down at her exhibit's feet. If she was not satisfied, her foot would move out and the leg would move back to the required position. Her hounds had very good temperaments and she could kennel several adult males together without any fear of troubles. She seldom accepted any judging appointments. Rumour had it that she received some adverse criticism for her decisions and decided that she would be happier in her showing career if she restricted it to exhibiting only.*

The Mythe Borzois were probably the most easily identified strain of all time. Many in the breed felt confident to say, on seeing a Borzoi in the ring, 'That is a Mythe Borzoi', and they were usually correct. The characteristics which made them easy to recognise were their deep chests and overall strength, with sound well positioned legs, with good angulation both of shoulders and stifles, and the resultant good movement which this construction helps to produce. They had good textured coats with very adequate fringes. Not the profusion which is seen in some modern day exhibits (1990s) and which can be imagined on a wet day's hunting would produce an unprintable stream of swear words from those serfs employed to keep a large kennel of hunting hounds clean.

Mr Guy wrote of Mazeppa at the LKA Show in 1936: *A very worthy champion, today better than ever. I understand it is 18 months since his last show, moved with such freedom that only a dog enjoying life can show. He is very compact, full of type hound, medium size, one of the nearest perfect Borzois in the fancy today, shown to perfection.*

Miss Murray considered him among the greatest Borzoi ever when asked in the early 1990s, but did mention the rather unusual fill-in under his eyes, *rather like a Bull Terrier. He reproduced it once in Ch Miss Mazeppa of Barnaigh, but it carried the risk with it of being undershot. It was his other excellent physical characteristics which gained him his championship, his great presence and beautiful balance between fore and hind quarters. He had a well angulated shoulder, matched with the correct amount of angulation behind with how hocks. Deep roomy chest. Dark eyes, strong jaw, proud head carriage, a good mover with a very nice temperament.*

Originally two Robinson sisters had the kennel: Miss Edith who exhibited the dogs and Miss Violet, *who was of a retiring nature, but had a gift for rearing puppies.* Mr Guy, who did not have an affix but named his hounds after leading race horses, lived nearby and had several Mythe hounds. His Ch Fet was the litter sister of Ch Mythe Molva and Ch

Mythe Marinsky. His post-war stud dog Challenge, sire of three champions that were made up in 1948, was of pure Mythe bloodlines. On the death of Miss Edith Robinson, Mr Guy published a book of photographs of her hounds as a memorial.

The Mythe bitch line went back to the first Mythe champion, Ch Mythe Mischa, born in 1905, and the best stud dogs were used. This bitch line descended from old English lines, the lines from the original Russian imports of the 1880s.

Ch Mythe Mazeppa.

Mythe Moya – his granddam

Mythe Moya was the product of a brother to sister mating. Mrs Harpur of the Barthill kennel described her as: *A beauty, all curves but was never shown as she fell playing in a muddy orchard and broke her hip. It set naturally, but she was never sound. A lovely type. I used to stay with Miss Robinson, and it happened the day before I arrived for a visit. Moya lay on a cushion for weeks until the hip mended.*

Gornostay of Addlestone – his grandsire

Moya was mated to Gornostay of Addlestone, from Mrs Vlasto's hugely successful kennel, to produce Ch Mythe Mazeppa, often considered the greatest of all the Mythes. Gornostay was Mrs Vlasto's personal companion and lived in the house, sleeping on a couch in his mistress' bedroom. His show career was cut short by a broken leg, but Mrs Vlasto considered him her best ever, and he was remarkable for his outstandingly charming disposition and quite exceptional intelligence. He was known as a wonderful guard because of the following story: *One night, while the family was at dinner Gornostay suddenly left the room and went upstairs. As he was often in the habit of taking himself to bed no one thought much of this until a terrific baying and uproar was heard proceeding from above. On reaching the stairs leading upstairs it was seen that he was trying hard to get into his mistress' room. The door was found to be locked. On entering it was discovered that a ladder had been placed against a window, entry had been forced and the greater part of Mrs Vlasto's collection of jewels had been stolen. It was thought from the fact that it had not all gone that the dog's intervention had scared off the thieves. At a later date they did try to rob Mrs Vlasto once again, but this time they were heard and Gornostay gave chase. They did not return a third time!*

Both his sire and his dam had imported sires with Perchino blood close up. There had been a great dispersal of Borzois after the Revolution with many hounds arriving in Belgium, Holland and Germany. Dogs of the finest bloodlines would find themselves no longer the property of Dukes, as their masters had to gain occupations, maybe as waiters or perhaps butlers.

Ch Aureola of Llanfair – his great-granddam

Gornostay's dam was Ch Aureola of Llanfair, bred by Mr Cramb and later owned by Mrs Addlestone. She was a self red with hardly any white, and her litter brother, Russet of

Boran.

Gornostay of Addlestone.

Llanfair, was noted to be 91cm (36in) to the shoulder. Their sire was the Dutch import Max, a great-grandson of the Russian-born hound Asmodey Perchino who was rescued from the Grand Duke's estate just before the Communists arrived (see chapter 1). Max also had a British line behind him to dogs exported from Major Borman's Ramsden kennel. Mrs Chadwick used to visit him in quarantine, and described him as *a beautiful dog with a delightful temperament but he was subsequently shared by Mrs Knapp and Mrs Alexander, the arrangement that each kept him in turn, for three months at a time. Not surprisingly, this ruined his temperament and he became very bad tempered.*

Aureola was an incredible brood bitch. She produced Gornostay when mated to Ch Podar of Notts and, when mated to Podar's sire, Chak Kozak of Shay, she produced Gordey of Addlestone, the sire of five champions to Gornostay's six. The finest hounds of the 'golden age of the Borzoi' often had both these half-brothers in their pedigree.

Going back to the pedigree of Kubans Almaz, through his dam he was the grandson of two Bransgore hounds. Mrs Lucy Gingold's Bransgore kennel rivalled the Mythes and the Addlestones in the 1930s. They were based on Addlestone, with two champion bitches as foundation: Ch Siegerin of Addlestone, a daughter of Gordey of Addlestone, and Ch Sandra of Addlestone, a daughter of Ch Podar of Notts.

Both of these bitches were mated to Gornostay, Siegerin to produce the wonderful Ch Brazhnik of Bransgore in 1933 and Sandra to produce Ch Ballerina of Bransgore, who became the first Borzoi to win Best In Show (BIS) at an all breeds championship show. Ballerina was described as:

... an extremely wonderful bitch with a very positive front, outstanding shoulders and neck, and stood over a lot of ground. Her brisket was deep and she had a beautiful neat hung tail and a gorgeous head. The Duchess of Newcastle (one of the most important of the original breeders of the 1890s) reported of her after judging at one show, 'A very perfectly made Borzoi, with great liberty of movement.' Mrs T A M Hill, at that time the senior breeder in England, also wrote of her after judging Ballerina, 'A beautifully balanced bitch of good substance, particularly sound, long quality head, very dark expressive eyes, very profuse coat.'

Many good days were spent coursing over the homelands of Bransgore and each Borzoi had hunting experience, but perhaps the greatest coursing hound of them all was Ch Ballerina. At the same time few could surpass her for disposition and lack of nerves.

Ch Braznik's son Ch Baraban of Bransgore is also considered one of the 'greats' of the breed. Even in the 1990s Miss Murray considered him among the top three Borzois of any time from any part of the world. In general, the Bransgores were noted for their *intelligence, robustness, soundness, self confidence and affectionate personalities.*

The Bransgore Borzoi had great evenness of type which would have satisfied the Russians, as would their size and soundness. They were clean-shouldered, big quartered and well ribbed up specimens that were not heavy boned giants that could not meet their natural enemy successfully. The coats always received a great deal of attention and they carried a sufficient quantity of coat of the correct texture. The inmates of Bransgore were far from numerous because Mrs Gingold demanded that each Borzoi received personal attention from the nest on.

When the war started Mrs Gingold closed down her kennel.

The 1930s really were the golden era of the breed. At The Kennel Club Show in 1938 (then quite separate from Crufts) the judge was Mr Bernard Timberlake. He started his report with:

I feel greatly complimented by such a splendid entry of my old favourites, not only as regards numbers, which, I understand, were an improvement on most of the shows of this year, but as regards the very high quality of the exhibits. It was indeed a first class collection and, with three full champions present, five other challenge certificate winners, of whom four were seeking their third, and a big batch of extremely promising youngsters, the competition was very keen all through, giving me plenty of food for thought in many of the classes.

Max.

It was some time since I had judged and I had seen only two of the dogs before. I was greatly impressed by the vastly improved general standard of type and soundness, exhibitors and breeders appearing to have arrived at a far more uniform opinion about these all-important points than used to be the case. Also I was pleased to see that more attention had been paid to correct tail carriage, only one exhibit curling its tail right over its back, in the faulty way, instead of at least half those present doing so as I have often seen years ago.

The entry included hounds from the best strains. The winner of Puppy Dog was one of Mr and Mrs George's Tangmeres, Figaro of Tangmere, *A very good, well reared, almost white puppy of lovely type, in superb coat and condition; showed and handled splendidly; first class quality all through, and, with maturity, his body properties and his general movement will improve and he should go far. He won the puppy class with ease.*

For Post Graduate Dog the winner was a Mythe: *First Mythe Peteroff, an extra good young hound of the best type, and very sound everywhere; his condition was hard as nails. He has an excellent head, was in lovely coat, showed well and is difficult to fault. He also won mid limit.*

In Open Dog the great Baraban of Bransgore had to take second place to an Addlestone hound.

Open dog: *This was my best class, and the hardest to judge, with most of the hounds having already won challenge certificates or good enough to do so. First Ch Alesha of Addlestone; I had not seen this famous dog before, but he at once filled my eye; of outstanding type, he owned the best head, eye and expression of the hounds present, was in gorgeous coat and condition, and showed marvellously; he is very well boned and has a perfect front and shoulders, nice short back, strong quarters, excellent depth of brisket with well sprung ribs; he moves beautifully with a full, free action, and the only fault I could find with him was that I thought him a trifle straight in the stifle. He could do the breed a lot of good.*

Second Baraban of Bransgore, another glorious hound of ideal type and quality, who, I was told, was wanting his third certificate. He pressed hard for the honour, but, in my opinion, was beaten in head, in arch and length of back, and, on the day, in general condition, though in lovely coat. He seemed a bit listless in the ring, but has ideal front, shoulders, quarters, and is absolutely sound everywhere; may he soon rank among 'the immortals' as I consider him well worthy to do.

If this was an excellent class, Open Bitch seemed like one from a dream.

Open bitch: *A wonderful quality class. First Ch Mythe Molva; I have never seen this famous black and white before, but she won comfortably and went on to be made the best Borzoi. In gorgeous coat and condition, like all the hounds in this kennel, as sound as a bell everywhere, with a lovely free action, well boned and coupled up, perfect arch, quarters and tail carriage. She owns a beautifully balanced head with nice dark eye and correct expression, full of quality, but it might possibly be slightly more 'inclined to the Roman' in profile. Very difficult to fault and well deserved her position.*

Second Kestor Nadine, a fine upstanding fawn and white of ideal type, with good head, eye and expression. I was particularly impressed with her lovely neck, shoulders, front, depth of brisket and her real true arch. She was not in her full coat but even so went on to win the reserve challenge certificate. She is one of the best bitches I have seen for some time, reminding me a little in shape and conformation of that lovely bitch Ch Mythe Maslova. In my opinion she should very quickly become a champion and I wished she were mine.

Just in case this report of the breed at the end of the 1930s gives too glowing an idea of the quality of the hounds, we can look at a more critical report written by Mr George after he judged at Richmond in 1939.

In most cases quality was outstanding and in some classes very little separated the winners. I thought that several of the exhibits were sadly lacking in size and substance, but as many were half-grown youngsters, time may improve this defect, though some I am sure will never get the size this breed should attain. Eyes seem to me to be very much better, I only saw about four exhibits with really light eyes. At this time of year it is hard to be critical about coats as nearly all the dogs are casting, but one or two struck me as not too good in texture, but on the whole they were not at all bad and some were in beautiful bloom. I saw several fronts that left much to be desired. There seems to be a tendency in the breed at the moment for 'turned in' front feet, as the ground in the Borzoi ring was very bumpy, and the board too wet and slippery to be used, it was not easy to come to any real conclusion as to how much was due to the dogs themselves and how much to the surface they were standing upon. Apart from the aforementioned tendency I thought that feet were far better than they have been, scarcely any were flat. I found several exhibits with very broad and coarse skulls, which is so much against a Borzoi. These coarse skulls seem to be on the increase at the moment, which is a pity for the breed had made very definite improvement in this respect of latter years. It seems to be a fault that is very predominant and breeders should use extreme care in their breeding operations; otherwise the breed will be back to where it was some years ago in respect to heads. I found no nervy or shy Borzois which was very pleasing and most of them showed plenty of character and spirit.

Baraban took the challenge certificate and so becomes a champion; but he had a hard fight to get first place, and it was a close thing between him and the young dog Molodetz. I finally put Baraban top on maturity and slightly better action. He has a superb head and good eye and expression. Have seen him in better flesh and coat, but he was hard and fit. His body properties are all good, and he is good and strong in legs and feet; his coat is of good texture and he had lovely long featherings; in moving towards me he was inclined to turn in one front foot, but did not do so when standing; apart from that he has a nice smooth and free movement; I consider him well worthy of his title, but as I have said before it was a very near thing.

Kester Nadine took the Challenge Certificate and also the cup for best of breed. She is a true Russian if ever there was one; she has a head that one strives after and seldom attains, and a neck that must be the envy of all. She is one of the few Borzois I have ever seen who has real 'head carriage', her body is good, nice arch and good quarters, good depth of brisket, nice feet and very good hind legs. Her forelegs are rather spoilt by having the dew claws on. Nadine has a nice coat of good texture and good featherings, to be extra critical I would like her a little finer in front and more free in action, but that is asking a lot for she is very perfect otherwise; she should soon get her title, and will do the breed a power of good as a brood.

Poor Nadine, she never gained her title, for she had only two Challenge Certificates when the Second World War was declared in September 1939. It seems she had not behaved well in the ring at her first shows. At the Big Breeds Show in 1938 the judge, Mrs T Hill, had written of her: *Although she is of the type I like, I could not place her. She is upright in pastern and weak in bone, besides being so shy. I could not see her properly.*

She was out of a Bransgore bitch but by an American champion imported by Mrs Gingold in an attempt to breed all-white Borzois that was ruined by the war. Her sire was Am Ch Bransgore Akuratni of Romanoff, whose brother, Am Ch Vigow of Romanoff, is illustrated and discussed in chapter 4. The price paid for Akuratni made him the most expensive dog imported to Great Britain, and unfortunately he died not long after coming out of quarantine. Nadine did not contribute to the breed post-war, but her litter brother was Bargany of Barnaigh, the sire of Mrs Chadwick's black bitch Astrakan of Barnaigh, who was the start of the post-war revival. Both Nadine and Bargany were bred by Captain and Mrs Maxwell-Hyslop, but at this time The Kennel Club allowed dogs to be re-registered under completely different names, so Nadine gained the Kestor affix of her owner Mrs Huth, and Bargany the Barnaigh one of Mrs McNeil.

Borzois have always had a tendency to be highly strung, and breeders have tried through the generations to reduce this. In 1938 Mrs Hill started her Big Breeds Show critique: *Quality all round was good and I was pleased to find a great improvement in the ring manners and deportment of the majority of the dogs exhibited. Contrasted with the appalling shyness frequently seen in the ring some years back, the cheerful friendly demeanour of many of the exhibits was most pleasing. I cannot stress too strongly the importance in my opinion of breeding Borzois with sound temperaments and freeness from nerves. Surely a Borzoi, aristocrat that he is, should carry himself with dignity and composure and not skulk into the ring like a frightened cur? It was heartening to see so many beautiful hounds with good sound nerves, and carrying and showing themselves as they should. I have never forgotten some years ago watching the famous American Champion Vigow o' Valley Farm* [who was in fact Nadine's grandsire] *winning a group class at one of the big American shows. Beautifully handled by his owner this grand dog behaved with composure, obeying his handler's every wish, and all with such evident understanding and enjoyment, that he was the cynosure of all eyes. Vigow was undoubtedly a pattern in manners as well as in looks, and if wishes could have transferred ownership he would have most certainly been mine that day!*

These critiques from the 1930s are more detailed and honest than those of today. Perhaps it was this greater honesty that helped to keep the standard of the breed high. Some people who go to shows have no perception of what a good dog is like, and there are many more of these today than before the war. The great increase in disposable income and leisure time from the 1960s onwards altered the profile of the dog show exhibitor, the relative price of a pedigree dog falling so that most could afford one.

The new generation of exhibitor has no connection with other livestock, most especially horses, and does not understand the fundamentals of soundness because they have not ridden a sound horse and stayed on and then had the uncomfortable experience of a ride on an unsound one. Miss Robinson's Mythes were sound because their mistress rode to Foxhounds and she had soundness as one of her priorities in breeding.

Critiques that miss out the bad points allow people to continue to believe that their dreadful hounds are the best and deserve to win. Such people do not take kindly to more honest, detailed reports, so these cannot be found in the dog papers. Often it is the editorial staff who emasculate the reports forwarded to them, fearing argument or even litigation. Should the progress of a breed be hampered by these considerations?

Ch Podar of Notts

This dog (pedigree overleaf) was bred by Mr H Thompson in 1925 and later owned by the Duchess of Newcastle, who had started in the breed in the 1880s. Ch Podar of Notts was a very important stud dog, as we have seen, helping to transform the rather plain, over-long, flat-backed dogs that were in the ring immediately after the First World War. He was three-quarters imported blood.

Chack Kozack of Shay – his sire

The imported dog Chack Kozack of Shay, born in June 1923, was described as *a charming dog with a blanket of brown markings.* He was a grandson of Asmodey Perchino, who was bred by the Grand Duke Nicholas and is illustrated in chapter 1 on page 27.

Bedin Achotnik – his grandsire

Ch Podar had as his grandparents the brother and sister Blanda Achotnik and Bedin Achotnik, whose grandsire again was Asmodey Perchino.

Bedin was imported to Great Britain from Holland by Major Borman, who had the Ramsden kennel. This had been one of the leading British kennels, but it was dispersed at the outbreak of World War I. After the war, Bedin was bought from Mr van der Berkoff because of the proximity of Perchino blood in his pedigree. However, after doing well at Crufts in 1923, he contracted distemper and died, having sired only one British litter to Marie of Haywra. This litter contained two influential bitches: Zigani of Vedman who became a champion and Achotnik of Shay, who was to gain fame as the dam of Ch Podar of Notts, Ch Dozar of Addlestone and Ch Lovkaya of Addlestone.

Bedin Achotnik.

King of Diamonds of Addlestone

This dog (pedigree page 85) is the connection between Ch Podar of Notts and the old British bloodlines, before their improvement with the exports Chack Kozack of Shay, Bedin Achotnik, Ivan Ivanovitch and Max.

The Mythes were easily identifiable because of the consistent bitch line, and

Ancestors of Ch Podar of Notts

- **Ch Podar of Notts** b: April 15, 1925
  - Chack Kozak of Shay (imp)
    - Podar vom Baikal
      - Ashmodey Perchino b: in Russia, bred by Grand Duke Nicholas
      - Vlasta Ural
    - Blanda Achotnik
      - Almadin Nikolskoi
      - Planja Pascholl
  - Achotnik of Shay
    - Bedin Achotnik (imported)
      - Amadin Nikolskoi
      - Planja Pascholl
    - Marie of Haywra
      - King of Diamonds of Addlestone
      - Vaynor Perfection

they were the best of the old lines, becoming even better when the imported blood was added in. Mrs Vlasto's Addlestones were of more diverse type because their owner was a very clever purchaser of breeding stock. In April 1925 Mr Thompson bred a litter from Achotnik of Shay that included Ch Podar of Notts and Ch Lovkaya of Addlestone, but by November 1925 Mrs Vlasto owned Achotnik, who had whelped a litter containing Ch Dozar of Addlestone.

Chack Kozak of Shay.

When Mrs Vlasto started in Borzois she vowed that she would have soundness and type with size and quality. In the same way that the superb Bransgores started with Addlestones, the Addlestones were based on the Ramsden line. By mating Ch Ramsden Rajah to Yenia, a daughter of

Ch Ramsden Ranger, Mrs Vlasto bred Ch Trumps of Addlestone, Ch Pavlova of Addlestone and Ch Queen of Hearts of Addlestone, all born in 1910.

Addlestone bitches often produced multiple champions. In a subsequent litter to Rajah's son Michael of Addlestone, Yenia added Ch Lotka of Addlestone to her champion offspring. The most successful Addlestone brood was Ch Marie of Addlestone, who was the dam of five champions, including Ch Zavist of Addlestone (a granddaughter of Chack Kozak), herself the dam of three, including the Bransgore foundation Ch Siegerin of Addlestone.

The most influential stud dog was Sparrowhawk of Addlestone, a son of King of Diamonds. Sparrowhawk was the sire of seven champions, four from one 1922 litter to Marie. All four of the dogs made up in 1924 were Sparrowhawk children, the only one not home-bred being Ch Mythe Valdina, a basically white bitch who gave her colour to many Tangmeres. Sparrowhawk was described as *one of the most famous stud dogs at the height of his form in about 1924. He was not shown very much as he was too busy with other duties. He was a fine dog, white with lemon markings, and his chief failing was probably his skull, which was a bit broad.*

In total Mrs Vlasto bred 30 champions, and for several

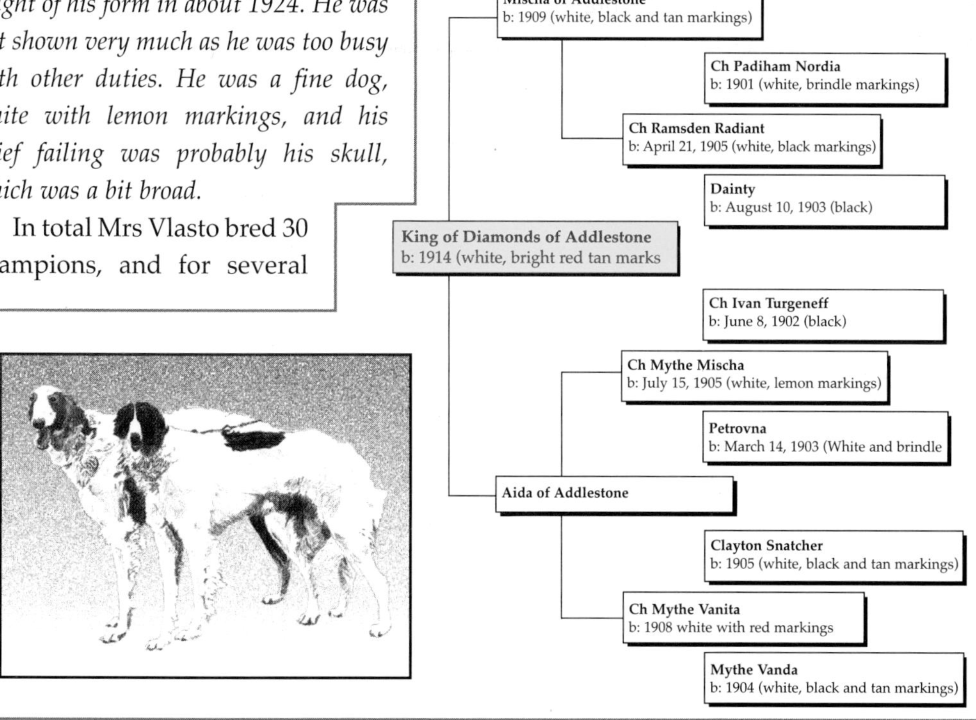

years hers were the only Borzois that won titles. Her first kennel was at Rivermead, Addlestone, Surrey in about 1905, moving to Bracknell, Berkshire in 1914 and finally in 1933 to Lavender Farm at Ascot, where there were 23 acres of exercising ground and the kennel range opened onto a 10-acre field. There was a kennel bungalow with an office in which one wall was covered with pictures of famous Borzois. The kennel kitchen and bake room had an Aga cooker and there was also a bathroom and storeroom in the bungalow.

The Borzoi Club was founded in 1892, and there was no jubilee show in 1942 because of the Second World War. However, a great celebratory show was held in Mrs Vlasto's grounds in 1952, with Mrs Vlasto judging the bitch classes. The grounds were compared to Kew Gardens in the show report and Mrs Hill, the dog judge, said that it was one of the nicest shows she had ever attended.

The Addlestone kennels were closed in 1945. Mrs Vlasto felt she could no longer carry on the kennel because her kennelman, Matthews, to whom she owed the superb bloom and condition of the Addlestone hounds, was too ill to continue, so she 'had to write an end'.

It was a point of pride that no small dog was ever killed at the kennels. The temperament of the Addlestone hounds was wonderful, and Miss Betty and Miss Pansy Vlasto's Pekingese never came to any harm from the Borzois.

The Addlestones started well, having as one of the foundations Ch Ramsden Radiant. Mrs Borman exhibited her first Borzoi from her Ramsden kennel in 1896 and, with her husband, bred six champions, though several more title-holders passed through the kennels. Dog breeding and showing was very different at this time; leading show dogs often had several owners, and The Kennel Club allowed the complete change of a dog's name. Today a dog carries the kennel name of its breeder as a prefix and, if the dog is sold, the new owner can apply to The Kennel Club to have his or her affix added at the end of the name. However, it is possible for someone who has bred both parents to name the dog as if he or she bred it.

Before the last war there were several great kennels who bred few of the champion dogs that carried their name. One big-name terrier kennel never bred a single puppy. A good eye for a puppy let these kennels pick up prospective winners, and a promising youngster was often bought at an open show. Kennel advertisements boasted about dogs that, unplaced by the judge on the day they were bought, went on under their new ownership to outwin every other dog in their class that day. In some breeds the highest honour was to have one of the senior breeders try to buy your dog. Lorna, Countess Howe, the main 'power' in the Labradors with three BIS Crufts winners in the 1930s, would eye up any dog that beat her stock as she stood in the line of prize-winners and, if she agreed with the judge, would try to buy the dog there in the ring.

Ch Ramsden Radiant – his granddam

A feature on the Ramsdens in *Country Life* in 1907 discussed the litter brother and sister Ch Ramsden Radiant and Ch Ramsden Ranger:

Another very beautiful bitch in the kennel is Ramsden Radiant, a rather heavily marked black and white, by Padiham Nordia out of Dainty. She has a wonderful outline, while her feet, legs and arch are good. Her head is a study. With her many fine points and beautiful colour she is one of the prettiest Borzois on the bench, and she attracts much notice whenever she is shown. She won her first challenge certificate at Crufts this year, and her second at Eastbourne, where she was also awarded the special for the best Borzoi in the show.

A very fine sable and white dog is Ramsden Ranger, litter brother to Ramsden Radiant. He is a very tall dog, standing 33in at the shoulder. He has a fine head and is distinguished by great depth of chest, while his hind quarters, arch and coat leave nothing to be desired.

Ch Miss Piostri – his great-granddam

The top winners at Ramsden were the home-bred Ch Miss Piostri and her son by Ranger, Ch Ramsden Rajah, both winners of 20CCs. Rajah was the most successful Borzoi ever at

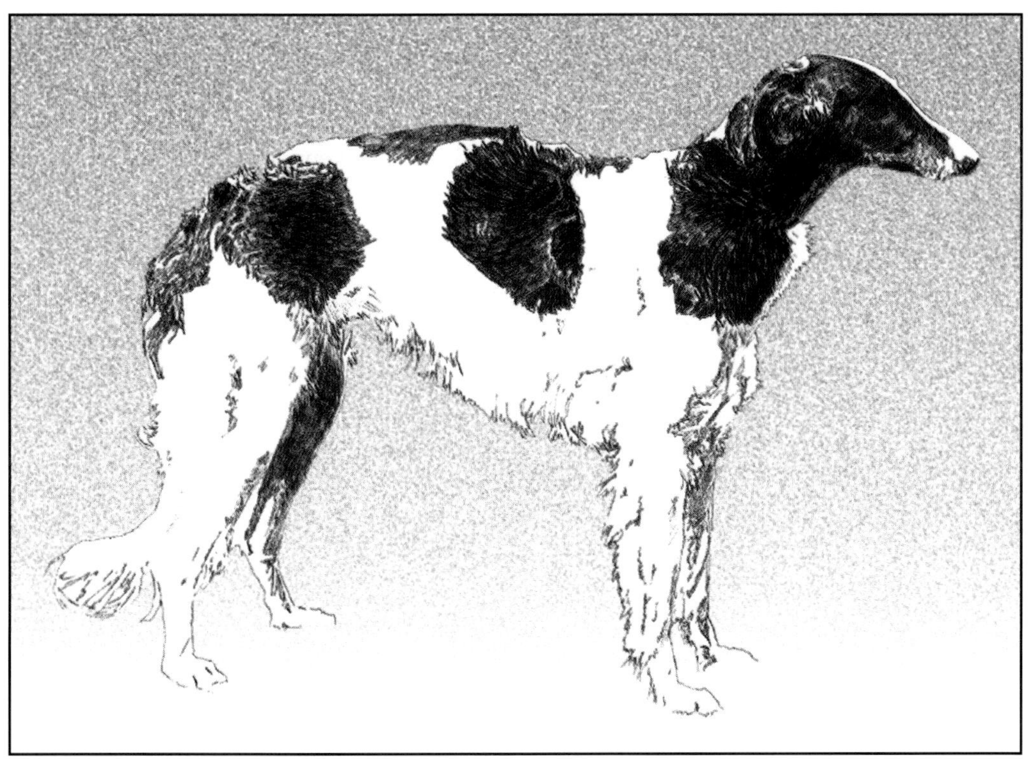

Ch Ramsden Radiant.

Crufts, winning the dog CC 1909–1912. A contemporary observer wrote: *It is not easy to say which holds pride of place, but Miss Piostri has very strong claims. She is by Piostri out of Princess Rubykoff, and is a beautiful white bitch with brindle marking. Some experts regard her as the most typical Borzoi bitch in England. Her head is of wonderful length and shape. She has great depth of chest, with splendid coat and hindquarters, and, for a bitch, a perfect arch.*

Her sire Piostri had a very fine head indeed for that time. There are worse heads than that in the ring today! Major Borman bought him from Dr Sydney Turner, then Chairman of The Kennel Club, to add qualities that the Ramsdens lacked. Piostri was not a great show winner himself because he covered too much ground and was lacking in substance, but he fulfilled the Major's hopes for him as a stud.

Ch Ramsden Rajah – his grandsire

Rajah was first shown at the Borzoi Club Show in 1908, when he was a 10-month-old puppy, taking six firsts and a collection of trophies. He was a white with fawn markings on the head and *he excelled in every feature, combining great substance and bone with perfect quality and with wonderful length of tail; his coat was beautiful.*

The Ramsden kennel was situated at Ivy House, Ramsden, Billericay, Essex, and many hounds were exported from there to Belgium, Germany, Canada and the United States. The bloodlines that went to Germany returned when Major Borman imported Bedin Achotnik. Ranger was exported to Dr Wegener of the Ural kennels in Germany.

Ch Ramsden Ranger

The pedigree of Ranger goes back to the original Russian imports that established the Borzoi in Great Britain.

Championship shows were started in 1893. Before that time various schemes were used to determine the champion. It is essential to be very circumspect about championship titles. Even in *The Kennel Club Stud Book,* titles are sometimes omitted or allocated where they have not been earned. As for kennel advertisements, remember that there were neither trading standard rules nor advertising standards in those days.

The only Borzoi to be made up under the old rules was The Hon Mrs Wellesley's Ch Krilutt, a Russian import, but he does not figure in our pedigrees. The first show with classes for 'Siberian and Russian Wolfhounds' was that run by the Crystal Palace Company in October 1889, and Krilutt won this class.

The show reports of the 19th century are a joy to read because they are so uninhibited. An anonymous ringstander at Brighton Show in 1890 wrote: A*lthough fifteen were entered only four were there for competition, of which Voorka, a very shelly one even for his age, was first dismissed. After Pagooba was awarded third prize the interest displayed by the onlookers was intense when the judge began comparing Krilutt and Zloeem. Undoubtedly the former is better in*

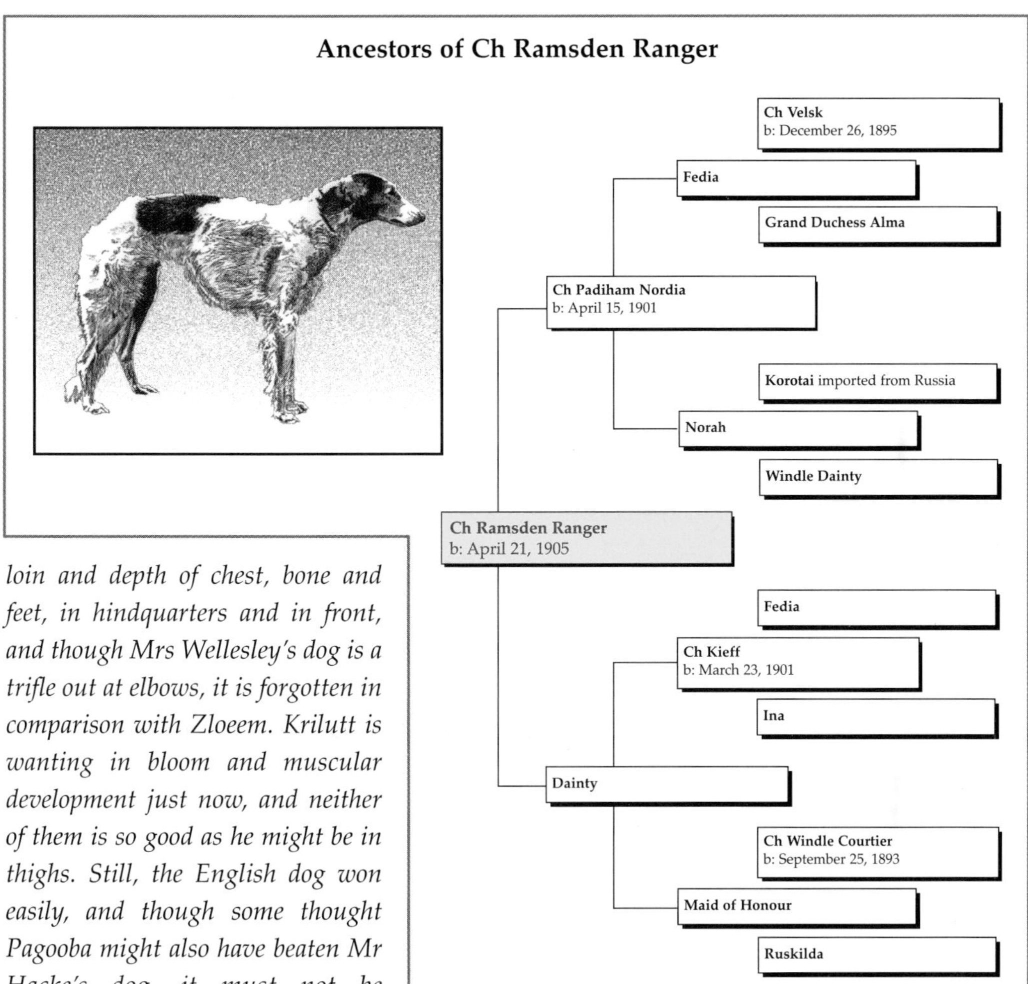

loin and depth of chest, bone and feet, in hindquarters and in front, and though Mrs Wellesley's dog is a trifle out at elbows, it is forgotten in comparison with Zloeem. Krilutt is wanting in bloom and muscular development just now, and neither of them is so good as he might be in thighs. Still, the English dog won easily, and though some thought Pagooba might also have beaten Mr Hacke's dog, it must not be forgotten that some little allowance should be made for the dog, as he was very badly shown in the ring.

Zloeem had been purchased by the American Mr Hacke, of Slatington, who had been told that the dog would beat Krilutt. The Brighton Show was the scene of the competition, with Mr George Krehl, a most respected judge of all breeds, officiating. Zloeem was defeated and stayed for a few more shows but, after coming third in a class of three to two much younger dogs, he set sail for the United States.

Korotai – his great-grandsire

At Crufts 1892 the Borzoi judging was reported to the dog papers by Captain Graham, the breeder who recreated the Irish Wolfhound. He wrote:

In these classes the excellence and number of the exhibits were simply outstanding, and the judge's task was a very trying one. Though they varied considerably in size, the evenness of type was remarkable and the quality, as a whole, undeniable, and no less than 16 had made the journey from St Petersberg and were necessarily shown at a disadvantage. They had noticeably improved by the last day of the show, when the best dog Oudar was purchased by the Duchess of Newcastle. Several others were also sold during the show.

Krilutt, in beautiful order, looking lovely, carried off the breeders' competition, the Challenge prize, and the stud dog medal and also headed the winning brace and team.

In the Open Dog Class Korotai, a truly magnificent dog of great size and length, took the first prize. He might be a trifle narrower and longer in head, and is also a trifle weak in limbs and feet; he was in splendid coat and condition. The second was awarded to Oudar, one of the imported team, a grand dog – perhaps better in head than Korotai – but not quite so symmetrical an animal. However, it is not improbable their positions may be reversed when Oudar gets into better condition.

It is interesting to note that the titled Krilutt is not in our pedigrees, but the two untitled Russians, Korotai and Oudar, are. Korotai was the foundation sire for the breed in Great Britain. He did have some minor show wins but, as reported at the Crystal Palace show in 1892, *He is a large and powerful hound, with a long head, perhaps a little wanting in the Roman curve of fore-face. He had one toe broken down, and in consequence turns his foot in, but this appears to have been through an accident, and, therefore, is open to lenient consideration. In colour and texture of coat he is good.*

Korotai appears once in Ch Ramsden Ranger's three-generation pedigree but, if we extended this further back, we would see that he was the sire of the Duchess of Newcastle's Ch Velsk, the grandsire of Fedia and also the sire of Ch Windle Courtier.

Oudar was the sire of Windle Earl, who was the sire of three champions, including Major Borman's Ch Statesman and Ch Sunbeam, bought by the Duchess of Newcastle to produce Ch Ivan Turgeneff, who was used in the Mythe breeding programme. The Duchess is reputed to have paid £200 for Oudar, a huge amount of money for that time. Eventually he was exported to the United States. He was described as *a big dog with tremendous coat and good arch, but poor head, light eye and thick shoulders. He was bred in the kennels of Mr Dourassoff and was born in 1888. He was white with a few markings.*

Ch Windle Courtier – his great-grandsire

Ch Windle Courtier was the first British-bred champion Borzoi, the first bitch champion having been the Duchess of Newcastle's imported Ch Milka. The Duchess had started in the breed with a bitch named Spain, so called because she was given to the Duchess' mother by a Spanish Grandee, the Marquis de Quandelmina. The Duchess, daughter of Major Henry Canby of the Ninth Lancers, married Henry, Seventh Duke of Newcastle in

Ch Windle Courtier.

1889. His ancestral seat was Clumber Park in Nottinghamshire, the estate that gave its name to the Clumber Spaniel and is just around the corner from the show ground where the Northern Borzoi Association still holds its championship show each year.

At first the Duchess did not use an affix, so none of the eight champions she bred between 1894 and 1904 has the 'of Notts' affix used by post-war hounds. After 1904 the Duchess put more emphasis on her other breeds, the Smooth and Wire Fox Terriers. Her breeding was even more important in these breeds than in the Borzoi, for every Wire Fox Terrier goes back to her Ch Cackler of Notts, and Fox Terrier registrations numbered thousands more than Borzoi ones. In most years from 1880–1914 first the Smooth and then the Wire headed The Kennel Club's registration tables. King Edward VII had as a constant companion Caesar of Notts, and this Wire Fox Terrier walked before nine kings in his master's funeral procession. Edward's consort, Queen Alexandra, had a Borzoi champion called Ch Alex when she was Princess of Wales and another called Ch Vassilka when she was Queen.

The Queen's kennels were situated at Sandringham in Norfolk, and champion dogs to hold this affix were her son George V's Clumber Spaniel Ch Sandringham Spark and the Field Trial Champion Labradors belonging to her great-granddaughter, our present Queen Elizabeth II. King George V also had a champion Labrador, Ch Wolferton Ben. Wolferton is the name of the station nearest to Sandringham, so George V used this name as an affix until the death of his mother.

The Windle kennel was owned by Mr R Coop and, although Courtier was the only champion made up from there, most of the early British-bred champions had a Windle in their pedigree. Courtier won 12 CCs, winning at Preston Show in May 1895, with Mr Walter Evans commenting: *He is one of the finest young dogs I have ever seen, has good legs, feet and head, with a beautiful expression. He would, however, be better if he could get a little more flesh on to fill up his gigantic frame.*

However, Courtier had a dramatic entry into the show ring at The Kennel Club Show in 1894, when Sir Everett Millais, who introduced the Basset Hound to this country, was the judge. Mr Coop played a leading part at the show.

Before I attempt to criticise these hounds I must in the first place tender my best thanks to the members of the Borzoi Club for entrusting such a fine show of hounds and such a task to an absolutely unknown judge, and in case I may, as I was told afterwards I did, have caused some dissatisfaction in my awards, I must inform the members and the other exhibitors, that I have my own views as to what Borzoi type ought to be, and that I did my best to judge according to those views. More I do not think a judge can say, but on this occasion I will plainly tell exhibitors that I did my best to get out of judging Borzois at the Palace [Crystal Palace], *and it was only after pressure that I consented, for although I felt that I could judge according to my own views, I at the same time felt they might not be palatable to others. Having made these few remarks, I will now proceed to explain my judging on this occasion.*

Novice class – *For third prize I selected Mr Coop's Windle Lady, one of a fine litter of young hounds. She has a sweet head, but is in poor condition, as all Mr Coop's were, and where such hounds as Borzois are kept (as objects of Beauty) condition is a consideration which cannot be overlooked. It may be said, and it was said, that it is difficult to get Borzois into condition as young hounds. This I am just as well aware of (as a breeder of them) as the gentleman who made the remark. Still it can be done, and if it is not, the exhibitor pays the penalty, as will be seen further on.*

Limit class – *Here in making the first two awards, I may at once explain matters by stating at the very commencement I had to choose between a magnificent and marvellously finished bitch of grand type, and what will probably be the best dog in England if he finishes as he ought to do, and I sincerely hope will. The bitch, Lebedeka by name, is very well known, and, as everyone will admit, has a most magnificent development; at the same time, she is out of coat, but sufficient remains to show what she is when furnished. Now I would ask anyone who weighs such a bitch in conjunction with an enormous puppy that is totally unfurnished, but which gives promise as to what he may be, how the scale ought to turn? We cannot take into consideration the puppy's possibilities. All we know is that he is not furnished, that he is miserably thin, that his chest is like a pigeon's, and that all he has to bring against such a hound as Lebedka is his coat and height, consequently with type equal and furnishing very much in favour of Lebedka, I do not think that I did wrong to give the bitch the prize. I refer to this at length, as owing to the judgement I regret to say that Mr Coop rather forgot his position in the ring, and refused afterwards to come for a special which was at his disposal, an occurrence I have never met with before and hope never to meet with again.*

Open dog – *In this class Ataman II stood out as winner at once. Again I say with such a hound and in such condition there ought to be no difference of opinion with him and an unformed pup such as Windle Courtier, to whom I gave second, although I was in some doubts as to whether circumstances ought not to justify me in placing Oudar in this position. I, however, thought that the pup stood better in the ring compared with Oudar, and on this point alone I relaxed my judgement, so Oudar came third. Very Highly Commended I gave to Korotai with Opromist under him. Had Korotai not the forefeet he has, I should have felt justified in placing him second, but one cannot even with the best of chests, the grandest of coats, and superb condition remain oblivious to feet that are undoubtedly 'gone'.*

Ch Velsk – his great-grandsire

The Duchess of Newcastle's home-bred Ch Velsk was the sixth Borzoi champion to be made up, and he was the winner of nine CCs. This son of Korotai was the sire of four champions, three to the Duchess' import Ch Tsaretsa, the last Borzoi to be imported into Great Britain before the introduction of quarantine. Tsaretsa was the winner of 17 CCs, a breed record until beaten by Ch Ramsden Rajah just before the First World War.

Velsk won the Dog CC at Crufts in 1901 and 1902 and was the best male Borzoi the year before when no certificates were on offer. He was famed for his long elegant head, which was 32cm (12½in) long. Born in 1895, he grew to 79cm (31in) at the shoulder and weighed 51.7kg (114lb). His colour was white with silver grey and the Duchess considered his best points to be *very dark eyes, well carried ears and stern, and he is the heaviest coated dog on the bench, also the strongest boned. He is absolutely perfect in expression.*

However, the Duchess did criticise the length of his back, saying it could do with *a trifle more arch, otherwise I can find no fault.*

His grandson, Ch Padiham Nordia, was the sire of the Ramsden pair, Ranger and Radiant, and was himself the winner of the dog CC at Crufts in 1906.

Ch Kieff, the maternal grandsire of Ranger and Radiant, was owned by the Bormans. The winner of six CCs, he stood 84cm (33in) at the shoulder and measured 32cm (12½in) in length of head and 81cm (32in) around the chest.

We have been to the origin of the breed in Great Britain through one pedigree line, so now we need to pick up other lines...

Ch Colhugh Valla

Valla was born in 1971 and her parents were Ch Grand Manner of Colhugh and Annikka of Greenhaven, the foundation pair of Mr Reg Bassett's phenomenally successful Colhugh kennel.

Ch Colhugh Valla had more influence than any other of the Grand Manner / Annikka progeny on the breed in the ring in the late 1990s. She produced three champion daughters, each of whom went on to found a new Borzoi kennel.

Ch Colhugh Collette of Olias was the foundation of Mrs Joan Mabey's Olias hounds. She won her title at the Welsh Kennel Club Show under Mr Bassett's nephew, Mr Graham Hill, whose Dimland Kennel has produced many champions and group winners. Mr Hill noted of Collette, *Red and white superior quality leading lady in gleaming condition, has an air of superiority, head is refined with all the feminine qualities, eyes are dark and of correct shape, graceful reachy neck and an elegant topline flowing to well let down hindquarters which are well muscled, mature lady which shows itself in body and depth of brisket, moved well as always with reaching front action and driving hind action covering the ground with ease, standing gives that desirable balanced appearance. Well deserved that long awaited third CC. Took best of breed on maturity and her precise movement.*

Collette was the dam of three champions: Ch Olias Crimson Queen, her litter brother Ch Olias Tangerine Dream and Ch Olias Oberon.

Ch Colhugh Chanel was the foundation bitch of Mr Roger and Mrs Ella Heap's Raes. She gained her title in 1983 at Belfast under Mr Tommy Agnew, who noted: *Red and white, no matter which way you look at her, true expression, dark eyes, rose shaped ear, good ribcage, nice straight front, strong well angulated quarters, combines elegance with style, in beautiful coat and condition, a credit to her owner, free elegant mover. CC, this gives her title.*

Chanel was the dam of three champions: Ch Rae Ravell, Ch Rae Rembrandt and Ch Rae the Revolution of Santerman.

Ch Colhugh Capucine was the initial bitch in Mrs Rose Mary Downes' Vronsky kennel. Her title came in 1984, under Mr Hill. Her first CC had been at South Wales in 1982 under Mr Douglas Appleton, most famous for his champion Beagles. He said: *The note in my judging book says 'simply gorgeous'. She hit the eye coming into the ring and the more I looked the better she became. As totally feminine as the open dog winner* [Ch Zomahli Udachnik of Colhugh] *was masculine – how nice!*

Her second CC came from the breed specialist Mrs Peggy Malone, who also gave the dog CC to Udachnik. She noted of Capucine: *Real charmer, not a big bitch but very feminine and so nicely put together. Good hind angulation, and just watch her go.*

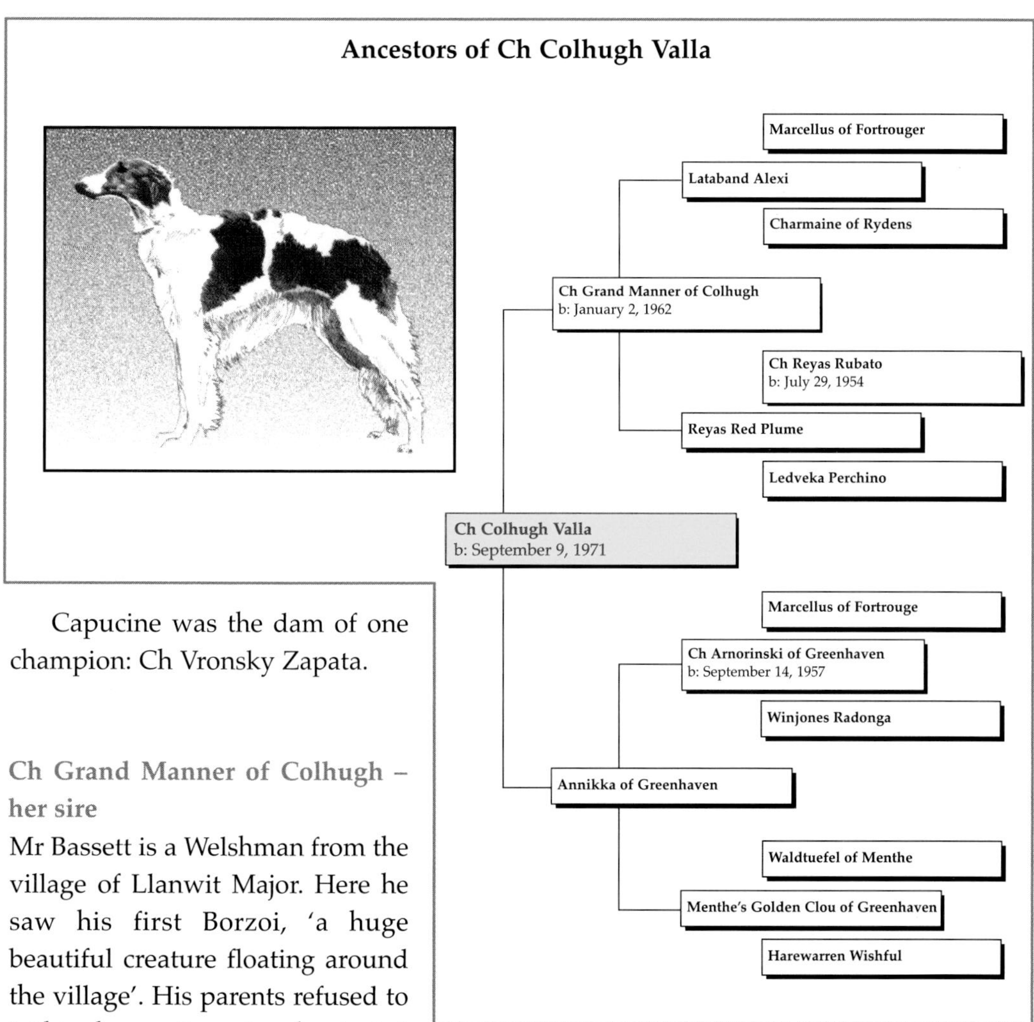

Ancestors of Ch Colhugh Valla

Capucine was the dam of one champion: Ch Vronsky Zapata.

Ch Grand Manner of Colhugh – her sire

Mr Bassett is a Welshman from the village of Llanwit Major. Here he saw his first Borzoi, 'a huge beautiful creature floating around the village'. His parents refused to let him have a Borzoi, so he started with a Corgi. At the age of 10 he had a very serious accident on roller skates resulting in three years in and out of hospital, so his interest in show dogs was fostered by his parents to encourage him to walk.

His dream of a Borzoi came nearer when he moved on impulse to Brighton after visiting a friend there. Just going to Brighton was quite an expedition for a young Welshman 'practically needing a passport to leave Wales'. His first livestock in his new home were tropical fish, and he paid for the electricity to heat the tank by selling fry. He won Fish of the Year at local shows with a Thick-lipped Gourami. When the fish began to take over he opened an aquarists' shop, giving up his regular job as the business started to do well. Five years later he heard from a customer of a Borzoi that needed re-homing

Ch Grand Manner of Colhugh.

and, since it was love at first sight, Lataband Alexi came to stay. He was never shown but, one day a year, he was borrowed by a fashionable lady who had a dress made to match him and took him to the local exemption show, where they won the *Best Dressed Lady and Dog* class every time.

On Alexi's death Mr Bassett bought one of his sons from Mr and Mrs Berney. This son was a very beautiful adult, but he was very stubborn and required a considerable amount of patience. All this bore fruit, as he became the group-winning Ch Grand Manner of Colhugh, foundation sire of the Colhughs.

Grand Manner's first CC came at Blackpool in 1967 under Mrs Bennett-Heard of the Keepers kennel. She said of him: *CC winner and best of breed, beautifully balanced, with no exaggerations, substance without coarseness, elegance with no loss of masculinity. His faults were quite outweighed by his other good qualities, beautifully presented, good feet, all his teeth and a sound mover.*

Mr Joe Braddon, one of the greatest all-round judges, gave him his second CC at Leicester a few weeks later. There was a ring-side report of the show from Mrs Beresford of the Yadasar kennel, who wrote: *taking his second CC and looking as usual in prime coat and condition. What a depth of brisket this dog has, this combined with his other many excellent points keeps him in the top flight.*

Mr R Yeoward gave him his third CC at the Ladies' Kennel Association, the final show of 1967, writing: *What a superb line of dogs! None deserved to be beaten, delighted to hear that not only was my first, Bassett's dog Grand Manner of Colhugh, a champion, but also that it was I who gave him his first first prize. I should have been happy to have had at least four CCs to award in this class, and several beaten dogs must be considered worthy winners. All dogs and champions have weaknesses and Grand Manner's is his front feet, but the rest of him is perfectly proportioned. This large red and white hound is first class.*

Annikka of Greenhaven – her dam

Annikka of Greenhaven.

Annikka of Greenhaven was the Colhugh foundation bitch, bred by Mrs Harrison. Mrs Harrison lived nearby, but Annikka and her sister were in kennels in Southampton where they were waiting to be rehomed. Mr Bassett and Mrs Harrison went to see them together and came back with the heavier-boned of the two.

The alliance of Grand Manner and Annikka was one of the most important in the breed. The first mating produced nine puppies, including Ch Galina of Colhugh, Ch Tina of Colhugh and Ch Alexi of Colhugh. A repeat mating produced Ch Sadko of Colhugh and Ch Sarclash of Colhugh. The third produced Ch Colhugh Mia and Ch Colhugh Valla.

Mr Bassett line breeds now, but at the beginning of his breeding programme he could not do so. Annikka and Grand Manner did have one ancestor in common in their two-generation pedigrees, however. Annikka was a quality bitch: an ordinary one could not have produced so many champion offspring. She was the winner of a Reserve CC at Blackpool in 1966 under Mr Fred Curnow, who wrote: *Free moving, elegant, feminine yet solid, deep in brisket, very good head, correct topline, well turned stifles and excellent legs and feet.*

Marcellus of Fortrouge

This dog was the common ancestor in the pedigrees of Ch Grand Manner of Colhugh and Annikka of Greenhaven.

The Fortrouge kennel of Miss Betty Murray was founded before the war. The name came from Miss Murray's homeland of Canada. Forte Rouge was the originally French settlement near her home which eventually became part of Winnipeg. Her family lived in Ireland for a time and she eventually went to study veterinary medicine in London, going to practise in Croydon where she remained until her retirement. At the outbreak of war her first two bitches were sent to Ireland for safety. However, she did not remain without a Borzoi for very long; she obtained the dog Moryak of Moscowa from Mrs Jenkins. Mrs

Ancestors of Ch Marcellus of Fortrouge

Marcellus of Fortrouge	Ch Eglon of Rydens b: December 14, 1946	Rimski of Rydens	Ch Mythe Marinsky b: May 12, 1936
			Mermaid
		Olga of Lenoken	Ivan of Lenoken
			Jewel of Lenoken
	Fleur of Fortrouge	Ch Eglon of Rydens b: December 14, 1946	Rimski of Rydens
			Olga of Lenoken
		Ch Folly of Fortrouge b: July 1, 1945	St Arvan's Moscow Moonlight
			Krown Khassia

Jenkins' kennel was in Folkestone, then right in the middle of the war zone, as it was surrounded by camps belonging to various forces and on the German bombing route. Mrs Jenkins lost her fences and her dogs were constantly running away. Her Afghan was taken to France with some troops who had adopted her as a mascot, so she felt Moryak would be safer with Miss Murray.

After the war The Kennel Club was keen to get championship shows started once again. As no benching was available in 1946, the only championship shows were those run by the various breed clubs. Often a few breeds would share a venue to reduce the expense of hiring the hall. However, the Borzoi Club had the Drill Hall at Buckingham Gate, London to itself. The judge was Mrs T Hill, and Moryak won seven first prizes, the dog CC and Best In Show. Miss Murray described these as her most exciting wins, the only negative point being that the wonderful array of cups she had won were still in storage.

The general championship shows started again in 1947 and the first to have Borzoi CCs on offer was Muswell Hill, no longer a championship show. Here Moryak won his second CC from Mr James Saunders and, five days later, at the Borzoi Club Show (held with Afghans, Chow Chows, Salukis and St Bernards), he gained his title, becoming the first post-war Borzoi champion.

Chapter Three

Moryak was born in late December 1942, luckily not in the hole his dam Moskowa Boryza of Bransgore had dug in the garden, ably assisted by his sire Ch Mythe Marinsky. After his show career he did some work as a photographic model, appearing on cans of Lassie dog food.

Ch Folly of Fortrouge – his granddam

Miss Murray's first bitch champion was Folly of Fortrouge. There was an act on stage called *Anna and Her Pals*, the 'pals' being two Borzois. Unfortunately, one died, and Miss Murray lent Moryak as a temporary measure. Anna was sent a bitch as a replacement, but she proved unsuitable for treading the boards, so she was sent to Miss Murray as a 'thank you' for the loan of Moryak. This bitch was Folly.

Folly gained her title in 1949, having won her first CC at the Metropolitan and Essex Show in 1948 under Mrs Vlasto and her second later that year at Southern Counties, the last time the Duchess of Newcastle judged. She was the foundation of Miss Murray's line.

Ch Eglon of Rydens – his sire

Marcellus was line bred to Mrs Young's Ch Eglon of Rydens, which affix was already famous for its champion Pugs. The mating of Eglon's parents had produced three champions: Ch Antoinette of Rydens in 1948, Ch Eglon of Rydens in 1946 and Ch Elegance of Rydens in 1946. All three were made up in 1949, Eglon and Antoinette doing the double at the Croydon Championship Show under Mrs Anstey.

The quality of the Borzoi was not as high as before the war as, with the terrible food shortages, breeders simply could not raise the hounds as they would wish. Food rationing for humans and dogs continued in Great Britain until the early 1950s and, though bread was never rationed during the war, it was soon after the end of hostilities. Looking at the photographs taken by Mr Chadwick at these early post-war shows, the overwhelming impression is of very thin hounds whose coats are not so profuse as those of the hounds of the 1930s and today.

Ch Eglon of Rydens.

Mrs Anstey wrote of her Croydon entry:

On the whole I thought quality was good, although in several cases not up to pre-war standard. The true Borzoi expression, with the veins and bone formation showing, are rare today. There are far too many hounds with light eyes; gay tails are prevalent, and one of the worst faults is bad movement, often caused by the handler using a tight lead, or by lack of training in ringcraft before exhibition.

Open dog – *First Eglon of Rydens, attractive hound, tremendous length of head, excellent quarters, he has size and substance, is sound and moved well. I would like a little more spring of rib.*

Open bitch – *Antoinette of Rydens, lovely well balanced black and white, beautiful outline with natural fall away and width of quarters, fine head, small ears, dark eyes, straight free mover with correct tail carriage. It gave me great pleasure to complete her title.*

Rimski of Rydens – his grandsire

Rimski of Rydens was the sire of these three champions, who were made up in 1949. That year was also a sad one for the kennel, as Rimski himself died, as did another of his sons, Balalaika of Rydens, full brother to the others and winner of two CCs. However, Mrs Young had been lucky in that Eglon was returned to her, having been sold as a puppy.

Rimski was a son of Ch Mythe Marinsky, and it was only through the line Ch Mythe Marinsky – Rimski of Rydens – Ch Eglon of Rydens that the beautiful, long Mythe head was passed on.

Ch Mythe Marinsky

Marinsky was one of Ch Mythe Mazeppa's six champion offspring. This number undoubtedly would have been greater but for the war. Marinsky became a champion in 1938, winning his third CC under Mr Guy at the Kensington Canine Society's Championship Show. Mr Guy wrote:

Limit and Open Dog – *First Mythe Marinsky; shown to perfection; also won the Challenge Certificate, which makes him a full champion and a very worthy one; won his others at Crufts and Birmingham; his faults are very few; a little plain in head, which is unusual to find in exhibits from the Mythe kennel; he has a perfect body, sound front, lovely quarters; fine tail carriage; quality, sound bone; moved easily and with life; stood away in show condition with his heavy silky coat; not yet two years old; same litter as Ch Mythe Molva, probably the best bitch living; a noted breeder's achievement.*

No wonder the rings of the 1940s looked ordinary: no Mythes, no Addlestones, no Bransgores, and dogs reared on a minimum of food.

When Miss Robinson realised that she had a terminal illness she rehomed her Borzois. Marinsky was sold to Mrs Hanson, who was going to India to start a kennel there. However, the entry of Japan into the war intervened, so Marinsky only made it as far as the Moskowa kennel belonging to Mrs Jenkins at Folkestone. Here he sired Miss Murray's Moryak of Moskowa to Moskowa Borzaya of Bransgore, who had been due to go with him to India.

Mrs Higgins of the Barinoff kennels went to Folkestone to mate her bitch to Marinsky just as Mrs Jenkins was beginning to feel she could keep him no longer. The combination of bombs and the constant gunfire across the channel discouraged people from bringing their bitches to him. Marinsky therefore accompanied Mrs Higgins home as a birthday present to her husband, 'where he was premier Borzoi and deeply loved not only for his matchless beauty but for his wonderful character, which he always passed to his progeny'. He died in 1947 at Barinoff, having been Mrs Higgins' companion to the end.

Ariane o' Valley Farm – his great-granddam

Marinsky had an American bitch in his pedigree: Ariane o' Valley Farm, bred by Mr Louis Murr. Ariane was imported by Mrs E Laurie and arrived in 1929 aged two. Her colour was 'mottled sable with white markings', and her sire was German-bred Asmodey Pascholl, a son of Bedin Achotnik, born before Achotnik was imported to Great

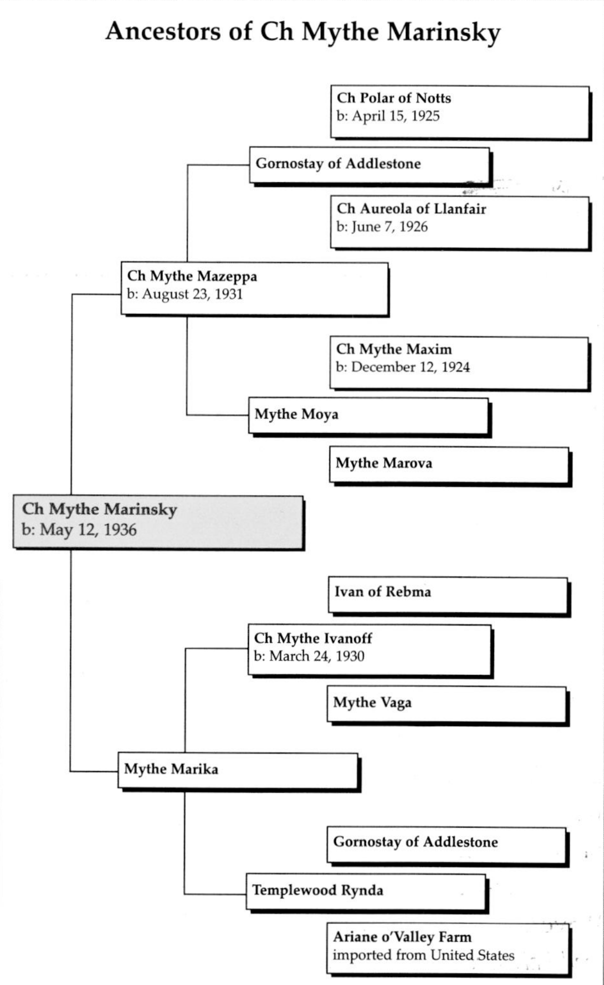

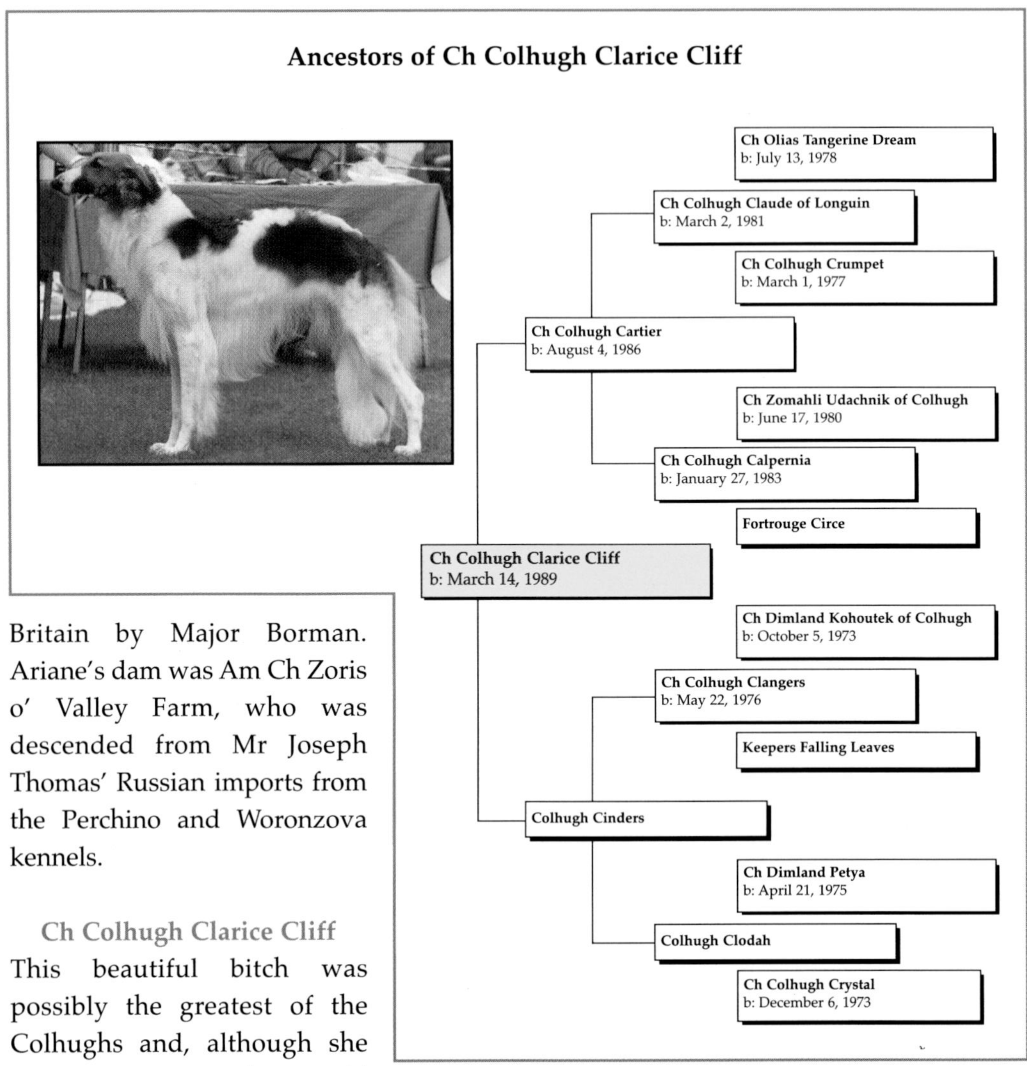

Britain by Major Borman. Ariane's dam was Am Ch Zoris o' Valley Farm, who was descended from Mr Joseph Thomas' Russian imports from the Perchino and Woronzova kennels.

Ch Colhugh Clarice Cliff

This beautiful bitch was possibly the greatest of the Colhughs and, although she won many CCs, she would have won many more were it not for the health of her breeder/owner, Mr Bassett. Her picture above must be one of the best photographs of front angulation in a Borzoi.

The Colhugh kennel took over the Addlestone record for the number of champions bred. Up to the end of 1997 there have been 34 home-bred champions, with others on the way, as well as dog and bitch CC record holders and the Borzoi with the greatest number of Group wins.

Clarice Cliff won her title in 1992 at Crufts under Mrs Claire Simmonds of the Waycross kennel, who wrote: *Stunning red and white. Very feminine but strong and elegant, well balanced and excellent type, just what I like. Shown in good coat and really hard muscular condition. Good, well balanced head, nicely set on good neck and well laid shoulders, good front, feet and bone. Correct, deep body with enough length of loin to give her balance and an excellent flowing topline. Good fallaway with super wide powerful quarters. Moved very soundly, did not put a foot wrong when challenging for the CC, she did all that was asked of her, and although I like some of her competitors very much, with her many attributes and lack of exaggeration I felt she was so outstanding that I awarded her the CC (her third) and later best of breed. It was a thrill later to see her shortlisted in the group.*

Ch Colhugh Cartier – her sire

Her sire, an outstanding dog, was Best In Show at the Scottish Hound Show in 1989. Mrs Denise Tyreman, breed judge at the show that year, wrote of Ch Colhugh Cartier: *Lovely quality sable and white, no jarring notes, everything flows beautifully, good head on nice reach of neck, shapely nicely angulated body, free and sound mover, top all of this with the Colhugh presentation and you have a well deserved CC best of breed and the delight of him going best in show.*

Ch Colhugh Cartier.
Photo courtesy Pedigree Pet Foods.

This was his second CC; his first was at Richmond in 1988, given by Mrs Peggy Malone, with the comment: Limit dog – *First Colhugh Cartier, tortoiseshell and white, well named for he surely must be another 'Diamond in the Crown', beautifully constructed young hound, long lean head, good reach of neck, nice fallaway together with good angulation and just watch him go! Floated effortlessly round the ring. CC best of breed and in the last five in the group.*

His title was won under Mr Vince Tyreman at the Southern Counties Show, with the comment: *How well balanced he is, shoulder angula-*

tion matches well his rear angulation, views from both front and rear are excellent, quality head, moved smoothly and freely covering the ground with drive. CC and best of breed, I was pleased he was in the last six in the group.

Ch Colhugh Claude of Longuin – her grandsire

Cartier's sire came from the original Colhugh lines – Ch Colhugh Claude of Longuin had five lines back to the Ch Grand Manner of Colhugh / Annikka of Greenhaven mating – but he also had the bought-in stud dog Ch Wellthornes Tilosky behind him.

Claude was owned by Miss Carol Broxup of the Longuin affix. He won his title at Driffield in 1986 under Mrs Ann Tomlinson of the Yadasar kennel. She wrote: *Grand dog, shown in first class condition, balanced head and eye, neck and shoulders were good, topline and body excellent, strong quarters, movement round and free, pleased to make him up.*

However, his four CCs paled into insignificance when compared with the wins of his litter sister, Ch Colhugh Caminickers (page 107). She remains the breed record holder with 40 CCs plus:

- Best In Show at Midland Counties in October 1985
- Hound Group at Manchester in March 1987
- Best In Show at the Scottish Hound Show in April 1987
- Best In Show at the Hound Show in August 1987
- Best In Show at the Ladies' Kennel Association in December 1987
- Hound Group at Crufts in February 1988
- Hound Group at Border Union in June 1988
- Reserve Best In Show at Blackpool in June 1989

At Driffield in 1986 she did the double with her brother and Mrs Tomlinson said of her: *Outstanding exhibit full of quality, really moved with style and has an easy flowing gait. CC and best of breed.*

The first of the three CCs to give her her title was at Midland Counties in 1982, under Mr Bill Siggers, a most respected all-rounder who had been the manager of one of the most illustrious Great Dane kennels, the Ouborough kennel of Mr James Rank. Her second was at Windsor in 1983, under the Finnish all-rounder Mr Hans Lehtinen, who said: *Superb bitch although she had left most of her coat at home. Perfect topline ending in excellent, strong and well angulated hindquarters, CC her second, the third cannot be too far away.*

The third CC came at the last show of 1983, the Ladies Kennel Association, under Miss Murray. The report read: *Red and white, lovely strongly built bitch, well proportioned outline, great width of quarters, deep chest, moved well, shown in excellent condition.*

Claude and Caminickers were not the only champions from that litter; there was also Ch Colhugh Crimebuster. The litter had comprised eight puppies. Of these, one bitch (Caminickers) was kept by Mr Bassett, one dog in a pet home (Claude) was not being well managed so was rehomed with Miss Broxup, and two were returned to Mr Bassett after a

Ch Colhugh Claude of Longuin.
Photo: Barry Greenwood

marriage break-up, one of which was Crimebuster. Also in this litter was Mrs Grist's Colhugh Calatka, the winner of the dog CC at Birmingham National Show in 1983 under Joe Braddon, and Miss Smith's Colhugh Corushko, who won the dog CC at Belfast that year under Mr Tommy Agnew.

Ch Colhugh Calpernia – her granddam

Cartier inherited his colour from his dam, Ch Colhugh Calpernia. Her sire was another truly great Borzoi bought in by Mr Bassett, Ch Zomahli Udachnik of Colhugh. The sable colour was a Zomahli trade mark, as were self blacks. Although he was not the most enthusiastic of stud dogs, Udachnik sired eight champions, four out of the bitch Fortrouge Circe. Udachnik came from the last British-bred Zomahli litter before Mr Prior emigrated to Australia.

Miss Murray lent Circe to Mr Bassett in a 'loan of bitch' agreement, for he had liked her very much when he had judged her. Circe was mated to Udachnik, but it looked as if she had missed. On returning from the Blackpool show Mr Bassett was surprised to find that she had given birth to a little bitch puppy who was to become Ch Colhugh Cyngle. As the litter had been so small, Miss Murray offered to let Circe stay to try for a larger litter and, in due course, there was a beautiful litter of coloured puppies. Calpernia was one of these puppies, as was Ch Colhugh Cuddles. The mating was repeated once again to produce Ch Fortrouge Ben of Longuin, winner of 15 CCs and Group winner at Bath in May 1988.

Calpernia was never beaten in her classes, winning six CCs before she died of bloat at the age of two, despite veterinary attention, leaving a six-week-old litter. Her first CC came from Mrs Sylvia Marston of the Falconcrag Borzois, who judged at Blackpool in 1984. Junior bitch – *First Colhugh Calpernia, superb, I found her entirely satisfying, her colour is glamorous, her flowing movement is a joy. CC and best of breed.*

Her title came from the all-rounder Dr Ben Raven, whose own breed was the Dachshund. His report from the Birmingham City Show ran: *Very elegant sable, good head carriage, noble bearing, excellent forehand, good topline, deep brisket, wide and strongly muscled behind, good turn of stifle, in good coat, moved and showed well, bitch CC, her qualifying third today.*

She lost out to her sire for Best of Breed: *Ch Zomahli Udachnik of Colhugh, showy sable, in excellent coat and bloom, well balanced head, dark oval shaped eye, shoulders sloped well back, good depth of body, great width behind with powerful hindquarters, good length of second thigh, moved with good stride.*

The bitch Reserve CC went to Udachnik's litter sister, Mr Michael Real's Ch Zomahli Ushmeka of Nakora: *Another elegant sable, well balanced in head, depth and body, in good coat, pleasing topline, good width behind, strongly muscled quarters, good turn of stifle, moved well.*

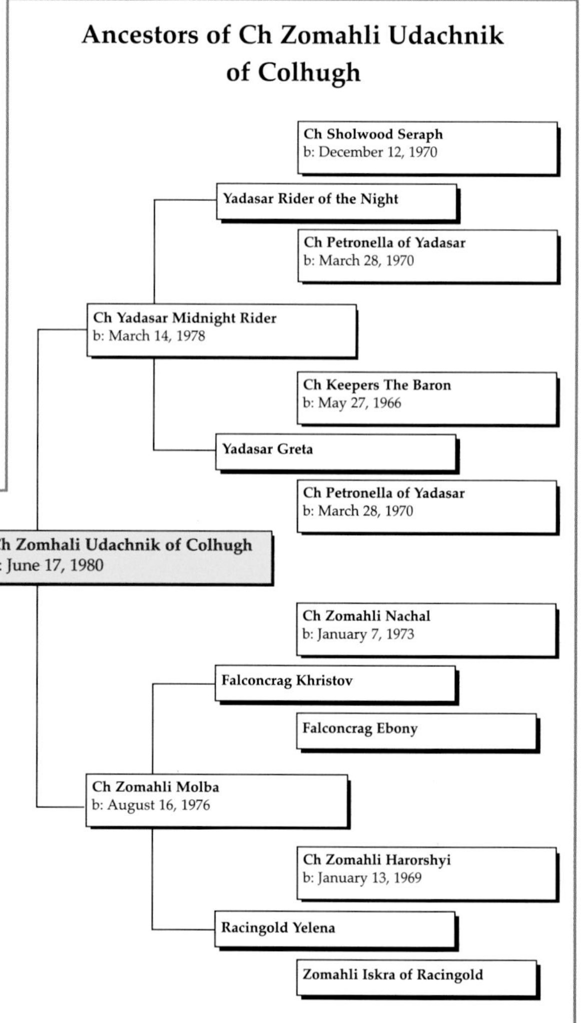

Ch Colhugh Caminickers, breed record holder with 40 CCs.
Photo: Diane Pearce

Ch Zomahli Udachnik of Colhugh

We have already discussed the beginning of Mrs Lillie Pearson and Mr Keith Prior's Zomahlis under Ch Zomahli Chernila on page 62.

Ch Zomahli Molba – his dam

Udachnik was a son of Ch Zomahli Molba, a self black bitch who won her title under Miss Murray at the Northern Borzoi Association Show in 1980. Miss Murray reported: *Well balanced head, sweet expression, dark eye, well angulated shoulders and hindquarters, deep chest, good coat, moved freely with good drive.*

Falconcrag Khristov – his grandsire

Although neither of Molba's parents carried the affix Zomahli, they were from Zomahli bloodlines. Her sire, Mrs Marston's Falconcrag Khristov, won two CCs and was the sire of four champions, three of them Zomahlis and one from Mr Michael Reals's Nakora kennel. Khristov won his first CC under Mrs Pearson at the Scottish Kennel Club Show in 1976, when she noted: *Big self black, in lovely coat and condition, very mature for age, beautiful head, excellent body and angulation, moved with drive on powerful hindquarters. CC and best of breed.*

His second came at the Southern Counties Show in 1979, from Mr Prior, who wrote: *An old favourite carrying a terrific coat, beautiful long fine head with well shaped dark eye, very well angulated, nicely bladed bone, moved with great drive. CC.*

Ch Zomahli Nachal – his great-grandsire

At this time The Kennel Club still allowed complete changes of name, and each hound brought into the Zomahli kennel had a name beginning with N. Nachal (Ch Zomahli Harorshyi ex Zomahli Iskra of Racingold) was bred by Mrs and Miss Dean. From Molba's pedigree we can see that Nachal was a full brother of Racingold Yelena, the dam of Molba.

Nachal was also the litter brother of the exquisite Ch Zomahli Nadesda who won 16 CCs and Ch Racingold Yasha of Lanclare. Nachal's first CC was from Mrs Marston at Leeds in 1776, who wrote:

Open dog – *First Zomahli Nachal. Black and white, beautiful coat and condition, powerfully built, well angulated, the desired width over the hindquarters, moved very soundly. CC and best of breed.*

Second – Racingold Yasha of Lanclare, self black, very little separated these two, the first scoring in balance and having the firmer front action. Reserve CC.

Mr Harry Spira from Australia gave Nadesa her first CC at Leeds 1974, commenting: *Superlative specimen, delightful Borzoi in all respects. Typical head properties in profile and when viewed from the top, feminine expression yet strong mandibles and deep muzzle, well shaped and properly placed dark eye. True front of adequate width yet not too wide, clean strong bone and excellent feet. Topline strong and roaching from withers to rump, this roach is present both when moving and standing. Despite strong competition, particularly in open bitch, went on to take the CC. At no time did she or her handler put a foot wrong, they worked as a team and thoroughly deserved best of breed.*

Nadesa's second CC came from the all-rounder Mr Bobby James, who had started with Whippets, and he called her: *A high quality tortoiseshell, at 17 months is surprisingly forward. Clean, fine head with veining (which seems to have virtually disappeared from the breed), good depth for age, correct bone and feet, very elegant, yet with the strength and power in her movement, presented and shown with aplomb. I should say will be an easy champion. A pleasure to give her the CC.*

Ch Zomahli Harorshyi – his great-grandsire

The next generation back was Ch Zomahli Harorshyi, owned by Mrs Barratt and winner of nine CCs, as well as a subsequent title in South Africa. Mrs Jill Chapman, daughter of Mrs Grace Beresford of the Yadasars, officiated at Cheshire in 1971 and said of him: *Most impressive self black, fabulous coat and fringing, put down to the minute. Well balanced throughout, good reach of neck, well laid shoulders, true front, grand compact body, firm well-angulated hindquarters, moved freely and with drive. I was pleased to award him the CC, his second, and best of breed.*

The Zomahli litters were named in alphabetical order and, as we are following pedigrees back, we go from the H to the G litter: Harorshyi's sire was Gordey, who was exported to the United Stares to win his title there. His litter brother and sister were Ch Zomahli Gueroy and Ch Zomahli Gratseeya, born in 1967 with Ch Black Diamond of Enolam (brother of Ch Angelola of Enolam, illustrated on page 60) as sire and Zomahli Nayada (sister of Ch Keepers Michael Angelo) as dam.

The G litter did well at Manchester in 1969 under Mrs D Whitwell, an all-rounder who had made up both Whippet and Greyhound champions. Her report ran:

Junior – *First and CC Zomahli Gueroy, truly great youngster, very hard to seriously fault and can improve only with age, excellent head, eye, neck, front, body, bone size and outline. Tremendous power behind, moved perfectly, good coat, condition, and feet. Will have a brilliant show and stud career.*

Novice bitch – *First Zomahli Gratseeya, litter sister of the winning dog, a beauty who should also go places when she gets confidence, lovely head, body, front and hind legs, balanced, good legs and feet, and the more she moved the better she went.*

Ch Yadasar Midnight Rider.

Ch Yadasar Midnight Rider – his sire

Udachnik's sire was among the most outstanding stud dogs from the Yadasar kennel that was started by Mrs Grace Beresford and continued by her daughter Mrs Ann Tomlinson. Ch Yadasar Midnight Rider won his first CC at Crufts in 1981 under Mrs

Sylvia Marston, who noted: *Self black, most handsome, stands over a lot of ground, has the movement I was looking for, a symmetrical, beautifully balanced Borzoi, very good in shoulder placement and hind angulation.*

Mrs Beresford married into Borzois by marrying Mr Stanley Beresford, who had the breed from the late 1920s. The name Yadasar came from a book about Russia called The Yadasar Fortress. At the time of the marriage Mr Beresford had a bitch called Eaton Emerald, and she was mated to a bought-in dog, a self red son of Petroff of Beechwood, winner of two CCs, who started off the Tangmeres. This dog was Wrays Golden Marquis, a dog of wonderful temperament, of whom Mrs Beresford said:

Nothing ever ruffled him. You could take him in the densest traffic loose and he would never move from your heel. He had a great weakness for potato crisps and a drink of beer. Once a publican tried to get him drunk by giving him two pints to drink. He lapped it up with gusto and the landlord of the pub came to watch him walk down the road but he was perfectly sober, walking along in his usual sedate manner.

Eaton Emerald, or Jennie, was just as calm. She always greeted friends with a terrific grin, which has come down to her children today. Jennie had pneumonia when two years old and never lay down for a month, just stood up the whole time. I fed her hourly on egg, milk and whisky and the vet came twice a day to inject her. Jennie's breathing could be heard all over the house but she pulled through and Duska was one of the puppies she had three years after.

Duska was in the pedigree of the first champion that Mrs Beresford made up, Ch Winjones Bolshia, bred by Mrs Chadwick out of Winjones Bistri, a granddaughter of Duska. Bolshia's litter sister was kept by Mrs Chadwick to become Ch Winjones Balviniza, and Bistri was also the dam of Ch Winjones Lebediska.

Ch Tessina of Yadasar was bought in. She was Best In Show at the Borzoi Club Jubilee Show in 1952 under Mrs Vlasto, who wrote: *This is a lovely bitch, shown in perfect bloom, very good bone, wonderful propelling power behind, hard to fault and went on to win the CC and best in show.*

Tessina was the product of a half-brother-to-half-sister mating, both of these from Mrs Harris' war-time Mantavani kennel. She had a line back to the Tangmeres and a number of Mythes behind her.

Ch Bolshia was mated to Ch Winjones Ermolai to produce Gay Cavalier of Yadasar, a self red dog who was an influential stud dog and the first stud dog that Ann Tomlinson remembers clearly. He was not campaigned at the shows because Mrs Beresford preferred to exhibit bitches, but he sired Ch Zomahli Nadia and Ch Nice Fella, both of whom won Crufts CCs.

Gay Cavalier was mated to Ch Tessina, giving Jonathan of Yadasar, another self red. Jonathan was doing well at shows, first in his class at Crufts 1955 under Mrs Diana George, who wrote of him: *Sixteen months dog, a bright self red, a very nice youngster indeed, good length of head of good quality, short coupled body and good quarters, plenty of heart room, he was well coated and in good condition, sound and a free mover.*

However, a flamboyant visitor arrived in Belper, Derbyshire, so flamboyant that she ended up in the Sunday papers. This was the Baroness von Thyssen, formerly the model Nina Dyer, and, when she returned to her chateau near Versailles, Jonathan went too. Before he went he sired Ch Reyas Sandra, probably the most important brood bitch in Mr Edgar Sayer's Reyas kennel. He also sired Lustre of Yadasar, the dam of three champions for the Barthill kennel of Mrs Harpur.

Ch Petronella of Yadasar – his great-granddam

Ch Petronella of Yadasar was Midnight Rider's granddam twice over. She was bred by Mrs Harpur and both her Barhill parents had lines back to Lustre. She was born in 1970, winning her first CC from Mrs Jackie Bennett-Heard of the Keepers affix at Richmond in 1971. Mrs Bennett-Heard wrote: *Exquisite self red, very feminine, beautiful head and dark eye, plenty of substance, moved and showed well, marvellous condition.*

Mrs Sylvia Marston gave her her second CC the following year at the Hound Show, commenting: *Self red, splendid shoulder and forehand generally, very good hindquarters, bend of stifle and low hock, sweet feminine head, has matured into a lovely exhibit, not a big bitch but she is so well balanced both in stance and movement, in good bloom. CC.*

When mated to Ch Sholwood Seraph, Petronella produced Yadasar Rider of the Night, a dog who tragically died at the age of two but fortunately after he had sired Midnight Rider.

Yadasar Greta – his granddam

When mated to a son of the Russian import Boran Petronella produced Yadasar Greta. As well as producing Midnight Rider, Greta won a CC herself. This was under Mr Keith Prior at the Hound Show in 1975, where the dog winner was Ch Sholwood Seraph. Mr Prior's report ran:

Open dog – *Sholwood Seraph, self black, old favourite of mine, showed and handled very well, in beautiful coat and condition, flowed round the ring, very hard to fault anywhere, CC and best of breed, I was delighted to learn later that he went on to best in show.*

Open bitch – *First Yadasar Greta, big powerful self black, in lovely coat and condition, well veined fine head, good shoulder and neck, excellent quarters which she used with drive, lovely straight front and good feet.*

Ch Sholwood Seraph

We have met many of the dogs in Seraph's pedigree before. It contains three of the greatest brood bitches in the breed, each of whom won her title as well. Seraph was a double

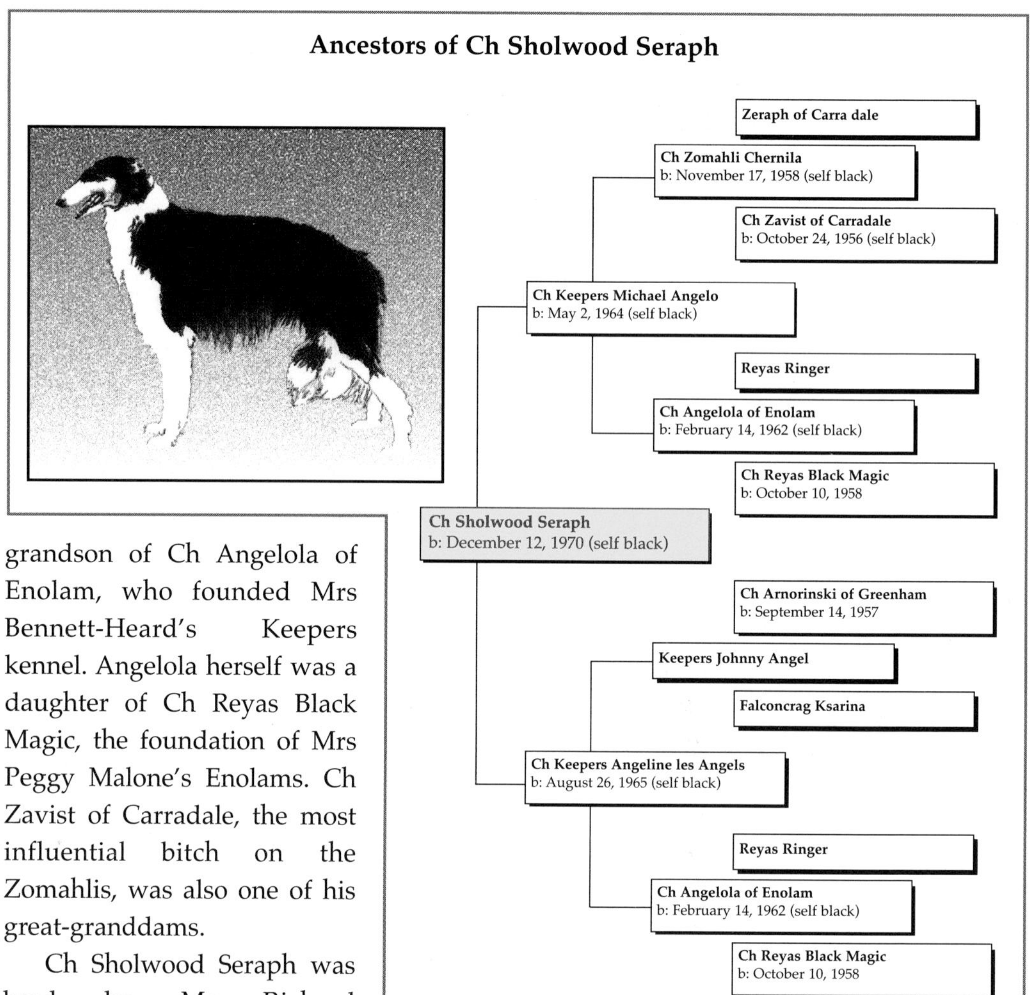

grandson of Ch Angelola of Enolam, who founded Mrs Bennett-Heard's Keepers kennel. Angelola herself was a daughter of Ch Reyas Black Magic, the foundation of Mrs Peggy Malone's Enolams. Ch Zavist of Carradale, the most influential bitch on the Zomahlis, was also one of his great-granddams.

Ch Sholwood Seraph was bred by Mr Richard Duckworth and, when he felt he could not do the dog justice, he let him go to Mrs Barbara Long as foundation stud for her Bacaret kennel. He won six CCs and BIS at the Hound Show 1975.

Ch Reyas Black Magic – his great-granddam

Ch Reyas Black Magic was the dam of five champions: three to Reyas Ringer (a son of Ch Reyas Sandra), one to Am Ch Jobi Reyas Rohan and the last to her own grandson, Michael Angelo.

She won four CCs, the first at Birmingham National in 1963, when Mrs Beresford commented from the ringside: *In excellent condition, lovely dark eye, neat well placed ears, is short, deep and of good shape.*

Her fourth came from Mr Leo Wilson, editor of the newspaper *Dog World* and a leading Fox Terrier breeder. Judging at the West of England Ladies Kennel Society Show in 1965, he wrote: *Heavily marked black, great size and length of head, remarkably well preserved for her six years and in lovely coat.*

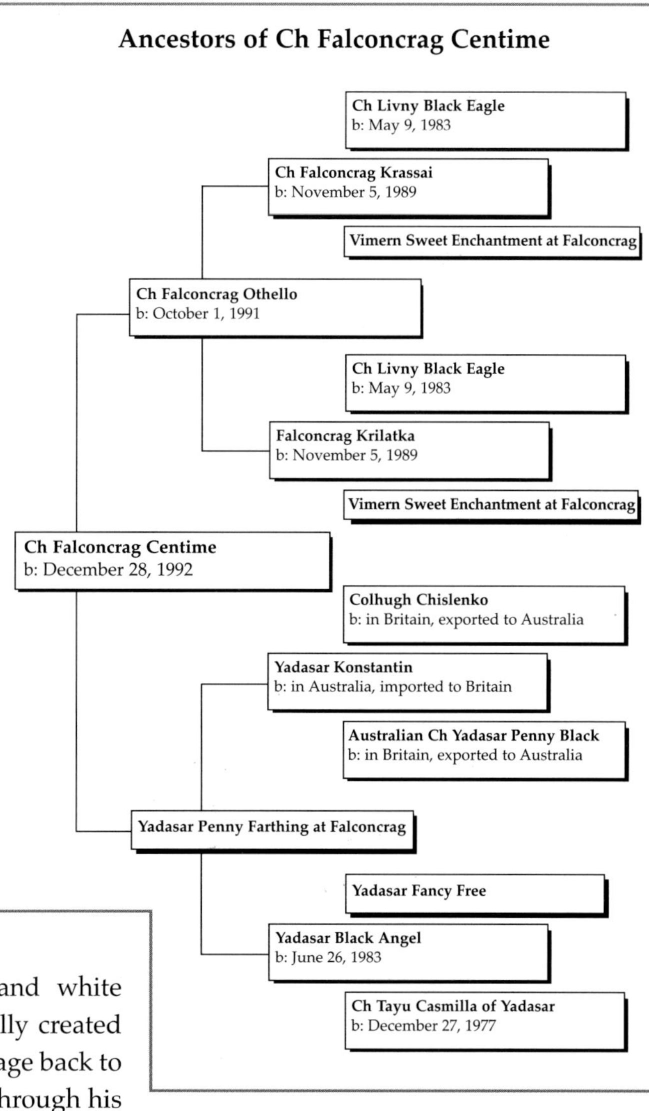

Ch Falconcrag Centime

If we look at the list of Borzois who have won CCs at Crufts in the period 1980–1990 we can see that there has been a 'revolution' in the type of hound winning. At the beginning we have self-coloured Borzois of ultra-houndy Northern British lines from the Yadasar, Zomahli and Barcaret lines. In 1985 both CC winners were of the stronger made Southern red and white bloodlines, a type of Borzoi really created by Mr Basset that traces its heritage back to Ch Grand Manner of Colhugh through his daughter Ch Colhugh Valla.

One of the few to keep to the Northern lines was the Falconcrag kennel of Mrs Sylvia and Miss Pamela Marston. The Falconcrags started in the late 1950s with Lataband Anita, a black and white who produced the first Falconcrag champion, Ch Falconcrag Zsa Zsa, who was made up in 1964. We have already met two of her grandparents: Lustre of Yadasar and Marcellus of Fortrouge.

Falconcrags appear in both Yadasar and Zomahli pedigrees, as can be seen in the section on dual-CC-winning Falconcrag Khristov, sire of four champions.

Falconcrag Centime is the most recent Falconcrag champion. She gained her title under Mr Trevor Jepson, the Secretary of the Northern Borzoi Association and breeder and owner of champion northern-type Borzois. He gave her her third CC at Leeds in 1996, writing: *Lovely self black bitch with a classic head, loved her as a junior and as a mature lady has not disappointed me. Has excellent angulation, lovely low hocks and moved very well with good reach and drive from behind. Pleased to give her her third and crowning CC.*

Ch Falconcrag Krassai – her grandsire

The first male Falconcrag champion, after a run of bitches, was Ch Falconcrag Krassai, a personal favourite of mine because of his sweet nature. His dam, Vimern Sweet Enchantment at Falconcrag, was a double granddaughter of Khristov, her sire being Ch Zomahli Ozopnik. Krassai won his first CC from Mr Michael Real of the Nakora kennel at the Ladies Kennel Association Show at the end of 1991, when he wrote: *What an eye-catcher, pleasure to go over, conformation is first class, classic head and expression with depth, totally in proportion, masculine, not a trace of coarseness, wonderful shoulders, excellent front and spring of rib, excellent topline, his outline both standing and on the move is flowing from nose to tail, when moving is a joy to watch, correctly made, movement is correct. To watch him, the drive with his super hindquarters on strong low hocks is obvious, wish he were mine, his crown will soon follow his first CC and best of breed.*

The third came at the next year's LKA show, this time under Mr John Stears who, with his wife Brenda, owned the Livny hounds. He noted: *This hound has matured fulfilling the promise he showed as a youngster. A pleasure to go over. Sound and as steady as a rock. Moved with purpose driving from his hocks, holding his perfect topline in the process at all times. Typical of his type CC and best of breed.*

Ch Falconcrag Othello – her sire

Krassai's son Ch Falconcrag Othello won all his CCs in 1994, his first at the Hound Association of Scotland under Mrs Jill Chapman. She wrote: *One that demands attention, true breed elegance with excellent head and eye, well placed shoulder, sound body and firm quarters, moved with drive, pleasure to watch moving. CC and best of breed.*

Ch Livny Black Eagle

Ch Livny Black Eagle was a widely-used stud dog who has had a profound influence on the breed through a number of bitches of varying bloodlines. He produced his first champion offspring for the home kennel when mated back to his dam to produce Ch Livny Winston. To the imported Ch Stillwater Virginia Reel there was Ch Sholwood Sonnet, an almost completely black bitch with no tan markings with her white ones. To a Fortrouge bitch he produced Ch Sholwood Sprig Muslin, and his next champion was

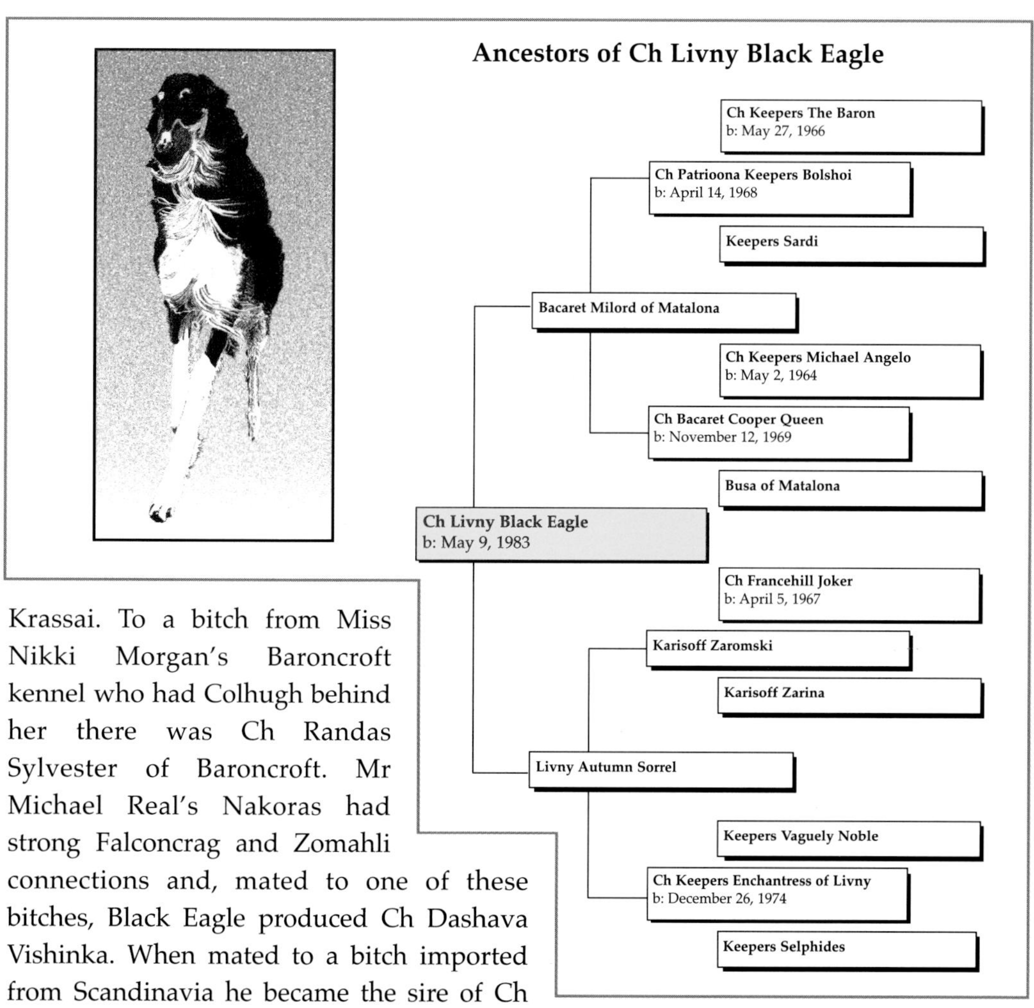

Krassai. To a bitch from Miss Nikki Morgan's Baroncroft kennel who had Colhugh behind her there was Ch Randas Sylvester of Baroncroft. Mr Michael Real's Nakoras had strong Falconcrag and Zomahli connections and, mated to one of these bitches, Black Eagle produced Ch Dashava Vishinka. When mated to a bitch imported from Scandinavia he became the sire of Ch Saringa's Angostura, and his final champion was Ch Lelant Galena, whose dam was a granddaughter of his own sire, Bacaret Milord of Matalona.

Altogether, Black Eagle won 18 CCs. His second came from the all-rounder judge Mr Terry Thorn, whose own breed was the Saluki, at the Welsh Kennel Club Show in 1984, with the comment: *Tall, elegant tricolour, super head and general forehand, nicely bodied with good depth for age, a dog of lovely balance and general outline. Moving very well indeed.*

He won BIS at the Borzoi Club Show, together with his fourth CC, under Mrs Penny Lamport, who said: *What a thrill to go over this handsome dog, such a beautifully proportioned hound, excelled in head, eye and neck and has all the essentials to make a great dog, covered the ground on the move with the utmost ease and precision. CC and best of breed.*

Bacaret Milord of Matalona.

Ch Keepers Enchantress of Livny

Mr and Mrs Stears' Livny kennel was founded on Ch Keepers Enchantress of Livny, the last champion from the Keepers kennel, bred by Mr Bennett-Heart. She was a self red, a granddaughter of Ch Keepers Michael Angelo and also with a line back to the Russian import Boran.

Her second CC came from Mrs Margaret Searle of the Francehill affix at the LKA Show in 1979 with the comment: *Beautiful dark self red, typical 'Keepers', excellent shape and being a tall elegant Borzoi, she has that look of quality that makes a CC winner, beautifully presented and shown to every advantage, I really loved her movement and shall watch for her to get the elusive third CC with eagerness.*

Bacaret Milord of Matalona – his sire

The litter born by Ch Bacaret Copper Queen to the group-winning Ch Patrioona Keepers Bolshoi in 1975 contained two important sires: Bacaret Milord of Matalona and Bacaret

Prince Noir. This mating was repeated in 1976 to produce Ch Bacaret Lord Super Tramp, who was later exported to Sweden.

Prince Noir won the reserve CC at the East of England Show in 1981 under Mr Keith Prior, who said: *Well bodied self black in excellent coat, good shoulder, nice flowing topline. I should like just a little more bend behind but he moved soundly.* He was the sire of Ch Swiftcroft Fleeting Spirit.

Milord, who was the sire of Ch Livny Whispering Windrush, older full brother to Black Eagle, won two reserve CCs, both in 1980. The first was at the West of England Ladies' Kennel Society Show under the all-rounder Mr Harry Jordan, who noted: *Built on nice classical lines, super head, very deep thorax, well coated, moved very freely.*

Mrs Barbara Long gave him a Reserve CC at the East of England Show. She commented: *My own breeding and proud of him. Self black, most attractive head and expression, correct bite and full dentition, dark eye, good shoulders, front and depth of body, strong flexible topline into correctly angulated hindquarters, with low hocks, hind movement strong and thrusting, his front long and free front extension covering the ground well. Not in the best of coats which matters when it comes to the CC. Had pleasure in giving him the reserve CC.*

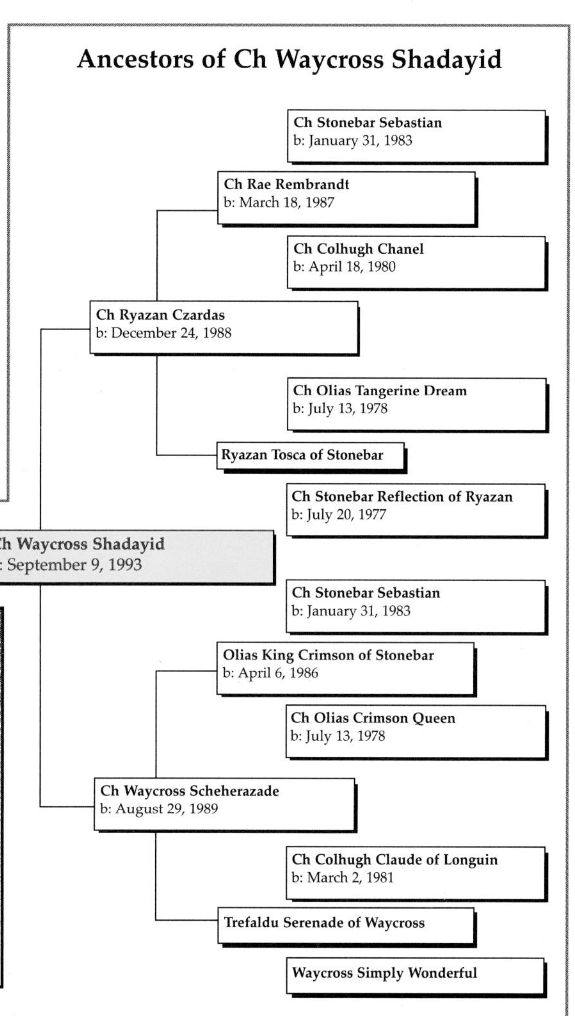

Ch Patrioona Keepers Bolshoi – his grandsire

Miss Annette Blair's Ch Patrioona Keepers Bolshoi was a grandson of the Russian import Boran through his sire Ch Keepers The Baron. His big win was at Cheshire Championship Show in June 1972, when he was reserve BIS under Mr Hawkin, one of the most senior breeders of the time, who commented: *Black and white, well balanced dog, good head, mature body, moved well.*

When he won his fifth CC Mr Bobby James wrote: *This black and white at six is right at his peak and it demonstrates how long the breed really takes to mature. Streets ahead of anything here in his sex, a dog of great quality and first class type, moves beautifully, retains his outline at any speed, correct topline, good depth, completely balanced, his quality head which is masculine yet fine, completes him.*

Ch Waycross Shadayid

The pedigree of Ch Waycross Shadayid draws together two lines descending from Ch Colhugh Valla, as she goes back to two of Valla's Daughters, Ch Colhugh Chanel and Ch Colhugh Collette of Olias.

Shadayid won her first CC at the Northern Borzoi Association Show under the American specialist judge Mrs Tamboer, and her title came at the Three Counties Show in June 1996 from Mr Reg Bassett. He said: *Nice head, good coat, moved well.*

Through her dam, Shadayid is from a line of bitches going back to the 1977 Crufts Group winner, the self black Ch Waycross Roksana, bred by Mrs Simmonds (then Mrs Anderson) and daughter of Ch Wellthornes Tilosky (see page 61). Roksana was BOB at Crufts in 1975 and 1976 as well as 1977. In an interview at the time, Mrs Simmonds said: *She was very like a Border Collie as a puppy being self black and a great lumping thing. Actually it was Reg Bassett who first liked her.*

The Group judge was Mrs Carol Appleton who had the Appeline kennel with her husband. They were most famous for Beagles, but they had also bred some German Shorthaired Pointer champions. Mrs Appleton wrote: *A bitch with whom I could find no complaint at all. A hound built to do the job for which she was bred, in superb condition and quite undismayed by the occasion. Her depth of brisket impressed me particularly.*

Ch Ryazan Czardas – her sire

Shadayid's sire was Miss Jean Clare's Ch Ryazan Czardas, grandson to Ch Colhugh Chanel and great-grandson to Ch Colhugh Collette of Olias. His first CC came at Windsor in 1991, under Mr John Stears, who noted: *White and red, exceptional dog of quality and substance, balanced throughout, well veined head, dark eye, good forechest and depth of brisket giving him ample heart and lung room, sweeping fallaway followed through to low set hocks. CC best of breed and short listed in the group.*

His second CC came at Bournemouth in 1991 from Mrs Gina Rose, whose Stonebar breeding figured in his pedigree. The foundation of the winning line in the Ryazan kennel was Ch Stonebar Reflection of Ryazan. Mrs Rose commented: *Red and white, good type of hound, good head, lovely dark eye, strong shoulders, well laid back, deep brisket, front feet well under him, firm loin, free moving with drive from behind.*

Ch Rae Rembrandt.
Photo courtesy Roger Heap.

Ch Rae Rembrandt – her grandsire

Czardas' sire, Ch Rae Rembrandt, won his title in 1991 under Mr Vince Tyreman, who noted: *A mature four year old fawn and white, well covered and presented. His overall balance and maturity won him the CC. Good set hocks and rear angulation.*

Ch Waycross Scheherazade – her dam

Ch Waycross Scheherazade won her title under Mr Reg Bassett at Manchester in 1991, when he wrote: *White and red, presented magnificently, whiter than white, nice head, quite nicely balanced, could have a darker eye but all round a super bitch. Nice angulation front and rear, decent shoulder, lovely back end, good fallaway, good depth, super bitch. CC and best of breed.*

Olias King Crimson of Stonebar – her grandsire

Scheherazade's sire was dual-CC-winning Olias King Crimson of Stonebar, a great-grandson of Ch Colhugh Valla through his dam Ch Olias Crimson Queen. Although neither he nor his litter sister Olias Ivory Queen won their titles they are both important influences on the Borzoi in the ring in the late 1990s. They made their debut at the Borzoi Club Show in 1986 under Mr Richard Duckworth, who noted:

Minor Puppy Dog – *First Olias King Crimson, beautifully constructed orange and white, very well grown and mature for age, masculine without coarseness, lovely forehand, depth and quarters. Best puppy.*

Minor Puppy Bitch – *A good class of promising young bitches. First Olias Ivory Queen, another quality one from this kennel, scored on her mature appearance and excellent construction, also in head, shoulder and outline, better feet than her brother but failed to him for best puppy on front action, however a very promising one.*

King Crimson won his second CC at Manchester in 1991 under Mr Reg Bassett. The critique ran: *Without a shadow of a doubt stood out in this class. Beautifully presented, nice head, lovely small dark eye. To be critical would have liked a finer skull and a bit tighter feet, but overall a lovely balanced dog. Just a little steep in the croup, but with lovely hind angulation and good muscling. A well deserved CC.*

Before King Crimson was exported to the United States he sired five champions. To Ch Colhugh Valla's granddaughter Vronsky Sweet Charity he sired Ch Vronsky Careless Whisper and Ch Vronsky Kindred Spirit of Tatiana. To Ch Ryazan Laura of Yadasar, four generations on from Valla, he sired Ch Yadasar Orlando of Labinska, Ch Yadasar Oprah and Ch Yadasar Odette of Ryazan. The last of these was from a litter bred by Mrs Ann Tomlinson as 'an experiment in the Southern bloodlines'. A rather successful experiment!

Olias Ivory Queen won the reserve CC at Leeds in 1989, the judge being Mr Robin Searle of the Francehill Borzois. He wrote: *Classic shape and type, good condition and sound mover.*

Ivory Queen twice won the Top Brood Bitch award. This honour has also been won by Miesque, the dam of multiple-CC-winners Ch Starborough Sharmanka and Ch Starborough Gorse at Redbanner.

Ivory Queen and King Crimson had a litter sister, Olias Queen Bee at Shelbor, who also became the dam of a champion: Mr Brian O'Callaghan's Ch Shelbor Gold Charm at Matford.

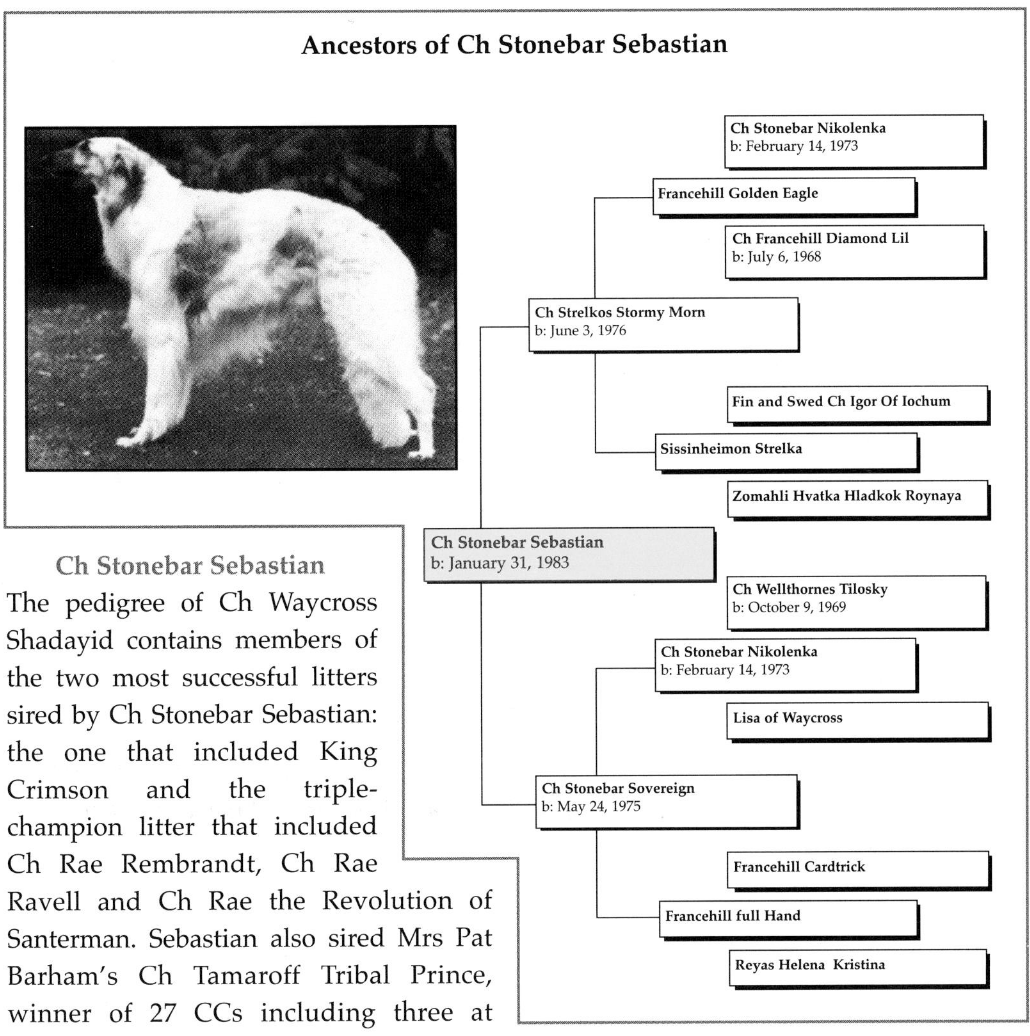

Ch Stonebar Sebastian

The pedigree of Ch Waycross Shadayid contains members of the two most successful litters sired by Ch Stonebar Sebastian: the one that included King Crimson and the triple-champion litter that included Ch Rae Rembrandt, Ch Rae Ravell and Ch Rae the Revolution of Santerman. Sebastian also sired Mrs Pat Barham's Ch Tamaroff Tribal Prince, winner of 27 CCs including three at Crufts.

In a poll for the greatest-ever Borzoi held in 1992, the centenary year of the Borzoi Club, Sebastian was the dog selected most frequently. He was one of the big winners in the group, and top-winning hound of all breeds in 1986, when he won the following awards:

- Hound Group at Three Counties Show
- Hound Group at Leeds
- Hound Group at Bournemouth
- Hound Group at the Welsh Kennel Club Show
- Hound Group at Birmingham City
- BIS at Border Counties Hound Show

Francehill Golden Eagle.

Mrs Barham was judging at Crufts that year, and she wrote: *Lovely, elegant, have always admired him, has matured since I awarded him a Reserve CC. Super head and expression, excellent shoulders and depth of brisket, correct stifle, well developed quarters, moved with plenty of drive, good feet, lovely silky coat texture, one I would like to own, CC and best of breed.*

Ch Strelkos Stormy Morn – his sire

Ch Strelkos Stormy Morn was the first champion bred by Mrs Christine Spencer, Secretary of the Borzoi Club, in her Strelkos kennel. He was the only puppy in the litter by Francehill Golden Eagle out of Sissinheimon Strelka. Strelka was bred by the Finnish couple Mr and Mrs Pellikka. Her dam was a Zomahli and her sire was a Finnish import who will be discussed in chapter 4.

Stormy Morn won his first CC at the East of England Show in 1979, under breed specialist Mrs Elizabeth Etheridge. She commented: *Has matured a lot since I gave him the reserve CC a year ago. Lovely flowing movement, beautiful head and coat, correct bite.*

Francehill Golden Eagle – his grandsire

Stormy Morn's sire was a CC winner. Francehill Golden Eagle won at Bournemouth in 1977. Mr Terry Thorn, the judge, wrote: *Striking fawn and white fills the eye for elegance and breed type. Lovely head and eye, perfect front and bone, good depth of brisket, correct arch, strong quarters, well angulated, completely free movement covering the required amount of ground in even and true fashion.*

Ch Stonebar Nikolenka – his great-grandsire

Golden Eagle's sire, Mrs Gina Rose's Ch Stonebar Nikolenka, appears twice in Sebastian's pedigree. Nikolenka was a full brother of the Crufts Group winner Ch Waycross Roksana, who beat him for BOB at Crufts 1977. Mr Stanley Young, the breed judge, wrote:

Open Dog – *First Stonebar Nikolenka, wonderful presence, a favourite of mine, good head, neck and shoulders, his arch starts in the right place and swings away to wide quarters, size and substance, his movement was a pleasure to watch.*

Open Bitch – *First Ch Waycross Roksana, superb bitch, sweet head, lovely bodyline, depth of brisket, nice turn of stifle, good short hocks, making her beautifully let down behind, I must congratulate her owner on the way she was put down and handled, second to none, my CC, BOB and the group winner.*

Ch Strelkos Stormy Morn.

Borzoi overseas

The first country to adopt the Borzoi as a show breed was Great Britain, so British-bred stock is behind Borzoi pedigrees in all countries except its homeland of Russia.

Dog illustrated

Ancestors of Am Ch Vinga of Seacroft

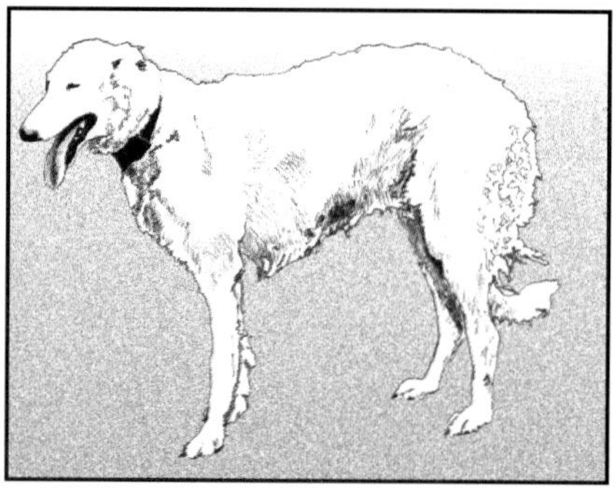

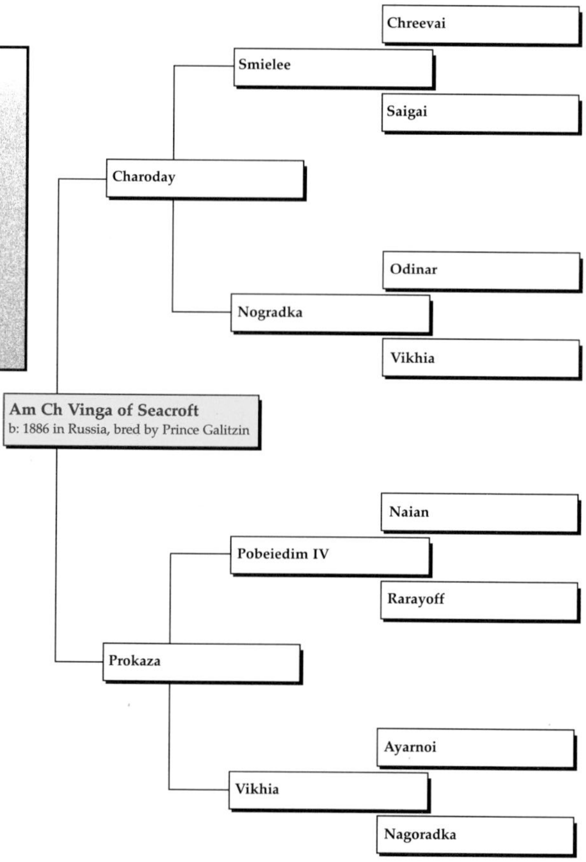

Dog	Parents	Grandparents	Great-grandparents
Am Ch Vinga of Seacroft b: 1886 in Russia, bred by Prince Galitzin	Charoday	Smielee	Chreevai
			Saigai
		Nogradka	Odinar
			Vikhia
	Prokaza	Pobeiedim IV	Naian
			Rarayoff
		Vikhia	Ayarnoi
			Nagoradka

Early American imports

The first British exports to the United States were a brother and sister, Vladimir and Princess Irma, who were registered in the 1892 volume of the *American Kennel Club Stud Book*. They were children of the first British champion, Ch Krilutt, imported by Mr William Wade of Pennsylvania.

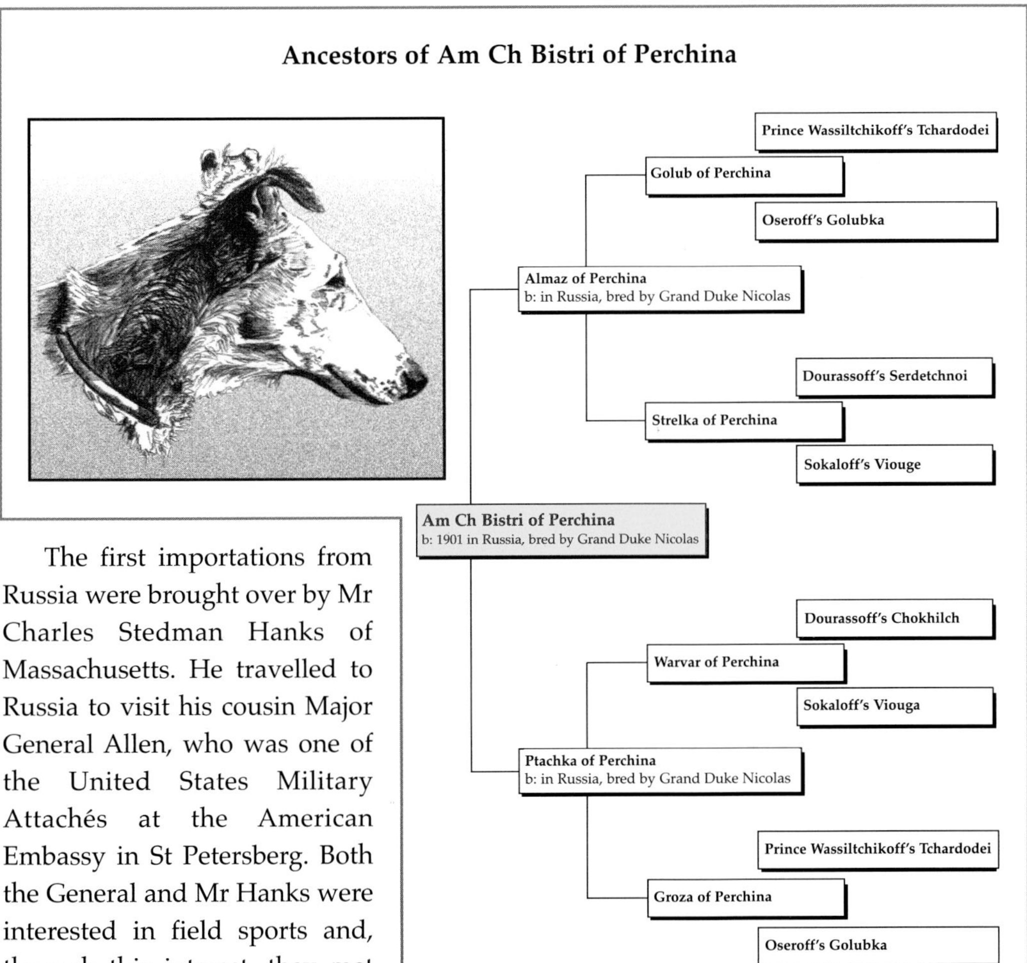

The first importations from Russia were brought over by Mr Charles Stedman Hanks of Massachusetts. He travelled to Russia to visit his cousin Major General Allen, who was one of the United States Military Attachés at the American Embassy in St Petersberg. Both the General and Mr Hanks were interested in field sports and, through this interest, they met those connected with the Imperial Kennels at Gatchina. They brought hounds over to America from 1890. These hounds were of the usual poor quality from this source and Am Ch Vinga of Seacroft, a white hound imported for Mr Hanks' Seacroft kennel, is pictured on the opposite page.

The first quality American imports were brought over by Mr Joseph Thomas after his visits to the Perchina and Woronzova kennels described in chapter 2. One of the finest of his imports was the hound who was to become Am Ch Bistri of Perchina. He was the best male Borzoi at the Westminster Show (the premier American dog show) from 1904 to 1906. Mr Thomas described Bistri's head as the ideal ancient type and greatly admired his sire, Almaz of Perchina.

A mating of Bistri with Rasskida of Woronzova, an import from Mr Artem Bolderoff's kennel, produced Am Ch Rasboi o' Valley Farm, who was Best Male Borzoi at

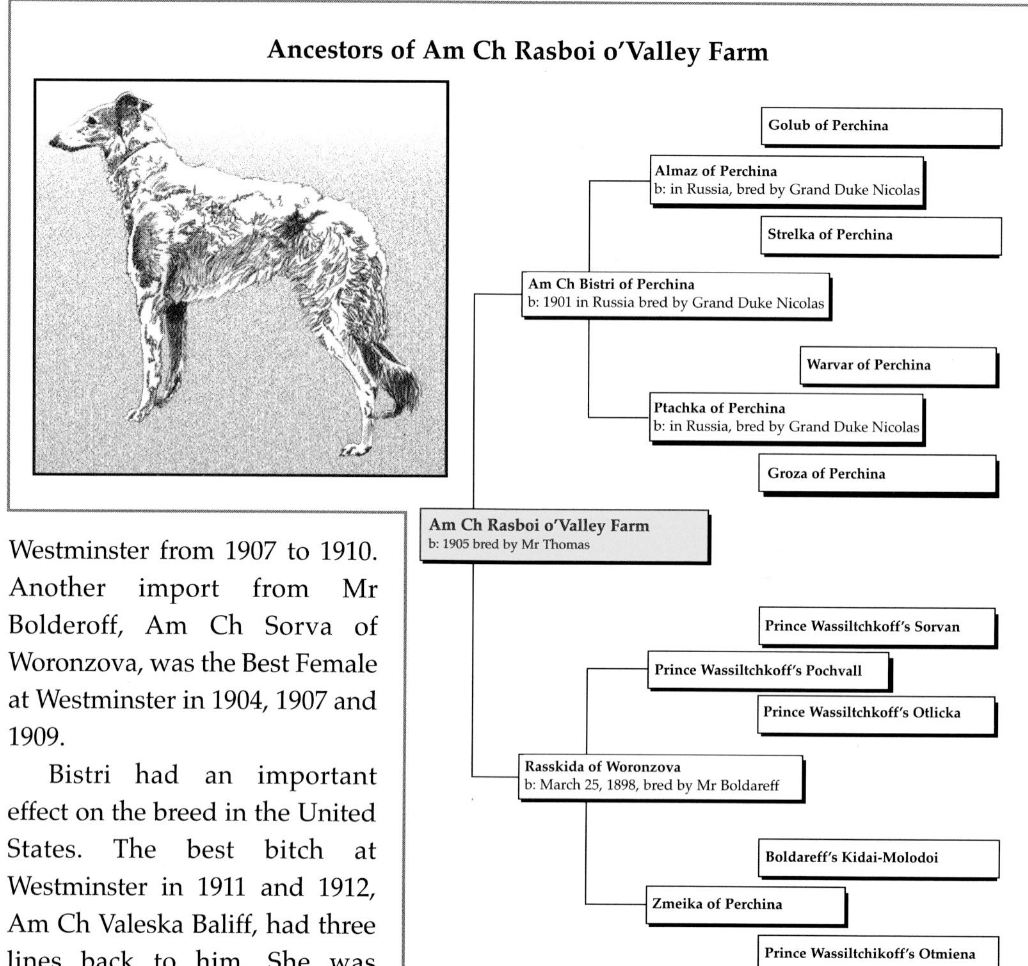

Westminster from 1907 to 1910. Another import from Mr Bolderoff, Am Ch Sorva of Woronzova, was the Best Female at Westminster in 1904, 1907 and 1909.

Bistri had an important effect on the breed in the United States. The best bitch at Westminster in 1911 and 1912, Am Ch Valeska Baliff, had three lines back to him. She was purchased from her breeder at the age of nine weeks by Mr J Bailey Wilson and became the dam of three champions.

Romanoff

The most successful American kennel in the 1920–1930s was Mr Louis Murr's Romanoff. Before being owned by Mr Murr it was owned consecutively by Mrs R C McAllister, Mr Leroy Pelletier and Mr Norman A Pabst.

Mr Murr did much to promote the breed and his hounds had a strong Valley Farm basis. Am Ch Tamara of Romanoff was the top winning American bitch of 1928 and, through her sire, she was four generations on from Bistri's son Am Ch Kopchic o' Valley Farm. She was also a great-granddaughter of Mr Murr's first Borzoi, Lorraine's Olga.

Am Ch Vigow of Romanoff was the most famous of the Romanoffs. He was never defeated in breed competition and was top American-bred dog of all breeds in 1935 and 1936, the only dog to win this award twice. He won 21 Best In Show (BIS) awards and had 67 group wins. His full brother, Am Ch Bransgore Akurtni of Romanoff, was imported into Great Britain by Mrs Gingold, but this was not until the late 1930s, so she was prevented by the war from breeding the all white hounds produced by this line (see chapter 3).

Mr Murr owned several Vigows, the first being Am Ch Vigow o' Valley Farm. This Vigow was out of the self red bitch Zohra du Zwaenhoek, bred by Mr and Mrs Beermaerts in Belgium. They took their kennel name from the Flemish word meaning 'the swans' because there were always swans on the pool of their home La Frondaire, near Ghent. Am Ch Appraxim o' Valley Farm was exported to the Beermaerts, to gain his title there as well.

The du Zwaenhoek kennel was set up before the First World War, and it was based closely on Perchino bloodlines. Mr Gustave Beermaerts purchased Ch Ugar Perchino from Grand Duke Nicholas, and it was through this dog that he met his wife. Her father gave her a Borzoi puppy as a birthday present and this puppy was sired by Ugar.

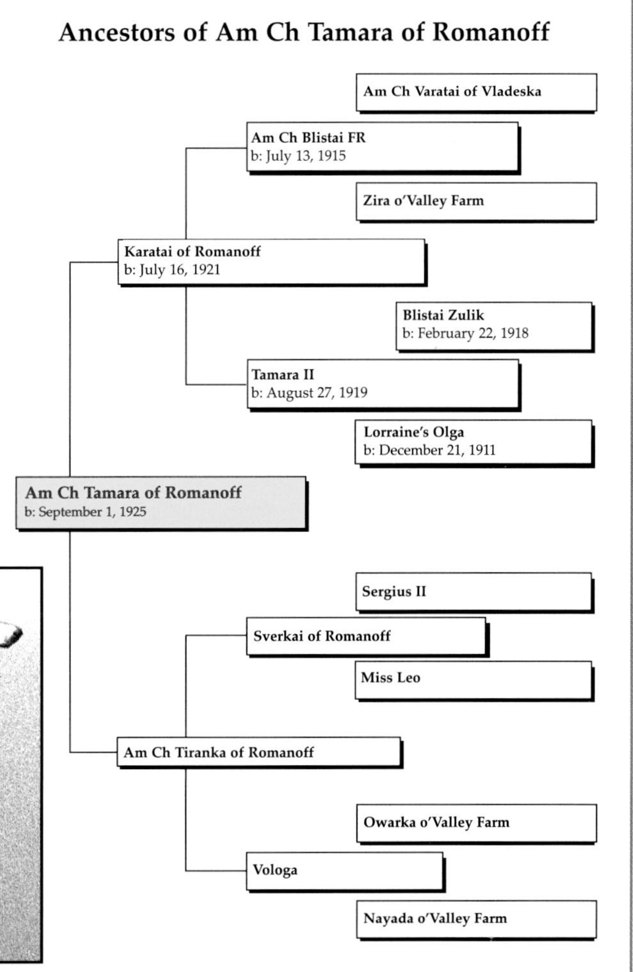

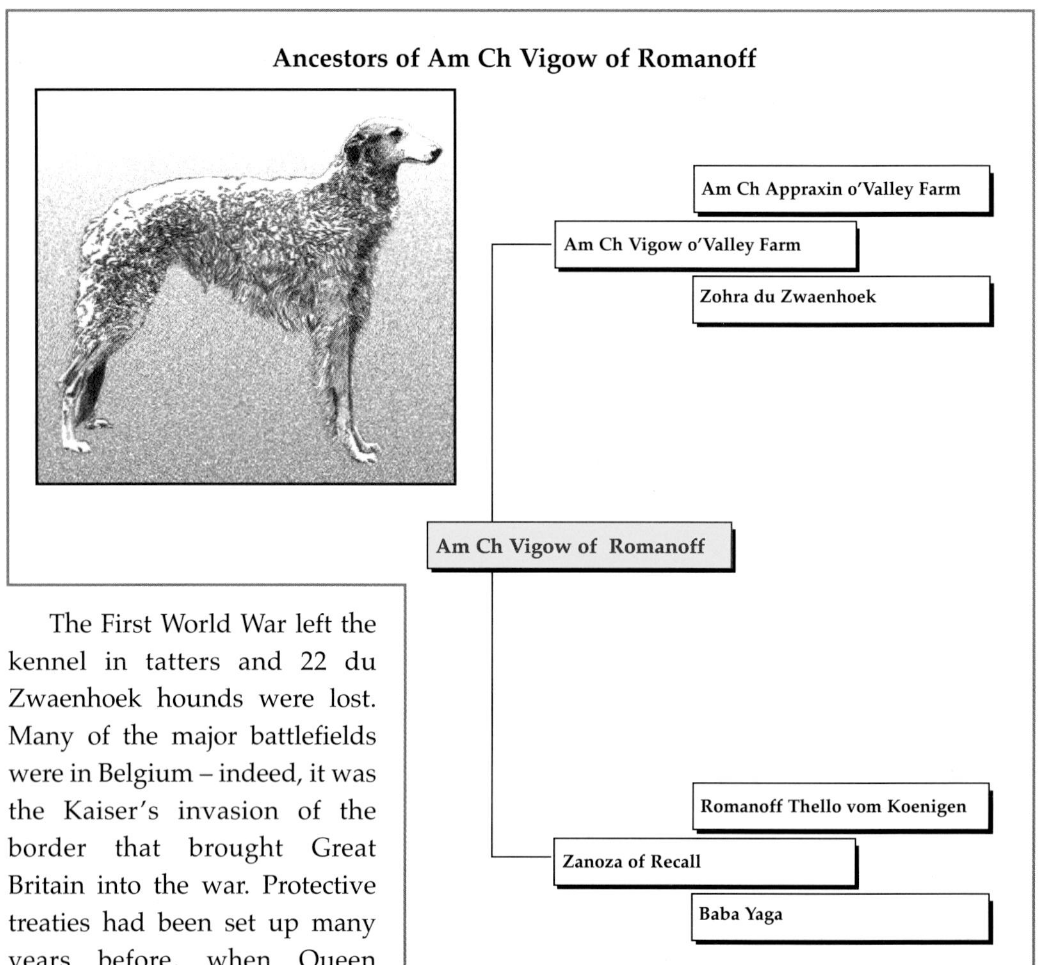

The First World War left the kennel in tatters and 22 du Zwaenhoek hounds were lost. Many of the major battlefields were in Belgium – indeed, it was the Kaiser's invasion of the border that brought Great Britain into the war. Protective treaties had been set up many years before, when Queen Victoria's Uncle Leopold was King of the Belgians. Rebuilding started in 1919 with the purchase of as many quality hounds as were available in Belgium and Holland. Through the purchase of Ch Volga du Nord there was a line back to the British champion Strawberry King. During the 1930s du Zwaenhoek usually housed 100 Borzois but, after Mr Beernaert's death, the Borzoi were gradually dispersed until in 1944 the kennel was bombed.

One of the last Borzoi owned by Mr Murr was Vigow of Romanoff II, a companion dog rather than a show dog. He was an important influence behind the Majenkir and Tamboer lines. The last hound to carry the Romanoff name was Am Ch Chudak of Romanoff, seen in the pedigree of Am Ch Majenkir Gyrfalcon. He was a son of the last Vigow, Am Ch Vigow of Romanoff III.

Mr Murr retained an interest in show dogs as an all-breed judge until his death in

1978. All Borzois purchased for the Romanoff kennel, from American and European lines, were acquired to consolidate the ancient type of Borzoi. In his day Am Ch Vigow o' Valley Farm was probably the best Borzoi in the world; certainly none of the British stock of that time could touch him and Continental Europe had just been ravaged by war. Mr Joseph Thomas visited the Romanoff kennel in 1934, when it was at its height, and commented: *Your dogs are uniform in type, size and quality and you have succeeded in retrieving some of the ancient type prized very highly in Russia for hunting and dog shows.*

Tam-Boer

The Tam-Boer kennel was started by Mr and Mrs Leonard Tamboer in New Jersey in the 1950s. Their first bitch was from the Romanoff kennel and, when they returned to the kennel to show how well she was doing, they noticed another bitch who won them over completely. This was Lady Gretchen of Tam-Boer, who gained great fame as a brood bitch. Her most successful litter was by Vigow of Romanoff II in 1955, comprising five puppies who all became champions. These were:

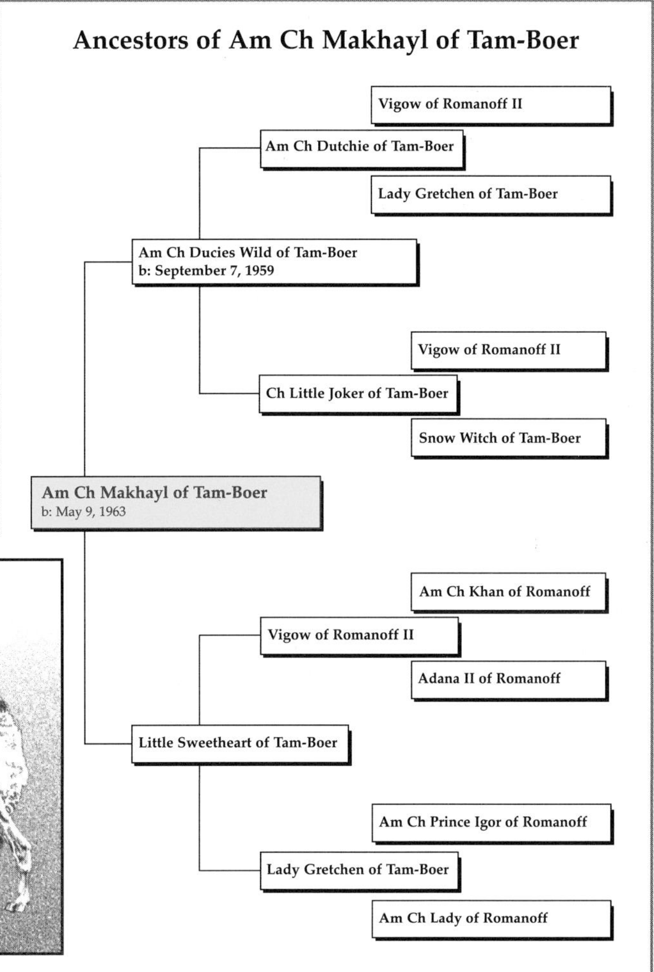

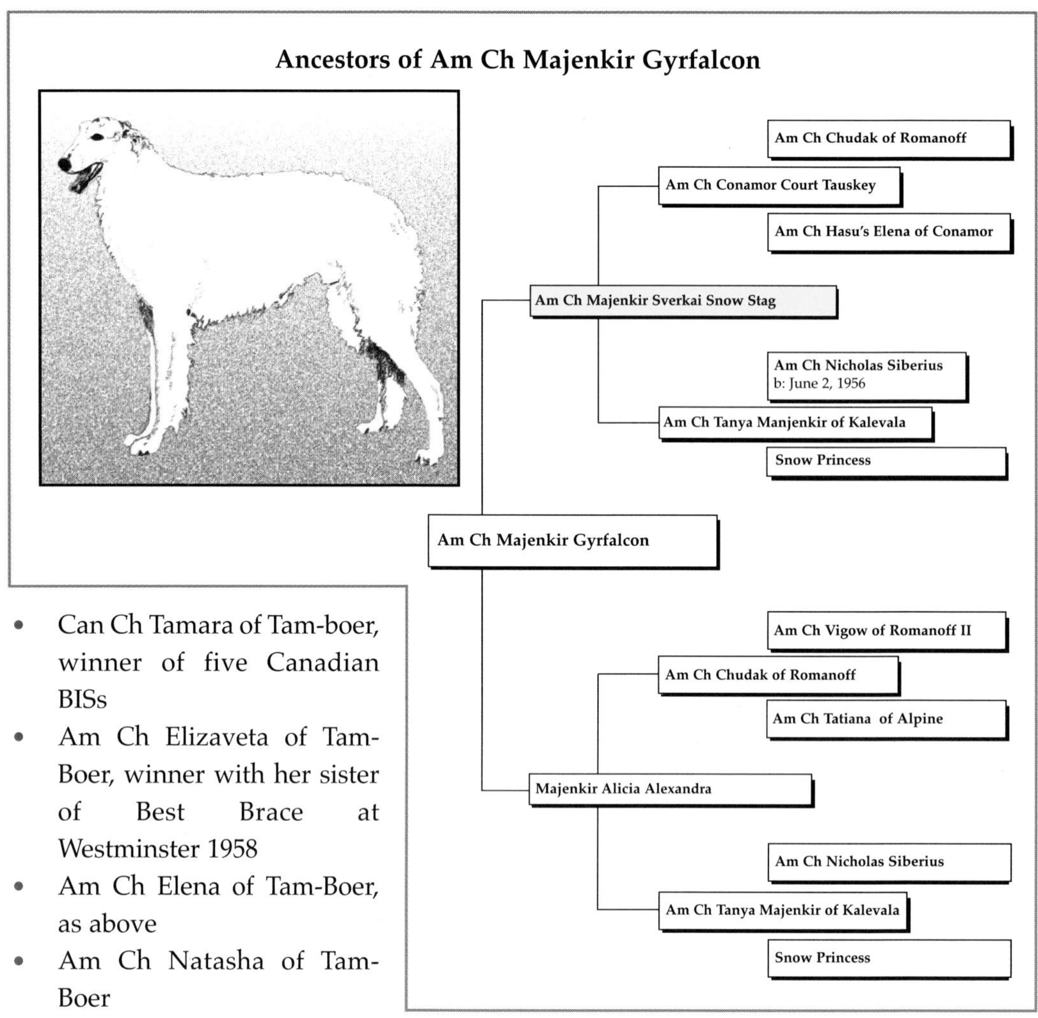

Ancestors of Am Ch Majenkir Gyrfalcon

- Can Ch Tamara of Tam-boer, winner of five Canadian BISs
- Am Ch Elizaveta of Tam-Boer, winner with her sister of Best Brace at Westminster 1958
- Am Ch Elena of Tam-Boer, as above
- Am Ch Natasha of Tam-Boer
- Am Ch Valia of Tam-Boer, BIS Borzoi Club of America 1956

The dog Am Ch Makhyl of Tam-Boer was Top American Borzoi in 1966 and in the top 10 in 1967 and 1968.

Majenkir

The Majenkir kennel of Karen Staudt-Cartabona was established in the early 1960s. Am Ch Tanya Majenkir of Kaleva was her foundation bitch. Tanya was from a brother to sister mating, Am Ch Nicholas Siberius ex Snow Princess, both being progeny of Vigow of Romanoff II.

This kennel has become famous for producing all-white stud dogs, the most notable being Am Ch Majenkir Sverkai Snow Stag and his son Am Ch Majenkir Gyrfalcon. Today, in the late 1990s, the kennel has bred many top-winning hounds; the Majenkir Internet pages tell of more than 300 champions produced.

Leicros

The Leicros kennel of Conny Croneryd and L Leifors is based in Sweden, but they have introduced the Majenkir lines through the Gyrfalcon granddaughter Astiafiev Snow Sybil. When mated to Leicros Russian Zovit she produced a litter of which two were imported into Great Britain. On this page is the pedigree of Leicros Zilver Shadow of Dimland, one of these imports, who has been used at stud in this country. This bloodline is controversial as the type of Borzoi produced is quite different from the true British lines.

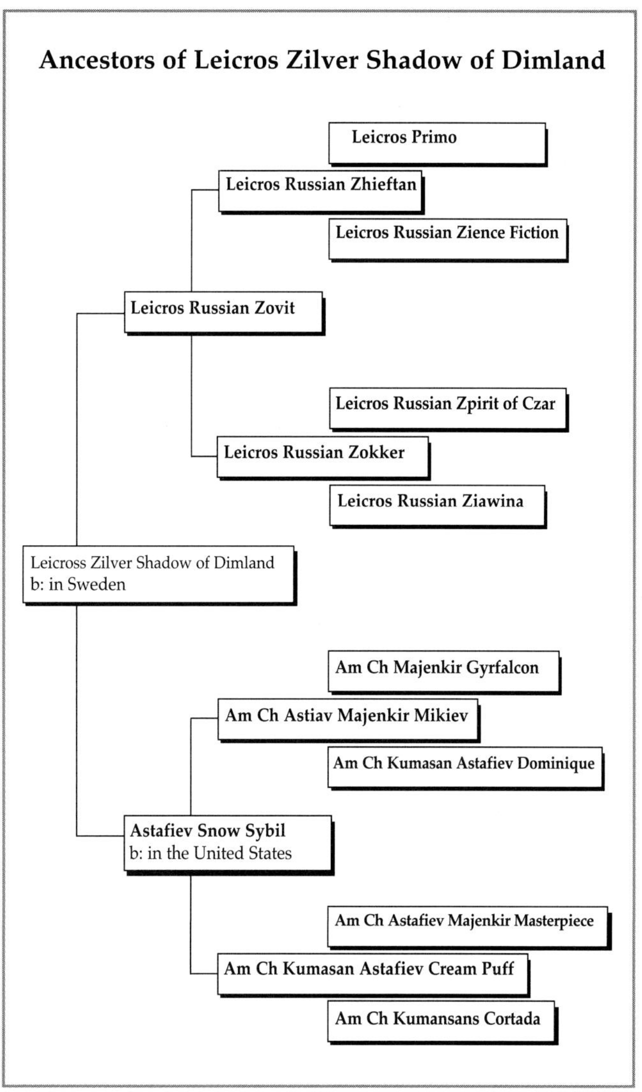

The Leicros kennel was based on two bitches: the American-bred Int/Nordic Ch V'Indras Vanity, bred by Charlotte Wheeler, and Swe Ch Ninotcka, bred by E Osterman. Ninotcka was out of a British-bred bitch and her sire was a grandson of Sadia of Whitelillies, a British export to Sweden. One of Ninotcka's puppies, the brindle and white Leicros Zandor, was exported to Charlotte Wheeler in the United States, where she gained her American title.

Leicros Zilver Shadow of Dimland is five generations on from V'Indras Vanity; Leicros Russian Zpirit of Czar was her grandson.

Fin/Swe Ch Igor of Iochum

Another Swedish line widely dispersed in British bloodlines is that of Fin / Swe Ch Igor of Iochum. He was the sire of two dogs found in British pedigrees: the dog Sissinheimon Sokol who is behind Mrs Rampley's Swiftcrofts and the bitch Sissinheimon Strelka, granddam of Ch Stonebar Sebastian (see chapter 3).

Ch/Am Ch Stillwater Virginia Reel

The most high profile American import into Great Britain was Mr Richard Duckworth's Ch / Am Ch Stillwater Virginia Reel, Group winner on both sides of the Atlantic. Her blue sable colour was quite different from the usual in the British show ring, and her construction was different, too.

The three Challenge Certificates (CCs) that gave her her British title came in 1987: the first from Mrs Eileen Ruggles at the Three Counties Show, the second under Mrs Elizabeth Whitehead at Windsor and the third at Paignton under Mr Vic Harrison. Mrs Whitehead wrote of her: *This bitch commands attention, classic outline, beautiful head, dark eye*

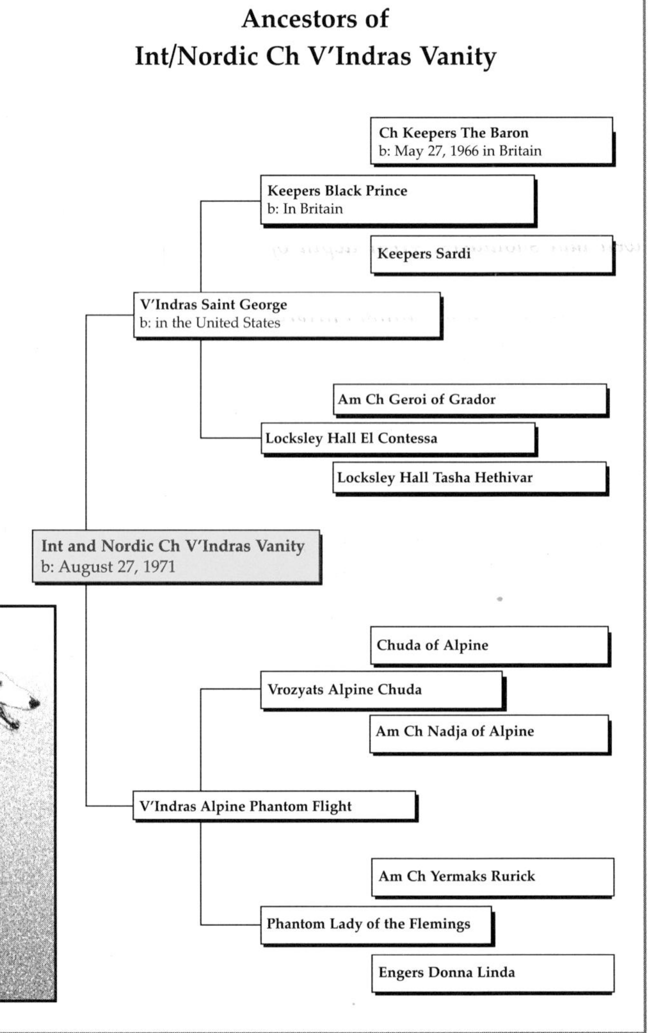

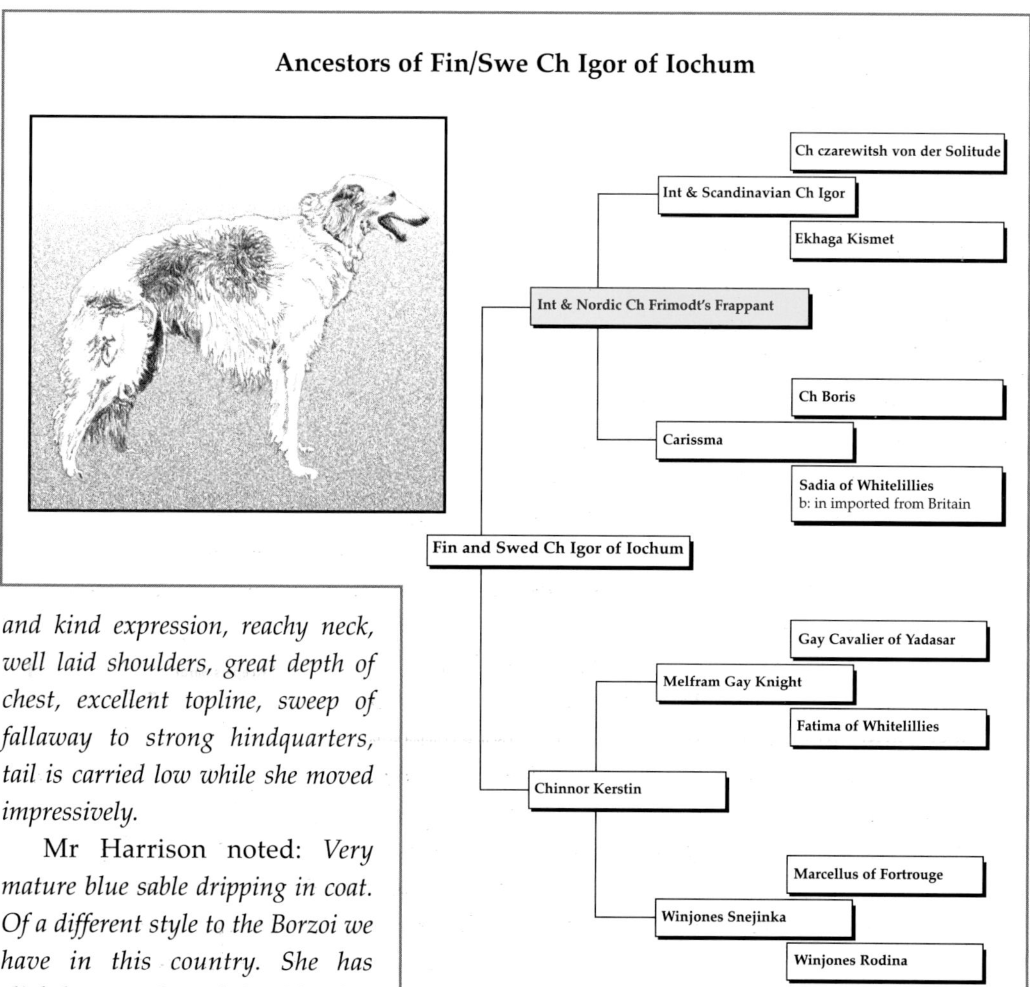

and kind expression, reachy neck, well laid shoulders, great depth of chest, excellent topline, sweep of fallaway to strong hindquarters, tail is carried low while she moved impressively.

Mr Harrison noted: *Very mature blue sable dripping in coat. Of a different style to the Borzoi we have in this country. She has slightly more lay of shoulder, but with increased hind angulation to compensate. Of excellent all over conformation, moved effortlessly. A little plain in head maybe, slightly wide front, nevertheless a worthy champion.*

Virginia Reel has some of the finest American and Canadian breeding behind her. The Sunbarr kennel of Mr James Barr of Winconsin was a very large affair. Sunbarr was a 300-acre ranch that had been laid out originally as a silver fox ranch. At the height of the Sunbarr operation there were 100–200 Borzois. There was much European blood behind the Sunbarrs: Virginia Reel's grandsire, Am Ch Thistle of Sunbarr, had a granddam from Mrs Betty Hargrave's British Shelbor kennel.

One of the most influential Sunbarr litters was the B litter named after saints. Romulus of Sunbarr was the product of the mating of two members of this litter, Malora's Bryan of

Sunbarr and Malora's Beada of Sunbarr. These were progeny of the German-bred Ilja v Bergland ex Scottish-bred Bright of Barnaigh, bred by Mrs Kathleen McNeill. Bright was a daughter of Ch Reyas Romancer.

Malora

Mrs Eileen Worthing's Malora kennel was started several years before the Second World War, the first litter being born in 1934. From 1949 she had an extensive programme of importation from Scotland, England and France. She worked closely with Mr Barr, as in the B litter mentioned above, and many of the same Borzois appear in both Malora and Sunbarr pedigrees.

Mrs Worthing wrote an interesting piece on her continental breeding plan and the differing behaviour of her imported Borzois:

In the last five years [written in 1963] *eleven Borzoi of European origin have come to make their home at Malora kennels. I have in this time had ample opportunity to view with intense interest certain factors in their characters and personalities that differ from the American Borzoi. I have not yet been able to reach any conclusion as to where the responsibility could rest; environment or hereditary. It has also been noted that the individuals that form the first generation of my continental breeding program have shared one trait in common, though they come from three countries, and that is, they possess to a most unusual degree, an air of self assured aloofness. In the adult Borzoi, whose background and environment in its native land conditioned it to this attitude, it can be understood, but what is puzzling is that I have found the same good natured but firmly rooted condescending aura in the youngsters of five and six months.*

I have seen an adult emerge from a crate at the airport with quite the gabbling circle of admirers, with nothing but a steady cool look and raised eyebrow. When I opened the door of the crate of the five month old Mara of Barinoff (English bred), she stood firmly on her sturdy little legs, and with the head up gave the customs man and two pilots who were standing near the same self assured look, and from the customs man came the remark, 'Snooty little thing, isn't it.'

The Scottish Borzoi have displayed a most endearing good nature but they will grumble if their routine is broken. They resent moving from one yard to another and complain loud and long if a kennel mate must be removed and another substituted.

The English Borzoi have displayed a gaiety and clownishness that is lacking in the Scots. They will enjoy thoroughly any trick they can pull on you, such as pulling off a cap and running madly around with it. In the showring the Barnaighs are business like and dignified whereas the English blend the dignity with a gleam in the eye. The English accept a new kennel mate with a playful skittishness, and a break in routine will be accepted with puzzled good nature. The French have presented a most puzzling and complex assortment of temperaments and behaviour patterns.

In the second generation I have had from the Scots and English blending, and the French and English mating, I have found that a most curious event takes place. The self-coloured puppies have invariably shown in their temperament and behaviour a distinct leaning towards the Scots side of their ancestry – and as this side is actually one-half German, I still do not know if these traits come from Barnaigh, v Bergland or Siberhof. The white puppies with varied markings have shown a strong, very strong dominance of their English background. When Kim, formal name Barinoff Ambassador, white with black markings and tan points, sired a puppy who is white with markings, that puppy invariably began to learn early signs of doing things just as Kimmie had done. It had that gleeful attitude, whereas the dark self colours, the mahoganies, reds, sables and blacks, though sired by Kim, will be but small editions of their haughty mothers.

To sum it up, I have found in these Europeans a vast field for future research as to try that elusive 'something' that makes them different from others of their breed. I have never found a single individual to have an unsound or sharp temperament. I have found them to be of above average intelligence, being able to be willing, and eager to learn what is expected of them. I have found them to be extremely sensitive to voice tones, and if they sense sarcasm or a too sweet overtone in the voice addressing them, they will, young and adult, turn upon the talker a cold, disgusted look and walk away. Dikky and Dione many times sat on the sun platform and deliberately turned their backs to people they did not like.

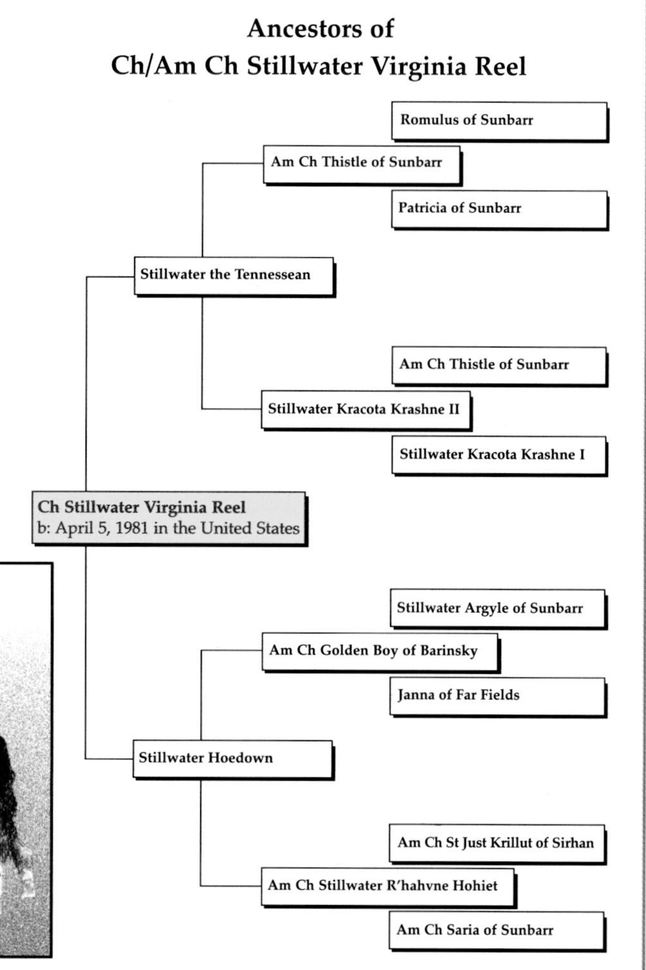

One more item, that might be of interest, is that the puppies I have sold, of the overseas line, for hunting, have proven themselves so efficient in this sport that it makes one wonder if the hunting instinct in European Borzoi is not still a dominant part of their hereditary force.

Am/Can Ch Sirhan Porchai.

Sirhan

Going back to Virginia Reel's pedigree we see the Sirhan affix of Mrs Audrey Benbow, who is based in Canada. The first Borzoi came to this kennel in 1960 and the foundation bitch was Can Ch Antigone of Tyree, who was from British bloodlines and a granddaughter of Marcellus of Fortrouge (see chapter 3).

The first litter from Antigone to Am/Can Ch Topaze produced five Canadian champions, three of whom also gained American championships. One of these was Sirhan Kaissack, who was an influential sire. The most famous of the Sirhans were Am/Can Ch Sirhan Porchai, Top Canadian Borzoi with many BIS wins, and Am/Can Ch Sirhan Poraschai, who went to California where he was owned by Mr Edward Abblett and Mr George Root. He was the Top Borzoi in the United States in 1971 and 1971, with many BIS wins.

Porchai and Paraschai were by Sirhan Podar of Sunbarr, who was obtained by Mrs Benbow as one of her prizes when her Am/Can Ch Sirhan Kaissack won at the Midwest Borzoi Club's Specialty Show at Detroit in 1967. Podar was a son of Malora's Bede of Sunbarr, another from the Sunbarr B litter.

Am Ch St Just Krillut of Sirhan was Virginia Reel's great-grandsire, and he was a son of Porchai.

Choosing and Training a Puppy

Before choosing a Borzoi puppy you must be sure that this is the breed for you. Borzois are completely unlike any other breed of dog, though sharing many behaviour patterns with close relations such as Afghan Hounds, Salukis and Greyhounds. The Borzoi's personality is complex, with at least two opposite thoughts running through its mind for each situation. Puppies brought up with well-behaved children are tolerant and even affectionate to 'their' children, but most Borzois prefer not to have much contact with children as they do not like their noise, quick movements and unpredictability. No Borzoi can tolerate badly-behaved children. Terriers and their like belong in the same category as children as far as Borzois are concerned and the fawning, noisy behaviour of gundogs seems to annoy them intensely.

Three quality puppies at seven weeks.

Even in puppies it is possible to see the difference in structure between the dog (front) and the bitch (rear).

Borzois love running free, and some love running free more than they love coming back. There are Borzois that take off for a few hours at a time. This is very dangerous; they may get into fields with livestock and, even if they make no attempt to harm the animals, the farmer may legally shoot them. Borzois do not have much road sense, and do get run over.

Borzois can be fussy eaters and derive great pleasure from watching you fret as you worry that they'll starve themselves. The more a behaviour pattern upsets you the more the Borzoi will show that behaviour pattern.

Any small injury brings on a performance better than most Oscar winners but, as long as you tell your dog how brave it is and what a terrible injury it has sustained and then 'kiss it better', the Borzoi goes off completely 'healed'.

A Borzoi will spend much of its adult life standing in front of the television set – but only at a point that is crucial to the plot.

As Borzois age (and old age starts at about eight or nine) the bitches in particular become grumpy and selfish, like the dowager duchesses of literature.

If you can cope with all these foibles you will get a spectacular dog, loving to immediate family but aloof with strangers. The Borzoi can curl up in a small space so that its presence may be forgotten, leaving you your personal space. In return, it likes to be given its own bed.

Where to get your puppy

I would certainly not recommend a pet shop or a large scale commercial breeder as a suitable source for a puppy of any breed, but fortunately such outlets ignore Borzois because they are not commercially successful.

A number of people have devoted much of their lives to breeding Borzois. Many of these advertise in the year books of the Borzoi Club and the Northern Borzoi Association. The addresses of the Secretaries of both these organisations are available from The Kennel Club. The advertisements usually include a picture and list the show wins of the kennel's current show dog so that you can get an idea of the different colours and types available. They also include telephone numbers to contact breeders. Even if the breeders you contact do not have puppies for sale, they may know of litters by their stud dogs or their bitches' relations.

Choosing your puppy

It is impossible to be sure of choosing a future champion as a puppy. It is a little easier to choose a good quality puppy from a litter, especially if you have bred the litter and several preceding generations. Such breeders will have seen so many puppies of their bloodlines grow up that they will have a good idea of how each puppy will end up. It follows that, to get a puppy that will almost certainly be of show quality, you need the help of the senior breeder of that bloodline. This breeder does not need to have bred the litter; perhaps he or she has bred the sire or dam and the litter's actual breeder may be a newcomer. However, if the breeder of the litter has followed the senior breeder's advice, the chain of breeding knowledge includes information about several generations.

An exceptional Borzoi puppy at seven weeks.

You can learn a little more about what to look for in a puppy by looking at the various photographs of good and poor quality puppies in this chapter.

What sex do you want? A **bitch** has the disadvantage of

coming into season twice a year, while the cynic might say that a dog is in season every day of the year! Dogs grow larger and stronger, but I consider bitches more conniving.

So we are now at the stage when you have decided what sex you want and are on the way to see the litter. All puppies are appealing but, if you want a show quality puppy, you should take the breeder's advice. The breeder's name goes in the show catalogue for all to see if you show the puppy. If the breeder says the puppy is not to be shown, this is not to deprive you of wins, but because the puppy is not up to show standard.

Preparations for the new puppy

At home, preparations should have been made for the new arrival. There should be a bed for the puppy's exclusive use, in a warm and draught-free location. Newspaper is a good lining to soak up 'accidents' and the easily-washed polyester 'fur' rugs are warm and reassuring. There should be newspaper around the puppy bed, too, for puddles during the night. Bed is a very important place for a puppy; it is its retreat from the world when things get too much. Borzoi puppies have a lot of growing to do, and most of this is done while they are asleep.

A few toys may help too, since this is the first night the puppy has been away from its family. Toys must be too big to get stuck in the throat. Some Borzoi pups are distressed by squeaky toys.

Collecting the puppy

At least two people should go to collect the puppy, especially if this is by car, as there should be someone to sit in the back with the puppy, who has left its litter-mates for the first time.

Documentation

The breeder should provide the following documents:

- the pedigree
- signed Kennel Club registration/transfer document
- receipt for puppy price
- insurance documents, if any
- a few days' supply of the food on which the puppy has been reared and a diet sheet

The breeder often takes out insurance for the pup for the first few months of its life. Insurance is a good idea throughout the dog's life, as a bill for a few pounds a month is much more pleasant than £300 or more for an emergency operation. The supply of food and diet sheet is important because a change in diet is likely to cause an upset stomach. Just moving home upsets eating, so try to make the transfer as easy on the puppy's tummy as possible.

Choosing a vet

Ch Desaev Baby Clair as a puppy.

The best way to find a vet is by personal recommendation. If you live near other Borzoi owners ask them about their vets.

It is a good idea if nothing terrible happens the first time the puppy visits the vet. A general health check, including weighing, is a good introduction. Some modern practices have puppy socialisation classes, and the vet can tell which puppies have attended these fun-packed sessions by their behaviour in the consulting room. Do not give your Borzoi any reason to begin the 'I'm at the vet's and it's the end of the world' routine.

New vaccination and worming products are being produced all the time. Indeed, the spectrum of disease also alters with time. The new killer disease of the 1970s was parvovirus, which killed many puppies before a vaccine was developed. Follow the up-to-date advice given by your vet for worming and inoculations.

The better the relationship with your vet the better the help he or she can provide. 'Vet hopping' from one practice to another gives less than ideal care. All veterinary surgeries have to provide 24-hour cover in one form or another. Find out how your practice does so. Borzoi emergencies are usually at 3.00 am.

The diet of the developing puppy

Borzoi pups have to do a lot of growing to attain adult size and it is the food they eat that allows this development. The diagram on page 142 depicts the skeleton of a puppy just before birth. The pink regions are those parts of the skeleton that are still cartilage at this stage. Compare this drawing with the skeleton of the correctly constructed Borzoi in

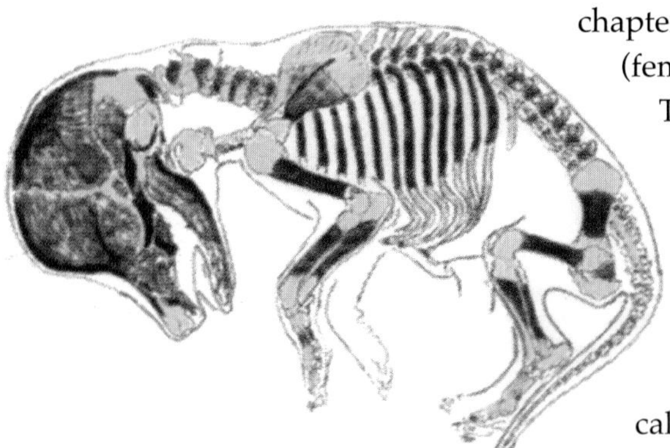

The skeleton of a puppy just before birth. The pink regions represent the parts of the skeleton that are still cartilage at this stage.

chapter 2. Only the middles of the long bones (femur, tibia) are bone; the ends are cartilage. The border between the cartilage and the bony shaft is the growth plate, and growth plates can be seen in various photographs of young puppies in this chapter.

Bones need calcium to develop and the balance between the right amount of calcium and not enough is very difficult. The easiest way to get this right is to use a complete premium diet. Home made diets with spoonfuls of bonemeal to make up the calcium can go either way. It breaks my heart to see a puppy carefully reared by the breeder sold to a novice who feeds it on substandard food. Puppies with lovely growth plates become starved of high quality nutrients and end up with matchsticks instead of correct bone.

Look at the puppy skeleton again. See how much of the bones is made of cartilage. This is another reason not to drop a young puppy. Full calcification of all these bones does not happen in the Borzoi until after two years of age. The final bone to finish growing is the lower jaw. This is how a mouth can 'go off': a previously correct scissor bite can become undershot. In humans the last part to finish growing is the joint between the scapula and the collar bone, which does not occur until about the age of 21. Dogs do not have a collar bone, but the scapula is one of the last bones to finish development, so a dog's final shoulder structure is another late feature.

Finer-boned puppies from the Northern lines. They show good bone – note the knuckle on the one looking at us.

Nowadays we have the luxury of several ranges of premium quality complete diets. These have revolutionised the feeding of dogs.

One of the finest of all dog breed books – indeed, it

would be one of my 'desert island' choices – is Bruce Fields' one about Cavalier King Charles Spaniels. Every Borzoi breeder should look at the extensive and sensible sections about the inherited diseases found in this breed: firstly to say, 'Thank goodness we are not plagued with these in Borzois!' and secondly to say, 'We must make sure that, should such diseases arise, they are stopped in the first generation'. However, it is his conversion in the field of dog feeding that I quote here.

I am a traditionalist from Yorkshire and so far as my own food goes, whilst I will readily try most dishes whatever their country of origin, I still retain a great fondness for traditional English dishes.

With dog foods I was also a strong traditionalist. Years ago I bought ox-heads from the abattoir and laboriously cut off the meat – about 9lb or 4kg from each head. I also bought the large 'green' unbleached tripes and cut them up in small strips. Then I would boil them up in a large electric boiler and the smell, particularly from the tripe, was awful. It was fed with good quality biscuit meal and the dogs loved it. I also fed 'supplement' tablets daily to ensure the dogs had all the necessary vitamins and minerals etc.

It then became impossible to buy ox-heads, as I was told they were all sold on a contract basis to the beef burger makers. Difficulties also arose in purchasing the fresh large tripes. Therefore about four years ago I spoke to several breeders and received good reports about 'complete' foods. For four years my Cavaliers have been fed on these foods and I am impressed. My son, who works and trials gundogs, has also been impressed with the zest and stamina his Labradors show on complete foods.

We wean both our Cavalier and Labrador puppies straight on to a complete food, and they thrive really well. All my dogs, whatever their age, are on it, including Ch Crieda Rosella aged 13. With the complete foods

Whippet puppies with great development of the growth plate at the end of the radius and ulna – the knuckle.

The top quality puppy on page 141 grew into Ch Desaev Baby Clare.

there are various grades, and protein levels, to suit dogs of different ages and with differing needs. For instance the elderly have a lower protein level, whereas the puppies, pregnant or lactating bitches, or highly active working dogs need a high protein product. The complete foods are said to contain everything a dog needs and do not need to be supplemented in any way. Palatability is high, in fact the dogs seem to really enjoy them.

It is possible to construct successful home-made diets with all the essential nutrients. However, a veterinary surgeon, Alison Bigg, wrote of these diets: *If you feed a correctly balanced home-made diet, they are often time consuming to prepare, usually need the addition of a vitamin/mineral supplement, and if prepared accurately can be expensive. Variations in raw ingredients will cause fluctuations in nutritional value. The only way to be absolutely sure that a home-made diet has the nutritional profile that you want is to mix all the food ingredients plus supplements, treats, snacks, scraps etc in a large pot, homogenise them and have a sample analysed chemically (this costs well over £100 for a partial analysis).*

The name 'complete' means just that. Not only is supplementing these diets unnecessary; it can be dangerous. The careful balance of minerals and vitamins is lost. The condition known as Hypertrophic Osteodystrophy is due to a diet too high in protein, calcium, phosphorus and vitamin D. This condition erupts suddenly, the puppy screaming with pain in the joints and running a temperature. X-rays show alterations at the growth plates, especially at the end of the radius and ulna, the 'knuckle' we have discussed before. Treatment, under veterinary supervision, is giving vitamin C and reducing the calcium, phosphorus and vitamin D in the diet.

Complete diets do not contain many bulking agents, so the faeces are of lower volume and easier to clean up.

The only point raised against these diets has been the inclusion of the preservative ethoxyquin, but many top-of-the-range formulations do not include this. Modern advice for feeding is therefore to choose such a brand and follow it though the stages of

**Beautiful bitch puppy with cross-breed friend.
Note the lovely bone on this pup.**

Best Puppy at the Borzoi Club Championship Show, 1997. This is a cousin of the pup in the head study on page 149.

puppyhood, adult dog and senior citizen, always following the manufacturer's guidance as to amount. Generally puppies have numerous meals, adults one or two and senior citizens need to go back to more meals. The expense of the foods is compensated by correctly-fed dogs who are easy to clean up after.

Put your puppy's food in a raised bowl. This reduces the amount of air the puppy swallows, reducing the chance of bloat, and helps the puppy's front to develop correctly.

Basic training

The secret of all training is to start at an early age, always to be gentle and to repeat things without letting the puppy get bored. Puppies who think that training is a game will have a more positive attitude.

It is also important for the puppy to understand the word 'no'. The owner should always be the pack leader and should not let the puppy think that it is dominant to any family member, even the baby. Remember that this cute puppy may end up bigger than you. It is important that dogs are not possessive about food and let you take their bowl away before they have finished. This may prevent a nasty incident in future.

Anticipate the destructive chewing during teething by providing tough dog toys instead of letting the Chippendale chairs being chewed.

Toilet training

Whenever a puppy awakes it needs to go into the garden to relieve itself. After every meal it needs to go into the garden again. All young animals have a gastro-colic (stomach/large bowel) reflex, which means they have to pass motions after eating. Those concerned with the changing of nappies will be aware of this. Taking the puppy out just before bedtime should cut down on night-time 'accidents'.

Toilet training involves positive reinforcement of good behaviour. If someone can observe the puppy when it is awake and put it outside every time it looks as if it is starting to squat, the time it takes to toilet train will be cut down considerably. The puppy must be lavished with praise when it goes outside and, if such words as 'busy' or 'puddle' are used, the puppy associates these with its natural functions. In future years, when you have travelled to the other end of the country to a show, it will be helpful if the dog has learned to pass water or motions on command.

The eight-week-old puppy has very little bladder control and it is unrealistic to expect complete day and night cleanliness before six months; remember, children take much longer. Never rub a puppy's nose in any mistake it's made – it is unhygienic, spreads germs, upsets the puppy and does not work anyway.

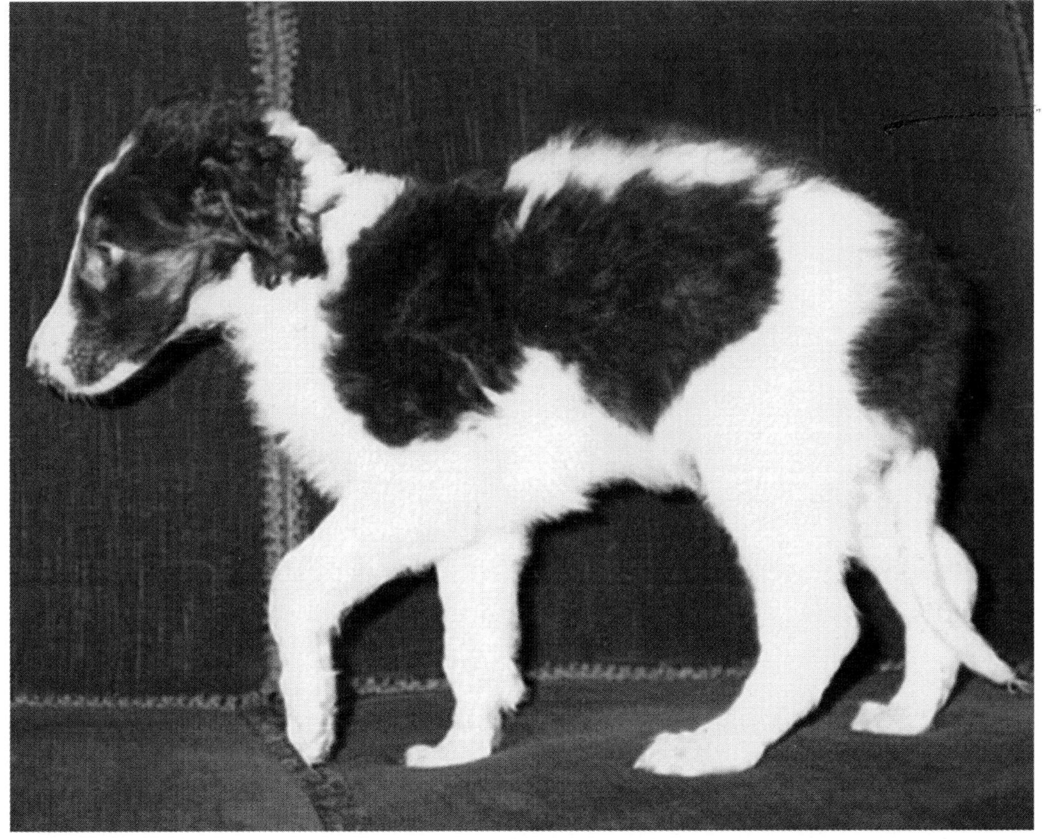

This puppy has not yet begun the massive growth spurt in its feet and legs, but the tail bones have been growing, making the tail disproportionately long.

This puppy has poor bone and, even at this age, it can be seen that the elbow is loose, so the action will always be faulty.

Lead training

Puppies need to be introduced to collars as soon as possible. Borzoi puppies do not like the first few (or many) times they are put on the lead; they scream like banshees and fling themselves to the ground. Patient and gentle persistence and reassurance that the lead will not kill the puppy (for, going by the noise Borzoi pups make, this must be the thought going through their heads) will help.

It is a legal requirement that all dogs have some means of identification attached to the collar when they are outside their home.

Obedience training

The Borzoi cannot really cope with more than basic obedience training. While not an unintelligent breed, it has been bred for chasing and hunting, and such concepts as sitting to order and retrieving are alien to its make-up. If you want an obedience champion, get a Border Collie.

The Kennel Club runs a Good Citizenship Dog Scheme that promotes a simple standard of training to which even a Borzoi should aspire. The dogs are tested on nine points:

1. The dog must be wearing a collar with identification and the owner must have some form of 'poop-scoop'.
2. The dog must let the owner put the collar and lead on it.
3. The dog must walk on the lead, ignoring its surroundings.
4. The dog must walk through a door or gate.

5 The dog must walk past people and other dogs while on the lead and behave when the owner holds a conversation for one minute.
6 The dog must lie down and stay there, though still on the lead.
7 The dog must allow its owner to groom it.
8 The dog must allow someone to examine its mouth, teeth, throat, eyes, ears and feet.
9 The dog must be able to distance itself from its owner while off the lead and come when called.

If you wish your dog to be a show dog, point 6 is not a good idea. It is better for the dog to think it must stand quietly when on the lead, as a dog that lies down all the time cannot be judged. Remember also that a Borzoi does not like to come when called if something interesting is happening elsewhere. With this in mind, make sure you are in a safe place, where your hound will not be in danger if it runs away, while rehearsing point 9. Otherwise, these basic skills will make your Borzoi a good citizen.

Head of a top quality youngster.
This is one of the newborn puppies shown on pages 203 and 205.

Borzoi Health

There are so many canine illnesses that they are beyond the scope of this book. Two up-to-date books that discuss illness in depth are *Doglopaedia* and *The Book of the Bitch*, both by J M Evans and Kay White. They are updated regularly, which is important, as veterinary medicine is changing constantly.

In this chapter I shall discuss:

- coat care
- nail care
- tooth care
- your veterinary surgeon
- giving a tablet
- breed-specific disease
- Kennel Club schemes for reducing genetic disease
- faulty dentition

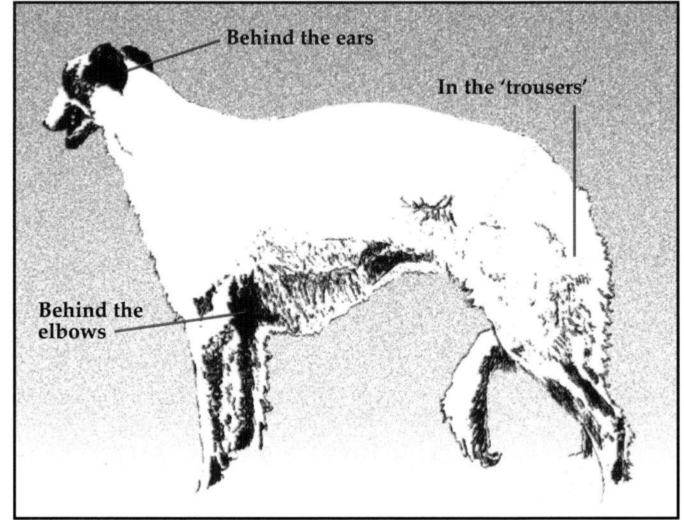

Where tangles are most likely to occur.

Coat care

The Borzoi has a long coat that needs to be brushed regularly. If it is not, the hairs will eventually tangle into a felted mass and the dog will need a general anaesthetic while it is clipped off. There is no need to panic if you miss the odd day's grooming, however. The areas most likely to tangle are behind the ears, behind the elbows and the 'trousers'. The best brush to use is a Mason Pearson and, because it is the best, it is the most expensive. However, the brush will last for many years if it does not go missing at a show.

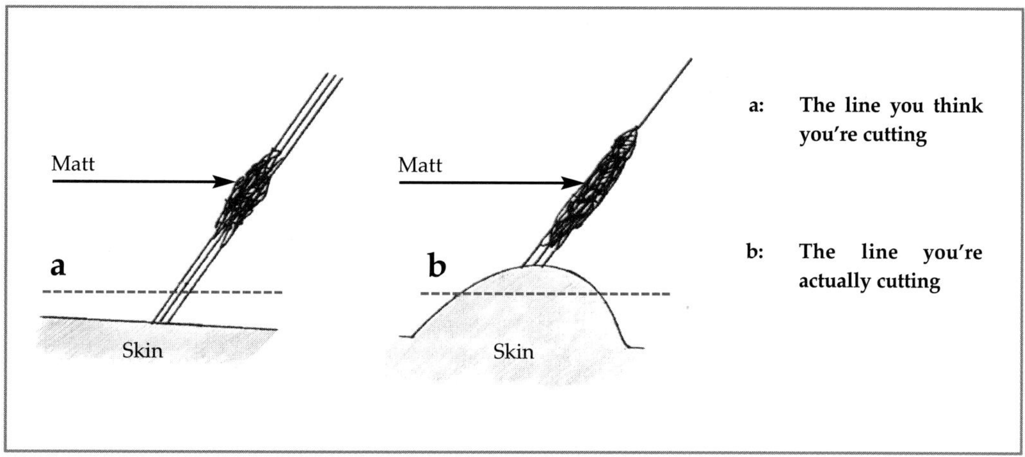

A little regular bushing, paying particular attention to the areas where matts are most likely to form, will keep the coat under control. If you do get matts, do not use scissors to remove them. Matts do not often go down to the skin; there is usually a little bit of unmatted hair between the skin and the matt. The temptation is to hold the matt and gently ease the scissors between matt and skin. The result is a hole in the skin, a screaming Borzoi and a groomer in a panic. The tool to use is a matt splitter. This has only one blade, which can be eased under the matt to cut from the coat like a scythe cutting a field of corn.

Trimming for the show ring

The Borzoi needs minimal trimming for the show ring. Hair between the toes and the fluffy bits on the back leg below the hock joint need to be neatened. Ordinary scissors will leave an obvious hard edge of hair. Use special trimming scissors that have blades that look like combs and the finished result will look as if the hair was never there in the first place.

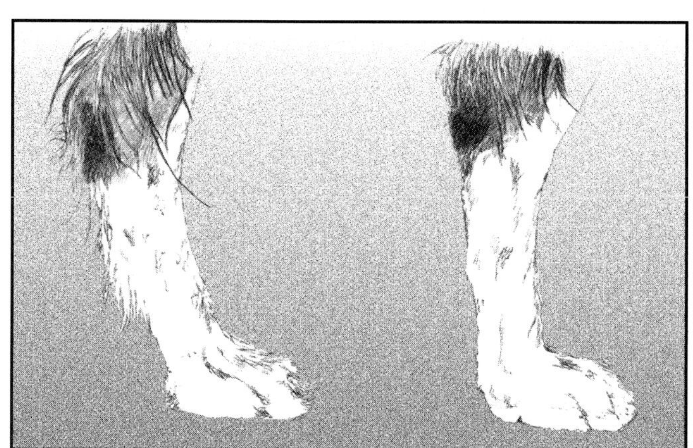

(Left) an untrimmed leg and foot and (right) the same leg and foot trimmed.

Bathing

In a luxury kennel, there would be a special raised dog bath with an integral shower. In reality, it is probably the human bath with a shower attachment that is used.

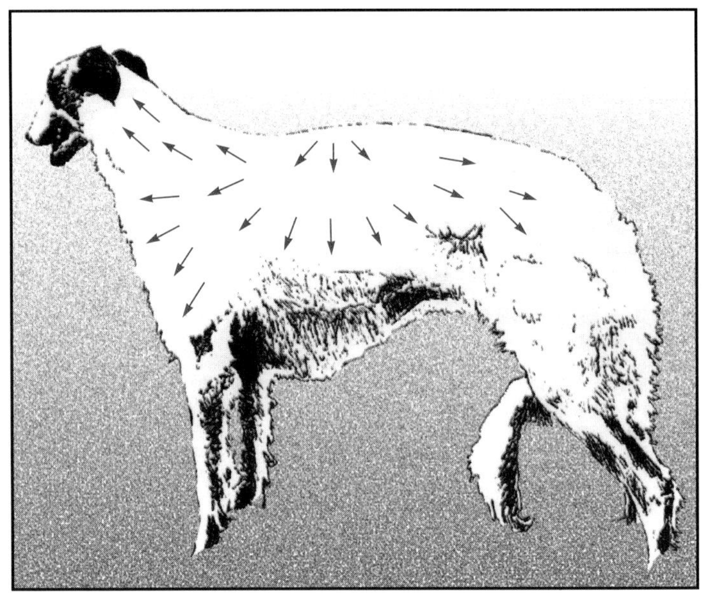

The pattern of hair growth in a Borzoi. Blow-dry in this pattern.

Poodles have a whole range of shampoos made specially for them with different formulations for different colours. Use a shampoo for black Poodles for a self black Borzoi and one for white Poodles for a basically white Borzoi.

Be very careful not to get shampoo into the Borzoi's eyes and be careful to rinse every trace of shampoo out of the coat. Any remaining shampoo may irritate the skin and become a focus for infection.

After rinsing, the Borzoi should be towel-dried to get most of the water out of the coat. Remember that, as soon as the dog steps out of the bath, it will shake itself vigorously and soak everything in range. Once most of the water has been wrung out, the coat can be brushed into shape and then blow-dried. The coat of a Borzoi falls in a different pattern from that of most breeds. It starts growing in the normal way but then curls over towards the head rather than the tail. This pattern starts from the shoulders (see above).

Nail care

A Borzoi's toenails need to be kept at the correct length. If the dog has plenty of exercise on a hard surface the nails may never need to be cut, as they are constantly worn down. If the nails are allowed to grow too long they will spoil the feet, as they spread the toes outwards. If they are badly neglected they may grow round in a circle and inbed into the pads of the dog's foot.

The nails of a Borzoi can be black or white. The white ones are easier to cut, as the quick can be seen on them, enabling you to avoid catching the quick in the clippers, thus causing much bleeding and Borzoi screaming. Borzois are very sensitive about their feet, even if you are not intending to cut their nails. Practise fiddling with the feet and nails of your puppy to help prevent nail-cutting from being a terrible experience for you, your Borzoi and the vet.

Tooth care

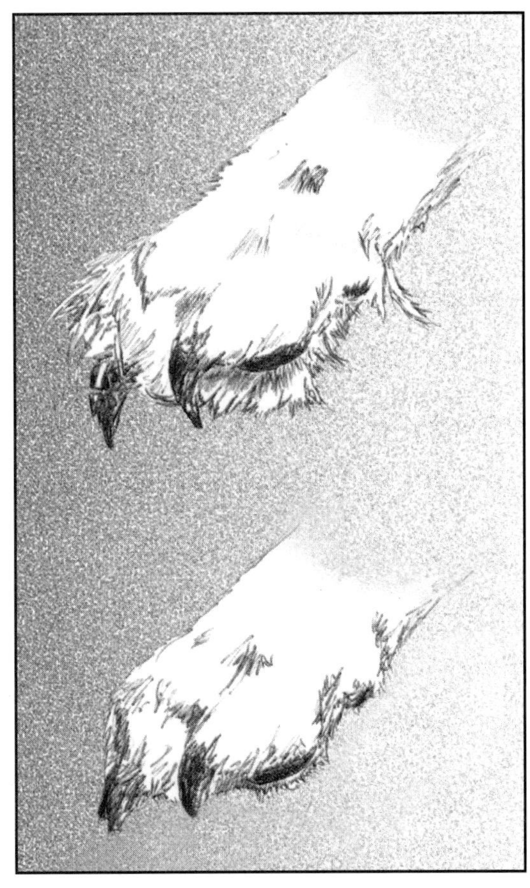

(Above) Before nails have been cut back and fur trimmed between the toes. (Below) After.

Dogs who have sufficient hard substances, such as real or synthetic bones, in their diet will usually have good teeth. Dogs fed on moist food only will have poor teeth and may end up with none at all. Regular brushing with dog toothpaste helps to prevent this. It can be brushed on with a human-style toothbrush or you can get a plastic one that fits over the finger.

Professional dental equipment is needed to remove heavy deposits of plaque and this type of fiddling often distresses a Borzoi so much that a general anaesthetic is necessary. While these are safer today than they were, the Borzoi is still one of the high-risk breeds when it comes to anaesthetics. Once the anaesthetic agent enters the body it is soaked up in the fat under the skin, from where it can come out gently at a steady rate. The Borzoi has little fat under the skin, so almost all the anaesthetic is in the system, which means it is difficult to keep a steady level in the blood stream. The Borzoi needs less anaesthetic agent than a dog of the same weight with a 'normal' amount of fat under the skin.

Since Borzois do not do as well under general anaesthetic as most other breeds, it is obviously unwise for them to be anaesthetised for such things as dental hygiene and removing matted hair when, with a little routine care and effort, the necessity could have been avoided.

Your veterinary surgeon

Your veterinary surgeon provides 24-hour veterinary care. If you are ever worried about your Borzoi's health, telephone your vet. Perhaps only a few words of advice are needed – or perhaps something is seriously wrong and immediate veterinary attention is needed. Do not gamble with a Borzoi's life.

Vaccination

It is important to keep your dog's vaccination programme up to date. Some vaccines are given annually, others every other year. Most vets have their records on computer so that they can remind you each year what boosters are due.

Worming

Worming is also important. At present worming every three months is recommended and the tablets available through your vet are more effective than those obtainable over the counter at your pet shop. Check with your vet what worming preparations he or she recommends.

Giving a tablet

If you have ever had occasion to give any sort of tablet to a dog you will know what problems it can cause. However, there could come a time when your dog would need daily medication to keep it alive.

Some of the new-generation worming pills have been manufactured with a flavour that appeals to Borzois. I had a puppy who ate everyone's worming tablets because he thought them a special treat. Apart from a night's vomiting, he was none the worse for his gastronomic adventure.

If your Borzoi will not eat the tablet you are trying to administer even when it is hidden inside a favourite food the best plan is surprise. Open the mouth, put the pill at the back of the tongue and push it. The dog will be so surprised that it will swallow. If you do not want to use your fingers to push the tablet down the throat a pen or pencil will do, but this does slow down the procedure.

It is good to be able to work with your dog's mouth, and the time may come when you need to remove something harmful. In any case, a prerequisite for the show ring is that the dog lets the judge examine its mouth.

Breed-associated diseases

The two conditions I shall discuss are associated with giant breeds such as the Borzoi. They are:

- Olecranon bursitis, or water on the elbow
- Gastric torsion, or bloat

Olecranon bursitis

The elbow joint consists of the humerus (upper arm) articulating with the olecranon process of the ulna. The two bones are separated by a sticky substance called synovial fluid that is kept in place by a bag around the joint called the joint capsule. Another much

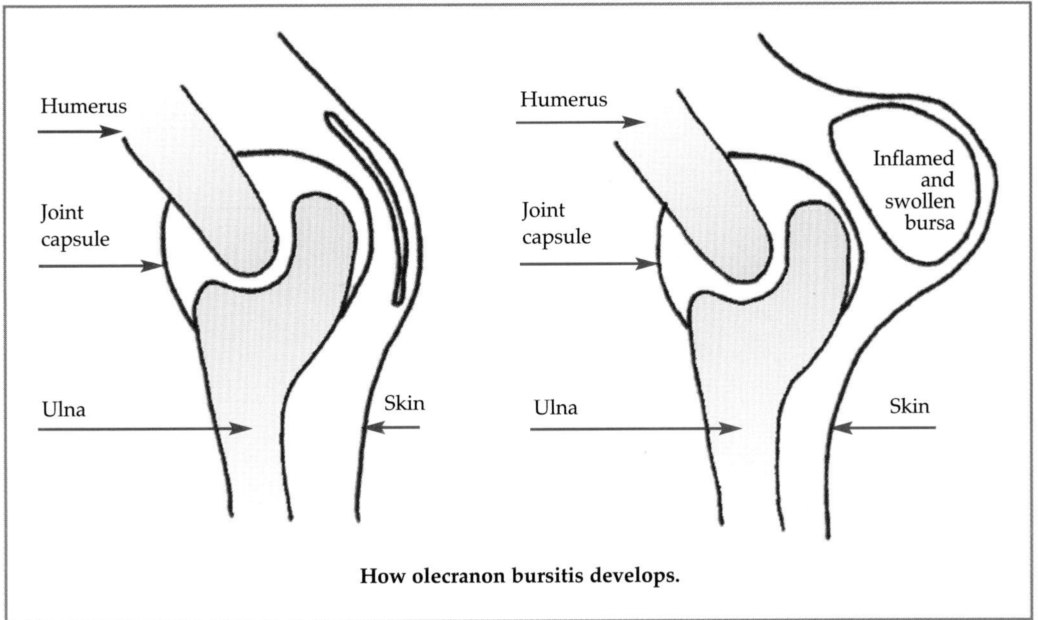

How olecranon bursitis develops.

more squashed 'balloon' next to the joint capsule is called the olecranon bursa. This too contains synovial fluid, but only a thin layer, so normally its sides are touching.

The olecranon bursa allows the skin to move smoothly over the muscle attached to the olecranon. If you put your hand on the point of your elbow you can move the skin about smoothly and easily. If you put your hand on the skin of your forearm it does not move easily over the muscle.

The Borzoi puppy is not very elegant. It tends to flop onto the ground, banging its elbows. If the ground is very firm, like a concrete floor in a run, this constant banging inflames the olecranon bursa, which swells with fluid. Housemaids who were constantly on their knees used to inflame the equivalent bursa over their kneecaps, getting the condition known as housemaid's knee.

The Borzoi pup's elbow looks very unsightly when it becomes swollen, but the condition does not seem to be painful. Gradually, the bursa shrinks down to its original size, usually needing no treatment; indeed, interfering by draining it can only make things worse.

Gastric torsion

This is a potential killer. One moment a happy Borzoi is in front of you; a few hours later it can be dead. The earlier the condition is diagnosed, the more likely your hound is to survive.

Gastric torsion starts as an accumulation of gas in the stomach. The stomach can then rotate, closing the entry point (the oesophagus or gullet) and the exit point (the duodenum or first part of the small bowel). The twisting increases the gas within the stomach and also twists shut the blood vessels to the stomach, and the increasing distention of the stomach wall further reduces the inflow of blood. With no blood supply, the stomach wall dies; once this has happened there is no hope of recovery. If the dog can be operated upon before the stomach wall dies it has a chance.

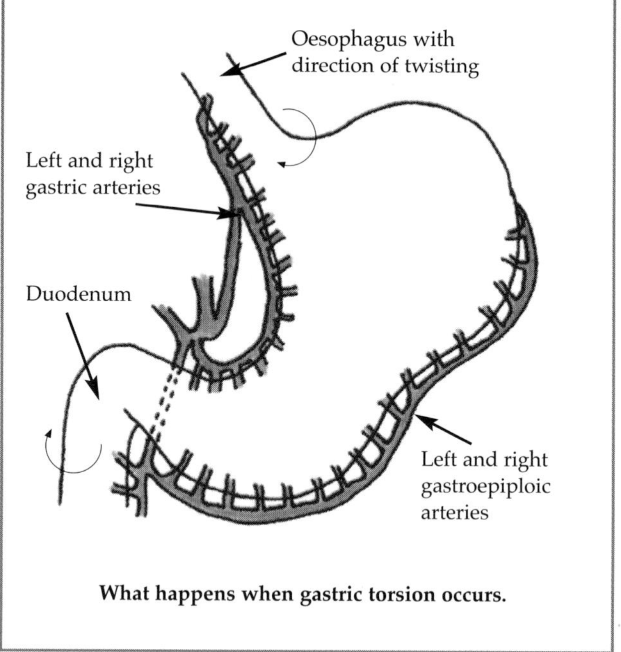

What happens when gastric torsion occurs.

When the stomach twists it is like a handbag, and everything at the 'two ends of the strap' is closed. The Borzoi has a deep chest, giving lots of room for the stomach to twist.

Symptoms: If the dog is at an early stage it has a chance of survival. If you think your dog is affected, telephone the veterinary surgery to say you are bringing in a dog with a gastric torsion. This gives them time to set up the operating theatre so that your sick dog goes straight from the car to the operating table.

I cannot stress sufficiently how much of an emergency gastric torsion is. Look out for:

- Abdominal distension. The gas makes the stomach of a dog with bloat very tense indeed; the abdomen is swollen and as tight and hard as a football.
- Dribbling, as saliva cannot be swallowed.
- Frequent attempts to vomit.
- Pain.
- Shock, due to an insufficient amount of blood circulating in the dog's system. The dog's gums and tongue will be white instead of pink, as there is not enough blood to colour them. The shock is just the same as if the dog's blood was pouring out onto the floor. As the stomach gets larger it presses on the major vessels that take blood back to the heart. If the blood is not returned to the heart it cannot be pumped around the body. The shocked dog has glazed, staring eyes. Time is of the essence in treating shock.

It is possible for a dog to have more than one incidence of gastric torsion, even if its stomach has been stapled in place to try to stop this.

Analysis of the gas in the stomach has shown that it contains a high percentage of air. This air has been swallowed when the dog was feeding. Greedy dogs who eat more quickly swallow more air than slower eaters. Putting a rubber ring in the feeding bowl means that a greedy dog has to eat more slowly, picking around the ring.

Minimising the incidence: No-one knows how to prevent bloat, but its incident can be minimised if:

- the dog is not exercised immediately before feeding.
- the dog is not exercised immediately after feeding.
- the dog is not fed on food high in cereals. High protein, low volume premium foods are the best.
- the dog is fed with its food and water bowls raised to reduce the amount of air swallowed.

Genetic problems

Hip dysplasia (HD)

The Kennel Club and the British Veterinary Association are involved in two schemes to try to reduce the incidence of genetic disease in pedigree dogs. The first of these relates to hip dysplasia, a condition in which the hip joint is not formed properly. There is a range of abnormality, from a dog hardly affected to one completely crippled.

A Dalmatian suffering from gastric torsion. Note the distended abdomen.

Hip dysplasia is not altogether a genetic disease; the environment in which the joint grows up is also important. Large, chunky puppies seem to be predisposed to the condition. Breeds with a high incidence include:

- German Shepherd Dogs
- Labrador Retrievers
- Golden Retrievers
- Rottweilers

Since Borzoi puppies are less fat than the puppies of these breeds, we do not know whether they carry the genes for hip dysplasia. Their comparative weight means that the hip joint is not in the environmental conditions that allow the illness to develop.

Inherited eye disease

The second Kennel Club/British Veterinary Association scheme is to reduce the incidence of inherited eye disease. At Crufts recently I asked one of the senior veterinary surgeons involved in the scheme if he had seen Borzois with genetic eye disease, and fortunately he had not. However, very few Borzois have been screened. The Borzoi gene pool is very small and few dogs are used at stud. If a stud dog with a genetic eye problem were widely used he could alter the whole situation. Blindness as a result of lens luxation (movement of the lens within the eye) is believed to have been introduced into the Tibetan Terrier breed by one stud dog, and the condition is now quite widespread within the breed.

Eye testing for inherited diseases involves instilling a drop of painless chemical into the dog's eyes to allow a specialist veterinary ophthalmologist to look at them through a special scope. It is worth considering how easy this test is to carry out, and how difficult it is to eradicate an inherited eye disease once it is widespread in a breed.

Dentition faults

Both dentition and bite faults can be found in the Borzoi. These are inherited, though not in a straightforward way like coat colour. Bite problems are complex, as tooth size may come from one parent and jaw size from the other. The sire may have a correct bite with big teeth in a big jaw; the dam may have a correct bite with smaller teeth in a smaller jaw. If the puppy inherits the dam's jaw with the sire's teeth, it follows that it will have a faulty bite. It may also have missing teeth because there is not sufficient room for all to erupt.

Overshot and undershot jaws put strain on the joint between the jaw bone (mandible) and the skull (tempomandibular joint). This can lead to pain in the joint. The ensuing abnormal tooth wear can lead to broken teeth – and further pain.

Dogs with a faulty bite should not be bred from. Dogs with missing teeth only should be assessed from the 'whole dog' point of view. An otherwise outstanding dog with one missing premolar may still have something to offer the breed as a sire; a mediocre dog with one missing premolar has nothing to offer.

Borzoi Genetics

The most difficult aspect of this chapter is to get you to start reading it. There is a scientific mystique about genetics that is quite unjustified. Yes, genetics is a huge subject, but we only know a very small part. Imagine a large library filled with a whole spectrum of books, from first readers to detailed analyses of advanced mathematical theory. The genetics we understand is equivalent to a first book of Disney stories, and Borzoi genetics to a few pages about Donald Duck.

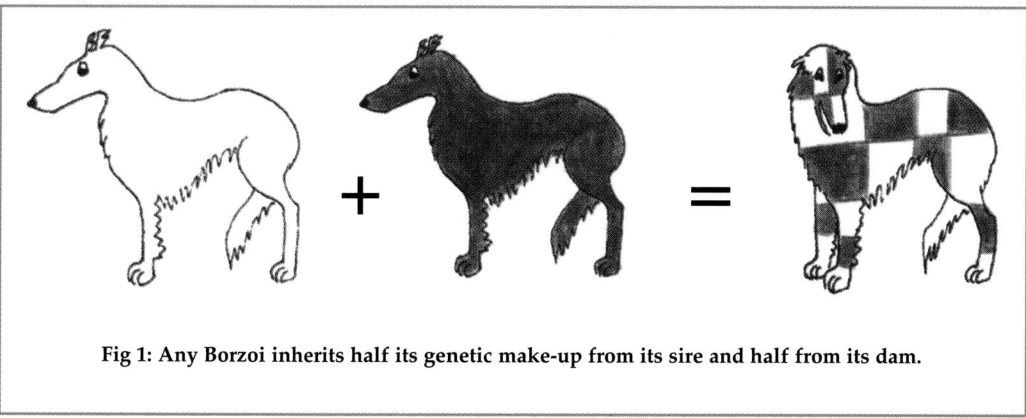

Fig 1: Any Borzoi inherits half its genetic make-up from its sire and half from its dam.

Coat colour is the only aspect of Borzoi genetics about which we can theorise with any degree of accuracy, so this chapter is confined to that topic. Colour is easier than the other aspects making up a Borzoi because we can see what colour a Borzoi is. Note that in all the diagrams in this chapter the colour is representative rather than naturalistic.

Any Borzoi inherits half its genetic make-up from its sire and half from its dam (see fig 1). The genetic material is inherited as little lumps of chemical called genes.

I find the best analogy for genes is to go back to considering books in a library. Each gene is a library book, a separate entity, but it also belongs to a group of similar books forming a category. Each category contains a different number of books; for instance, the Westerns section has rows and rows of books but the section containing travel stories from Outer Mongolia is much smaller.

In the Borzoi there are seven categories of coat colour (see fig 2 overleaf). Each pile of books is called a gene series.

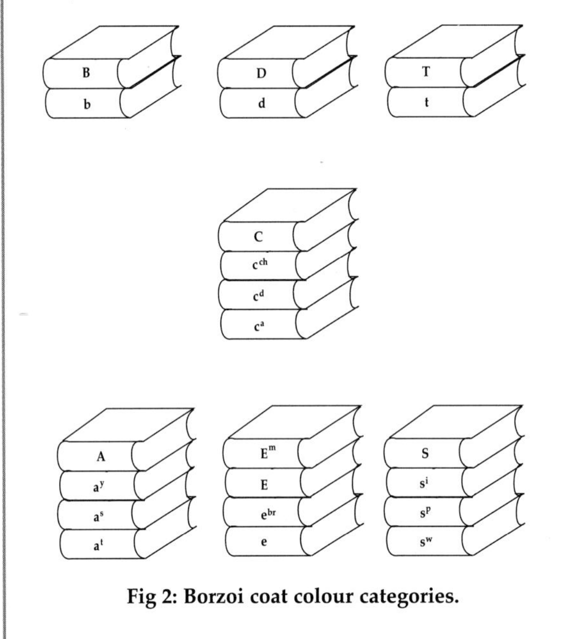

Fig 2: Borzoi coat colour categories.

By the rules of this library, from each series a borrower has to take one book as a present from his mother and one book as a present from his father. In other words, the Borzoi inherits one gene from each series from its father and one from its mother.

To make things more interesting, the library borrower is permitted to take two copies of the same book, one from each parent. In other words, the Borzoi can inherit the same gene from its mother and its father. In this case it is said to be *homozygous* for this gene (*homo* meaning same, *zygous* meaning new individual).

The library borrower may also take two different books. In other words, the Borzoi can inherit two different genes from the same series, one from each parent. In this case the Borzoi is *heterozygous* for this gene (*hetero* meaning different).

The B or black series

The first category is the B or black series. The gene b is rarely present in Borzois; most are BB. The gene B must be present for black pigment to be made. When B is present we see the colour black in the Borzoi. This gene is expressed as black nose, black lips, black eyelids and any black in the coat.

The gene B covers the presence of gene b. In genetic terms, B is dominant to b; b is recessive to B.

A Borzoi that happened to be Bb would be indistinguishable from the BB dog in appearance. It would still have a black nose, black lips and black eyelids. However, a Borzoi that was bb would be incapable of making the colour black. Anywhere that should be black would be liver or chocolate, so it would have liver nose, lips and eyelids.

Liver-coloured Pointers and chocolate Labradors have this bb conformation. Liver-coloured dogs cannot have black noses. As some-one should have explained to the overseas Bearded Collie breeder who coloured his brown dog's nose black for a series of photographs, it is genetically impossible.

The colour liver is a fault in the Borzoi.

The D or dilution series

The next category is the D or dilution series. There are just two genes in this series: D is dominant to d, and d is recessive to D.

If a Borzoi has the gene D the pigment will be seen at its full intensity; in other words, black will be black. The Dd dog will be indistinguishable in appearance from the DD dog.

A Borzoi that is dd has the pigmentation in each hair reduced. There is not full colour, but dilute colour. Black appears as blue and liver appears as yellow. Liver is almost unheard of in the Borzoi and I have never heard of the dilute form yellow in one.

The genetically black dog that is also dd cannot have the black nose, lips or eyelids but has blue nose, blue lips and blue eyelids.

There are two genetic types of black-pigmented Borzoi: the homozygous form (DD) and the heterozygous form (Dd). There is only one type of blue-pigmented Borzoi: dd.

To plan what could possibly happen at a mating it is best to write the genetic possibilities on a grid called a punnet square. If a dog that is DD is mated to a dog that is dd, only one colour type can be produced:

		blue (dd)	
		d	d
homozygous	D	Dd	Dd
black (DD)	D	Dd	Dd

All of these appear black just like the black parent, although they are heterozygous. However, if two of these puppies are mated together, the odds are that 25% will be blue, as can be seen from the punnet square below:

		heterozygous black (Dd)	
		D	d
heterozygous	D	DD	Dd
black (Dd)	d	Dd	dd

This brings us to the problem of population genetics. The very first genetic experiments were done by an Austrian monk called Gregor Mendel, who used pea plants. He carried out thousands of pea matings before publishing his original paper in 1865, which was shamefully disregarded in his lifetime. The first experiments involved crossing round-seeded and wrinkle-seeded peas. From these he bred 7324 pea seeds, of which 5474 were round and 1850 were wrinkled. This gave the ratio 2.96:1, which has been interpreted as 3:1; in other words, 66$^{2}/_{3}$% of the peas were round. However, figures will only work out like this if experiments are carried out on a large scale. This is not possible with Borzois; even the most widely used stud only sires a few hundred puppies. In a litter of eight puppies we will not get perfect ratios. We cannot predict the numbers of each colour, but we can predict which colours are possible.

Therefore, when two heterozygous blacks are mated together, all that we can say for certain is that the mating could produce homozygous black, heterozygous black and blue puppies. The two groups of blacks appear exactly the same in colour, and probably there will not be many blues.

The T or ticking gene

The next category is the T or ticking series. There are just two genes in this series. T is dominant to t and t is recessive to T.

A Borzoi with the gene T has small spots over its body, like the belton colouration of an English Setter. Sometimes these spots are only apparent on the front legs. This is a fault in the Borzoi.

- The Tt dog is indistinguishable from the TT dog.
- The tt dog has no spots.

As it is obvious which dogs carry the gene T, it is relatively easy to breed it out. In the United States they have managed to do this quite effectively in the English Springer Spaniel.

Let's consider the D and T series together. This means a much larger punnet square. Crossing a non-spotty homozygous black (DDtt) with a homozygous spotty blue (ddTT) we have:

		homozygous spotty blue (ttDD)			
		dT	dT	dT	dT
non-spotty	Dt	DdT	DdTt	DdTt	DdTt
homozygous	Dt	DdTt	DdTt	DdTt	DdTt
black (DDtt)	Dt	DdTt	DdTt	DdTt	DdTt
	Dt	DdTt	DdTt	DdTt	DdTt

The options down the side of the square are calculated as shown in the table at the top of the opposite page.

It follows that all the puppies produced by crossing a non-spotty homozygous black (DDtt) with a homozygous spotty blue Borzoi will be heterozygous black and heterozygous spotty (DdTt). If we mate two of these together:

d d T T = d T

d d T T = d T

d d T T = d T

d d T T = d T

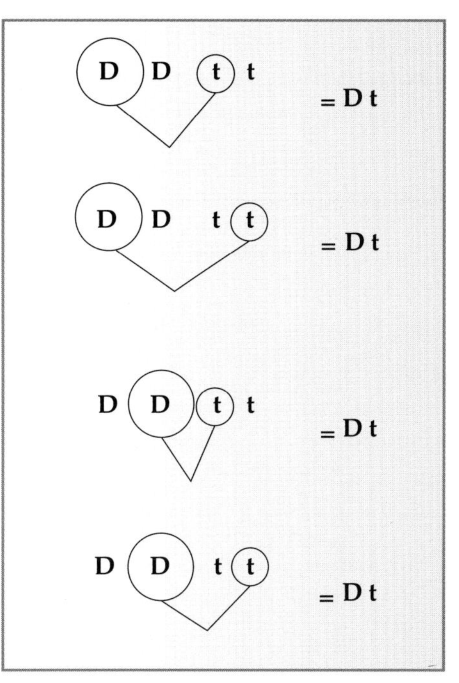

heterozygous black heterozygous spotty (DdTt)					
		DT	Dt	dT	dt
heterozygous	DT	DDTT	DDTt	DdTT	DdTt
black	Dt	DDTt	DDtt	DdTt	Ddtt
heterozygous	dT	DdTT	DdTt	ddTT	ddTt
spotty (DdTt)	dt	DdTt	Ddtt	ddTt	ddtt

Of these 16 puppies:

Q: How many will be spotty? To be spotty the puppy needs at least one T.

A: 12 out of 16.

Q: How many puppies will be black? To be black the puppy needs at least one D.

A: 12 out of 16

Q: How many will be non-spotty and blue (that is, ddtt)?

A: 1 out of 16.

Since the bitch is unlikely to have 16 puppies, all we can predict is that most puppies will have black pigment and most will be spotty.

The C or colour series

The C series is a little more complicated than those we have looked at so far because there are four genes available to choose from, though each individual Borzoi still has only two from this series, one from each parent. This is the albino series and its four genes are:

- C, which is dominant to the other three genes
- c^{ch}, which is recessive to C but dominant to the others
- c^d, which is recessive to C and c^{ch} but dominant to c^a
- c^a, which is recessive to the other three genes

If a Borzoi is c^ac^a, the dog is albino and has no colour at all. In this case it does not matter what happens in the B and D series; c^ac^a prevents colours from being shown.

The c^{ch} gene means that the hairs are pale coloured with a tip of a darker colour like the coat pattern of a chinchilla or a chinchilla-coloured cat. If a Borzoi has BD as well as c^{ch} the tips of the hair are black.

The c^d gene means that the Borzoi is white with a coloured nose, lips and eyelids and dark eyes. The colour of the nose depends on what is happening at B and D, but the coat colour given by B and D is hidden and the dog appears as a self white.

The C gene means that what is happening at B and D can be seen and expressed.

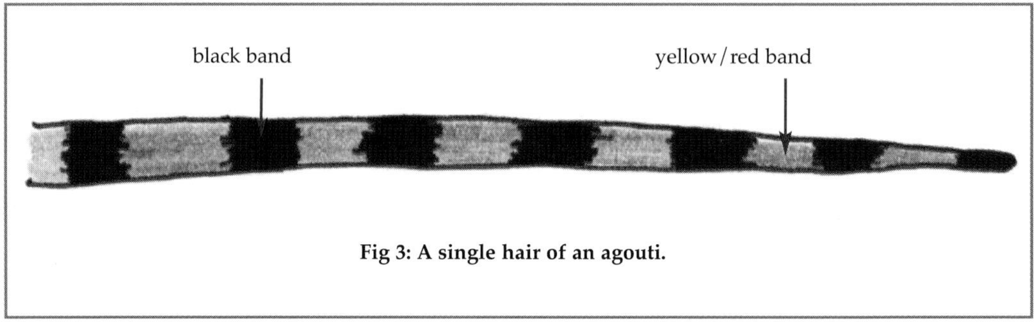

Fig 3: A single hair of an agouti.

The A or agouti series

The next category is the A or agouti series, named after a South American rodent called an agouti that looks rather like a giant guinea pig. The agouti has hairs that are banded alternately yellow/red and black, as shown in fig 3. There are four genes in this series and their effects are illustrated in fig 4:

- AA – the hair is completely black
- a^ya^y – the hair is completely yellow/red
- a^sa^s – black hair on saddle but the rest of the coat is yellow/red
- a^ta^t – tan markings of a Dobermann

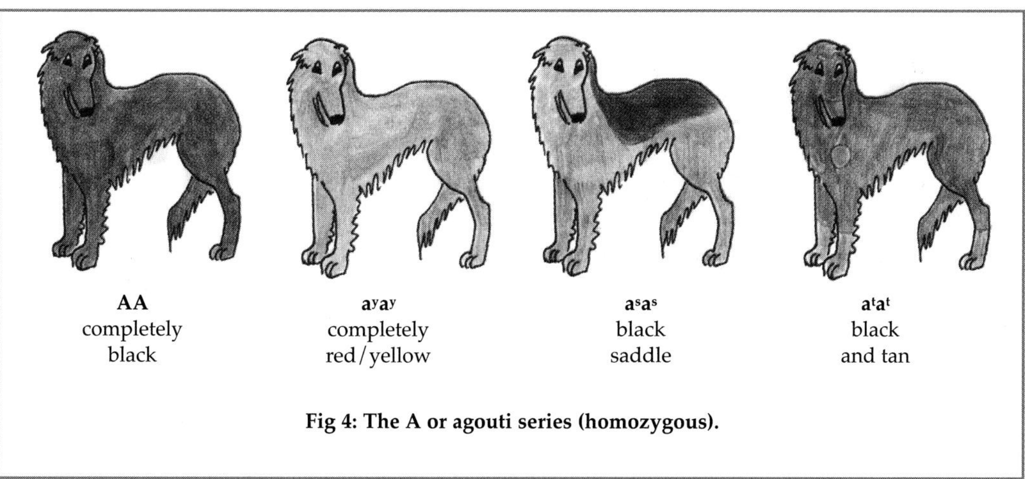

Fig 4: The A or agouti series (homozygous).

The dominance is in this order but, when the Borzoi is not homozygous for its genes in this series, we have more colour patterns, as illustrated in fig 5:

- a^ya^s – lightly shaded sable
- a^ya^t – shaded sable
- a^sa^t – black and tan

Fig 5: The A or agouti series (heterozygous).

If the Borzoi does not have a D gene (in other words, is dd) there will be no black colour, just blue. This means we will have:

- dda^ta^t – blue and tan
- dda^sa^s – blue sable

The E or extension series

To understand this series we have to assume our Borzoi has

- B – so that black pigment can be formed
- D – so that the colour is of normal intensity
- C – so that the coat colour is not hidden by white
- a^ya^y – so that the coat is completely yellow / red

The genes in the E series, illustrated in Fig 6, are as follows:

- E^mE^m – red with a black mask. The red colour of a Boxer is due to E^mE^m.
- EE – red without a black mask. The red colour of a Basenji is due to EE.
- $e^{br}e^{br}$ – red brindle.
- ee – yellow. The yellow colour of a Labrador is due to ee.

Dominance is in the following order:

- E^m is dominant to the other three.
- E is dominant to e^{br} and e.
- e^{br} is dominant to e.
- e is recessive to the other three.

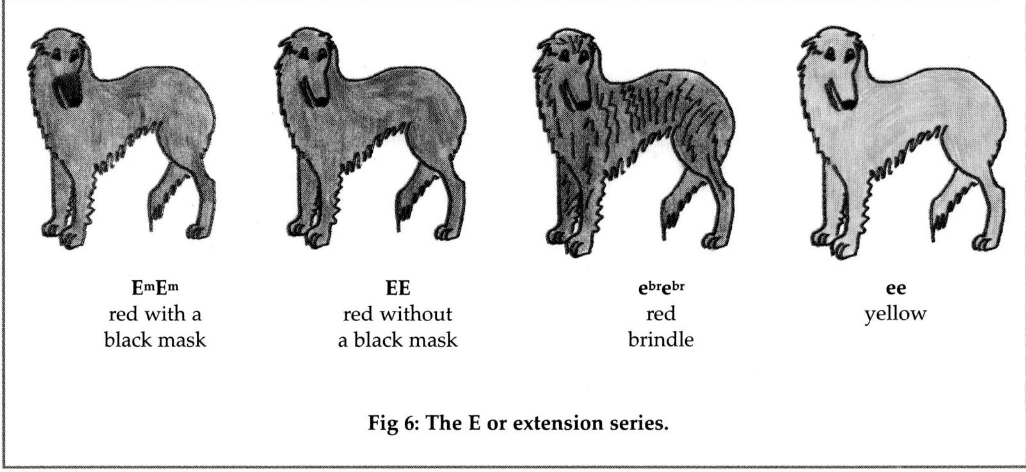

Fig 6: The E or extension series.

The S or spotting series

The last series that is important to Borzoi colour is the S or spotting series. This governs the size of white markings. The genes in this series, illustrated in figs 7 (red), 8 (black and tan) and 9 (black saddle) are:

- S – no white areas
- s^i – Irish pattern of white
- s^p – a substantial amount of white
- s^w – mostly white

Dominance is as follows:

- S is dominant to the other three.
- s^i is dominant to s^p and s^w.
- s^p is dominant to s^w.
- s^w is recessive to the other three.

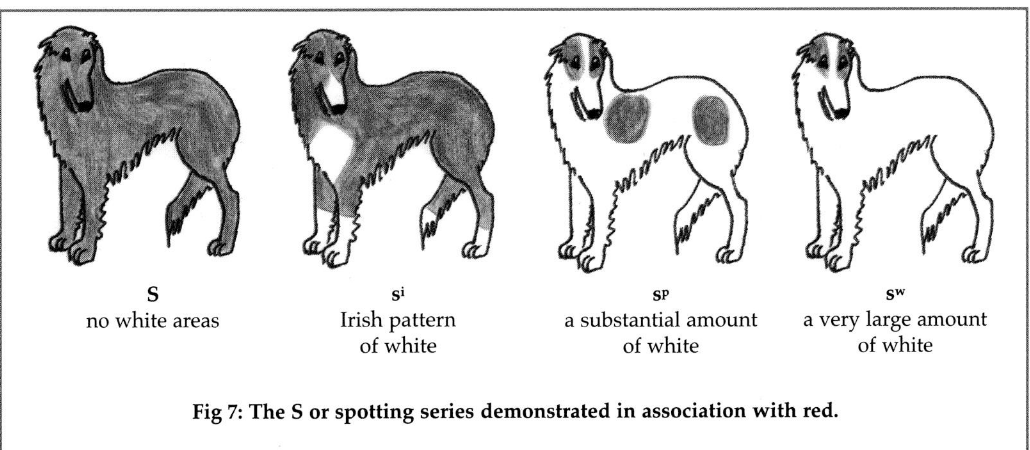

Fig 7: The S or spotting series demonstrated in association with red.

The S gene is uncommon in the Borzoi as most have some white somewhere. By mixing the combinations of s^i, s^p and s^w we get the different amounts of white seen on Borzois:

- s^ws^w would have the most white.
- s^ws^p would have more white than s^ps^p.

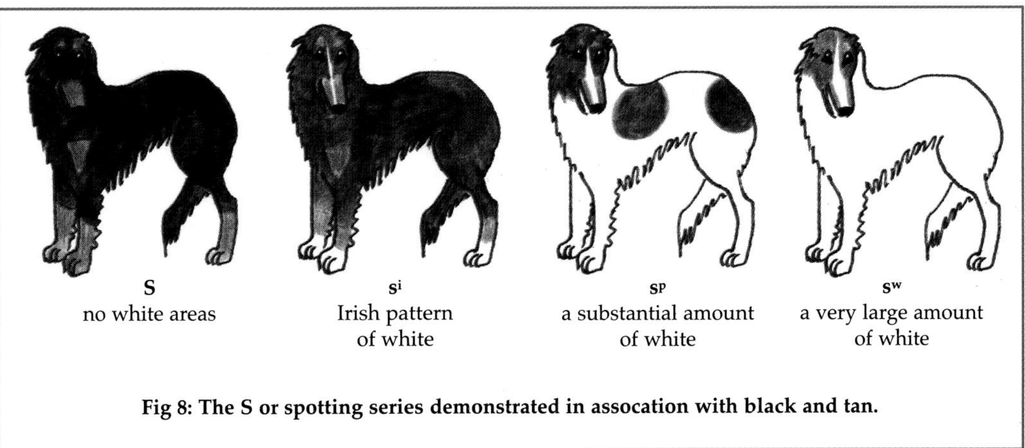

Fig 8: The S or spotting series demonstrated in assocation with black and tan.

It is very unusual for the Borzoi to have no white markings at all and, although the vast majority of dogs with black as their main colour also have tan markings, they are generally called 'self blacks', disregarding the tan and the small amount of white marking.

As the amount of spotting with white increases the dogs are called white and black, again disregarding the tan. In the set of red dogs with increasing white the red dog with Irish spotting would be a self red.

Going through the series again, this time with a sable (black saddle) dog (see fig 9), we have:

- s produces self sable with no white markings (very unusual)
- s^i also produces self sable, since the presence of the Irish white markings is disregarded.
- s^p and s^w are both known as 'tortoiseshell', the markings produced by extensive white on sable being reminiscent of those on tortoiseshell cats.

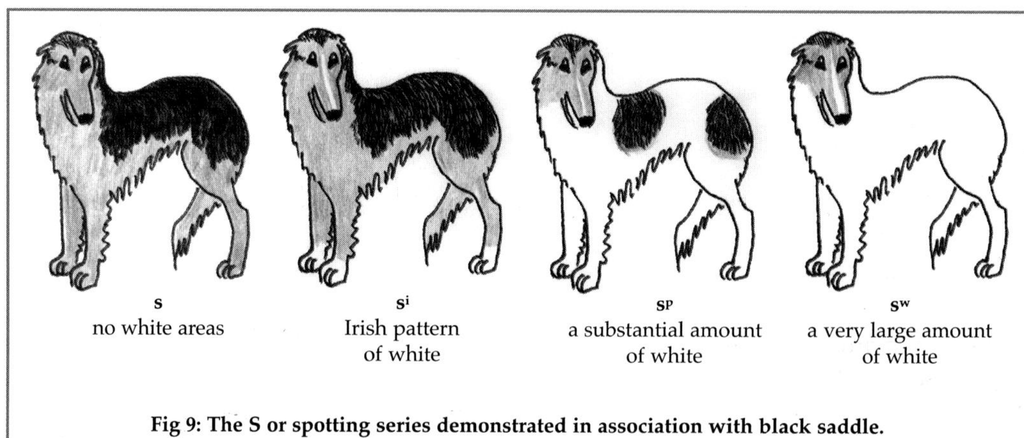

Fig 9: The S or spotting series demonstrated in association with black saddle.

Undesirable colour patterns

Not many colour patterns are considered undesirable in a Borzoi. Apart from ticking and liver, the only other problem is the distribution of white markings. These should be symmetrical, especially over the head. A patch of colour over one eye and not the other is ugly, as are heavy, isolated patches of colour on legs, separated from the main body colour (see fig 10).

Fig 10: Undesirable colour patterns.

The Borzoi rainbow

By mixing the gene combinations together we can get the rainbow of colours characteristic of the Borzoi. To finish this section, here are some examples of famous dogs and their genetic patterns. Where it is not possible to work out the exact genes I have inserted asterixes.

Ch Colhugh Caminickers (see page 107)

Ch Colhugh Caminickers, the breed record holder, is red and white with no black mask and no ticks.

- B series must have at least B
- D series must have at least D
- T series must be tt
- C series must have at least C
- A series must be a^ya^y
- E series must have at least E and definitely does not have E^m
- S series probably has something like s^ps^p

  This gives us B*, D*, tt, C*, a^ya^y, E*, s^ps^p.

Ch Colhugh Clangers (see page 58)

Ch Colhugh Clangers, the dog record holder, was a heavily-shaded mahogany with a black mask, no ticks and the Irish pattern of white markings.

- B series must have at least B
- D series must have at least D
- T series must be tt
- C series must have at least C
- A series is probably a^ya^t
- E series must have at least E^m
- S series must be s^is^i

  This gives us B*, D*, tt, C*, a^ya^t, E^m*, s^is^i.

Ch Zomahli Chernila (see page 62)

Ch Zomahli Chernila, the previous breed record holder, was a self black: that is, black and tan with the Irish pattern of white, no ticks, no black mask.

- B series must have at least B
- D series must have at least D
- T series must be tt
- C series must have at least C
- A series must be a^ta^t
- E series must have at least E and definitely does not have E^m
- S series must be s^is^i

  This gives us B*, D*, tt, C*, a^ta^t, E*, s^is^i.

Borzoi Showing

Let us imagine that you are sitting at home with a lovely puppy, the pride of its breeder, and you wish to share the beauty of this puppy with the world. The best way to show your puppy to all those interested in the Borzoi is to enter it at a dog show. The puppy has to be at least six months old to be entered at a show, and the best one to start with is the one nearest to your home. Going to a show is very tiring for a puppy; the shorter the time away from home, the better.

There are many different types of dog show in Great Britain. In the first place, there are all-breed shows and shows for Borzois only, the latter run by the Borzoi Club and the Northern Borzoi Association.

All-breed shows are run by such societies as the West of England Ladies Kennel Society (WELKS) and the Land o' Burns Canine Club. WELKS holds an annual championship show in April, located at Malvern. An all-breed championship show is a very large event with thousands of entries from all breeds and from all over the country. People travel many miles to championship shows because Challenge Certificates (CCs) are awarded at them. One CC is on offer for the best of each sex in each breed. The CC is the most sought-after award as three of these, each awarded by a different judge with at least one when the dog is more than a year old, mean that the dog can be called a champion.

The Land o' Burns Canine Club holds open shows. An open show typically has a few hundred entries from all breeds. Popular breeds like the Golden Retriever have two or three classes. Borzois may occasionally have a class of their own but they usually have to be entered in the Any Other Variety Hound class.

The show closest to your home is most likely to be an open show. Only 24 societies run all-breed championship shows, with another 12 holding group championship shows, but hundreds hold open shows.

Other types of show are limited, sanction and primary, but these are restricted to members of the club holding the show.

Filling in the entry form

You will need an entry form to enter a show. The secretary of the society holding the show will send you a little booklet called a schedule, which contains an entry form. Addresses of all show secretaries can be obtained from The Kennel Club or from advertisements for shows in the two dog newspapers, *Dog World* and *Our Dogs*.

It is important to get all the details correct on the entry form. If your dog wins but there is a mistake on the entry form your dog's award can be taken away. A one-letter mistake in a Wire Fox Terrier's name caused the dog to lose the CC it had won. The award was reinstated after a great deal of protests, but it is easier to fill in the form correctly in the first place than to persuade The Kennel Club to change its mind.

On the entry form you will need to fill in the following information:

- Puppy's name
- Puppy's date of birth
- Breeder's name
- Puppy's father (sire)
- Puppy's mother (dam)
- The numbers of all the classes in which you are entering the puppy.

If your puppy does not yet have an official Kennel Club registration document you must add the letters NAF (Name Applied For) after its name. In the 1980s, before The Kennel Club's system was computerised, there was a point when the registrations were so delayed that two Groenendael champions called Ch Sonmar I Remain Nameless and Ch Sonmar I'm Nameless Too were made up!

If you do not yet have an official Kennel Club transfer document saying that you are the owner, provided that the puppy does belong to you and not to the breeder you must add the letters TAF (Transfer Applied For) after its name.

The puppy cannot be shown at a show licensed by The Kennel Club if it is not Kennel Club registered. You should get the registration certificate with the transfer section signed by the breeder when you take the puppy home. This document should be sent to The Kennel Club with the correct fee to register transfer of ownership.

It is important to get the class numbers right as you will not be able to transfer to the correct class on the day.

The schedule will have a closing date on the front. Remember to post your entry before this date, enclosing the correct entry fee. Often it is possible to buy a catalogue at the time of making your entry, and the catalogue will be cheaper than on the day of the show. The catalogue contains all the details taken from the entry forms about the dogs entered at the show.

The entry form also contains a declaration that you have to sign to confirm you will abide by Kennel Club rules and that, if your dog comes into contact with an infectious disease, you will not take your dog to the show to pass on the infection. Before effective vaccines were developed many dogs died from illnesses picked up at shows.

Dog show classes

All-breed open shows

At an all-breed open show there will not be many classes that your Borzoi can enter. It is unlikely there will be a Borzoi puppy class, so the options will probably be:

- Borzoi
- Any Variety Hound
- Any Variety Hound Puppy

Borzois are slow developers and go through a long ugly duckling stage, so it is unlikely that your puppy will win against mature Borzois. The best choice of class is the Any Variety Hound Puppy, with the hope that there are separate Dachshund classes. Small hound breeds, especially Miniature Dachshunds, mature far more quickly than Borzois. A Miniature Dachshund will be almost mature at seven to eight months, giving it a great advantage over the Borzoi puppy.

All-breed championship shows

There is a greater selection of classes in which you can enter your Borzoi at all-breed championship shows. There will be a Borzoi Puppy class, which is the best one for your puppy. The usual Borzoi classes at an all-breed championship show are:

Puppy: for puppies of six and not exceeding twelve calendar months of age on the first day of the show.

Junior: for dogs of six and not exceeding eighteen calendar months of age on the first day of the show.

Post Graduate: for dogs that have not won a CC or five or more first prizes at championship shows in Post Graduate, Minor Limit, Mid Limit, Limit and Open classes.

Limit: for dogs who have not won three CCs under three different judges or seven or more first prizes in all at championship shows in Limit and Open classes.

Open: for all dogs of the breed for which the class is provided.

Puppy and Junior are determined by the age of the Borzoi and the higher classes are divided by the number of wins. Keep an accurate record of your dog's wins. If you enter your dog in a class for which it is no longer eligible any awards will be disallowed.

Borzoi-only shows

Borzoi-only shows may be open or championship shows. They have many more Borzois entering them than all-breed shows, so there is a larger selection of classes. There will be two puppy classes, the addition being:

Minor Puppy: for puppies of six and not exceeding nine calendar months.

Other classes available are likely to be Beginners, Novice, Undergraduate and Graduate. The specific regulations for entering these can be found in the schedule.

Junior Warrant

This is an award granted to young dogs who have had a certain number of wins. However, the conditions for awarding it changed in October 1997 and the new conditions have not yet been published in full.

Stud Book entry

Every year since 1874 The Kennel Club has produced *The Kennel Club Stud Book*, which contains details about the dog winners of the previous year's championship shows. Each dog entered has won his Stud Book number, a number of four figures followed by a two-letter code for the year.

At present a Borzoi gains his Stud Book number if he wins a first or second prize in the Open class or first in the Limit class at a championship show where CCs are on offer for the breed. The two CC winners win their numbers whatever breed class they won, as do the two Reserve CC winners.

A Stud Book number is a prestigious award. If there was only one entry in an Open class, and this was a hound of poor quality, the judge should withhold the first and second prizes in this class, as such a dog should not get his Stud Book number.

Qualifying for Crufts

Crufts is the largest dog show in the world, and it is held by The Kennel Club in March every year. This is the only British dog show for which a dog has to qualify before it can enter. The necessary wins for qualification alter every year, and they are detailed in the schedule for the show.

Preparing for your first show

Preparation for a day at a dog show should take into account that most of your time will be spent sitting around while you wait to go into the ring. All shows have catering but this is often very expensive. If you do forget to bring something it is more than likely that you can buy it at one of the trade stands at the show, but you should try to remember the following essentials:

- water bowl for dog
- cups for humans
- bottle of water for dog
- flask of tea or coffee for humans
- dog food
- human food
- rug for dog to sit on
- for a luxury show, chairs for humans to sit on

The class winner: the judge approaches, book in hand, to present the first prize rosette to the CC-winning Borcho Miss Havisham, with owner/breeder Edward McKenzie.

- schedule with the classes you have entered marked so that you do not forget which they are
- show lead
- brush
- clip for ring number

It is a good idea to practise with the clip for the ring number before you get into the ring, as it is a fiddly little thing, and all your concentration should be on the judge once you enter the ring. At an open show the ring steward hands you your number as you enter the ring; at a championship show your number will be lying on your bench. Benches are formed by a raised wooden platform with metal partitions to separate the dogs and, at a championship show, your dog should be sitting on its bench when not in the ring.

Let us assume that your first show is a local open show. You arrive and collect your pre-paid catalogue from the secretary's desk and then find the ring in which your dog's class will be judged. Find a seat and sit and wait, breaking the monotony with a quick brush of your dog's coat, taking care to pick up the hair. If a venue is filled with rubbish

– including a large proportion of your dog's coat – it is unlikely that it will continue as a show venue.

Your class is called, and you enter the ring, collecting your number from the steward. You will know your number from the catalogue. Do not go into the ring first – if possible, be the last to go in, so that you can observe what the other exhibitors are doing. They will be doing what the judge asks them to.

The judge in the ring

The judge will be observing the dogs as they enter the ring. In the ring, after fixing their ring numbers on their clips, the exhibitors stand their dogs in show pose. The judge will then ask them to walk their dogs around the ring, one after the other, either once or twice, so that he or she can observe the dogs' movement from the side. After the circuit, all the dogs stop and the first dog is taken out of line up to the judge for individual assessment. The first dog is posed in the manner in which it looks at its best, standing square.

Standing an exhibit for the judge.

For the rest of this chapter I shall refer to the judge as 'he', simply to avoid the clumsiness of 'he or she'.

Going over the dogs

The judge then goes over the dog. Starting at the head, he will open the dog's mouth to check that it has the correct scissor bite and complete dentition. Looking at the correct, dark, almond-shaped eyes, the judge may gently stroke the head, especially if there is a lot of coat on it, to feel the elegant shape of the back skull.

Running his hands down the neck, the judge then checks that the neck is not cylindrical but laterally compressed and that it flows gently into the shoulders.

The judge starts by looking at dentition.

Now we are at the scapulae (shoulder blades). The judge checks that these are two fingers' breadth apart and then runs a hand down the upper surface of one of them to the shoulder joint, then back along the humerus to end up under the rearmost part of the scapula. The judge has now assessed the angle of the shoulder with the dog standing.

Assessing the head.

The judge's hand is now at the elbow, and this should also be the level of the lowest part of the rib cage, with no more than two fingers' breadth from the rib cage. The hand is now run down the front legs to see if the bone is bladed, and then taken back to the shoulders so that the judge can feel for the spring of rib. The rib cage must be neither too laterally compressed nor too rounded and barrel-like. The judge will place his hand between the front legs, checking for chest development.

Passing his hands back, the judge will assess the length of the rib cage and thus establish the proportion in length of ribs to loin muscles. The loin muscles should be short and well developed. The hind legs should be very well muscled indeed. They must not be laterally compressed, but rounded and well developed. The judge should also check that the muscles attached to the tibia (muscles of the second thigh) are well developed.

Having gone down the neck and shoulders, the judge assesses the bone in the front legs.

The tail is now assessed. Its length is measured by pulling it gently through the legs to the iliac crest (crest of the hip bone), not to the tip of the hock. The iliac crests should be at least 8cm apart.

Movement

At this point the judge has finished examining your dog and now needs to see it move. The traditional British way is to do a triangle but it is important to do whatever the judge asks. This is where being the last to enter the ring pays dividends. Do the same movement pattern as the exhibitors in front of you.

The triangle shows the hind movement as the dog goes from the judge, side movement as it passes him and front movement as it comes towards him. At the end of the triangle the dog stops in show stance.

The final line-up

Once the judge has gone over each dog in the class he will have a good idea which one is going to be awarded first prize. If he likes two dogs equally he may go over these two again and ask them to move again. Once he has decided, he will indicate which is first, and this dog will come out from the line of dogs to start a new line. The next dog to be pulled out has won second, and the next third. The next award is called Reserve, then Very Highly Commended, Highly Commended and sometimes a Commended award is given. The final line-up can be altered right up to the time the judge hands out prize cards and rosettes and marks up the numbers of the winning dogs in the judging book. The judge then either writes down or records on a dictaphone a few points about the winning dogs: the first at an open show, the first and second at a championship show and first, second and third at Crufts.

The first part of the triangle.

The dogs now leave the ring – hopefully to an enthusiastic round of applause.

All the dog class winners compete for the Dog CC.
This shows the winners of Open and Limit Dog.

Awards

At an all-breed open show with only one Borzoi class the winner of the first prize is also Best of Breed (BOB).

At a championship show all the winners of the Dog classes compete ('challenge') for the dog Challenge Certificate (CC). After this has been awarded the Reserve CC is awarded. The dog that was beaten by the CC winner, coming second in the class, may be invited to compete with the winners of the other classes for the Reserve CC. These are both very special awards, although it is only the CC that counts towards the title champion. In each case the judge has to sign the declaration:

I am clearly of the opinion that .... is of such outstanding merit as to be worthy of the title champion.

A dog may be worthy of first prize, even the best male in the show, but not of such outstanding quality as to deserve the title champion. In this case the judge must withhold both CC and Reserve CC. If the CC winner should be disqualified for any reason the Reserve CC winner would receive the CC in his place, so both must be of championship quality. For this reason, there are occasions when the CC is awarded but the Reserve CC withheld.

The CC procedure is now repeated for the Bitch class winners, and the Dog and Bitch CC winners compete for BOB at all-breeds championship shows, which is also Best In Show (BIS) at breed championship shows. At an all-breed championship show the Borzoi BOB winner goes on to compete with the other BOBs in the hound group for Best In

Group, with first, second, third and fourth prizes being awarded. The final round in the show is the competition between the winners of the (at present) six groups for the title Best In Show (BIS). From 1999 there will be seven groups, as the present huge working group will be split into *working* and *pastoral*.

At some open shows the group system is used to decide BIS, but at others all the BOBs compete together for the honour.

Avoiding bad behaviour from your puppy

In my description of judging procedures I presented the ideal scenario. In the real world, your puppy is very likely to refuse to stand still for more than a moment at its first show, and I dare not mention the acrobatics that could occur when the judge tries to look at its teeth! Your puppy will not show its teeth if you have not practised this at home. When the puppy moves it is supposed to have all four feet on the ground. Often it will skip along on its hind feet, buck like a horse, go on strike, lie on the floor or slip out of its collar and run under the judge's table. However, practice and some luck should prevent the worst of these disasters.

Marking up the awards from the award board.

A good judge is especially gentle and patient with a puppy so that it is not frightened. A terrible experience at a show could mean that the puppy will never let a judge near it again. Judges allow for bad behaviour in Puppy and Junior classes but, as the dog gets older, it will lose out to a less well constructed but better behaved hound.

Many of the clubs that run open shows have classes once a week for you and your puppy to learn ringcraft. These are not always the best places for sensitive Borzoi puppies, especially if they are filled with gundogs and gundog people. A gundog is the antithesis of a Borzoi, enjoying bustle, noise and hearty patting.

However, such classes can be useful for puppy socialisation. Provided the other people there realise how sensitive a Borzoi is and make allowances, ringcraft classes could help to prevent your public humiliation by your Borzoi.

Which judge to enter under

Since the finer points of the Breed Standard can be interpreted in various ways, different judges have different ideas of Borzoi perfection. Some prefer the Northern British type: finer-built hounds with beautiful curves and a tendency towards self black in colour. Others prefer the more strongly-built Southern British type that tends to be red and white in colour. It is not a good idea to take your fine Northern hounds to the other end of the country to exhibit under someone who prefers the Southern type.

No judge can please every exhibitor at a show because not everyone goes home with a first prize. There will always be grumbles about the integrity and knowledge of judges. One of the finest pieces on the subject was written by Lady Wentworth for *Country Life* in 1950 and then reproduced in the *Irish Setter Association Annual Review* in 1996. I make no apologies for reproducing it yet again here.

The man who has tasted the excitement of exhibition will seldom really give it up again; it is closely allied to the gambling instinct, and, let him lose ever so often, a fatal attraction lures him back once more. When he can no longer afford to be a breeder or owner, he will hang about disconsolately, watching other people in the ring with envious eyes. As an old fancier once said to me when I talked of giving up my dogs: 'When you once get bitten by the show microbe, the disease generally lasts your life.' It certainly has done so, for, although I no longer show dogs, I show horses.

Feeling runs higher in dog shows than it does even over elections, and apparently it is only the shadow of Rule 17 which prevents exhibitors from assaulting each other with dead cats and rotten eggs – only I am afraid it would be dead dogs in these cases.

Exhibitors of either sex are seldom friends for long, like the lady who, speaking rapturously of her fiancé, exclaimed: 'Oh, we have such quarrels – but such reconciliations!' What, then, is the lure of the show ring?

Horse and dog exhibitors have to reckon with many kinds of judges.

1 *The weak-minded, well-meaning man, who can never make up his mind and gets hot and flustered and nervous, and makes the exhibitors cross and takes all the life out of the exhibits by having them sent round and round the ring 50 times when once would suffice. This kind of judge almost invariably ends by awarding the prizes to the wrong ones because, by looking at them too long, he loses the invaluable general impression of shape, style and outline, and eventually makes his decision on questions of minute detail, a white hair in the coat, a microscopic splint or uneven teeth, none of which matters a scrap. Looking too long and too closely at a thing tends to destroy all sense of proportion.*

2 *The unscrupulous old hand who is open to adapt his decisions according to the advantage he thinks he is likely to get, either in hard cash or in other ways.*

3 *The equally [unscrupulous] old hand who has a kink in his temper, who will put you up today and down tomorrow out of pure spleen and biliousness, who is insulted if he is bribed and more insulted if he is not.*

4 *The sensationalist, who likes to turn everything topsy-turvey, and his opposite number, the timid man to whom precedent is as Holy Writ.*

5 *The ostentatious and self-righteous prig who is always blowing his own trumpet and adopts the attitude, 'What I have written, I have written,' yet never bred a good animal in his life.*

6 *The rare judge who knows his business, who is firm, courteous and dignified in the ring, and punctual in getting there, who is rapid and decided in his awards, and perfectly consistent and reliable.*

7 *The irritating, happy-go-lucky man, who is always late, arrives in a breathless haste, with a flushed face and eager eye, and has to catch an early train home. He hurries through his classes, loses his pencil, mislays his judging book, awards the stud dog prize to a bitch, gives the hack prize to a brood mare, thanks everybody profusely, and vanishes in a whirl of flurry, taking the slips of the last class with him, and leaving everybody bewildered and gasping.*

8 *The bully who swears at the ring steward, insults the secretary, orders the exhibitors out of the ring if they dare so much as to sneeze without leave, frightens the grooms, reduces novices to hysterics, yet awards prizes to the right animals and departs saying he never saw such a cussed lot of wastrels in his life.*

9 *The ill tempered woman who considers herself infallible, speaks sharply, will not wait for anybody, is impatient with exhibitors for things they cannot help and bullies everyone within an inch of his life.*

Ring stewards should never by any chance give an opinion on the exhibits. Exhibitors enter under an advertised judge and expect his unbiased judgement; they emphatically resent the ring steward butting in and influencing the judge's decision. Yet many of them do it.

The judging ring is not the right place for good nature or social amenities or for the settling of old grudges. With few exceptions, each exhibitor truly thinks his exhibit the best, and it is the judge's business to decide on the matter and not be influenced by the desire of his friends to secure first place. Yet there are some who 'good naturedly' favour friends by giving them undeserved prizes. These same judges would no more dream of taking £5 belonging to a stranger and bestowing it on a friend than of robbing a mail coach or burgling someone's plate chest. This, however, is exactly what it comes to. Often people say: 'Oh, I put down A because B needs encouragement.' Now this kind of generosity with other people's money is robbery, pure and simple. After one show, where some outstanding exhibits were put back, I asked the judge to tell me why and he replied, 'Well frankly so and so has got such very good ones that he can afford to lose, as they will always go up again,' which was perhaps the oddest explanation that it has ever been my lot to hear.

If a horse or dog has an unbeaten record, some judges will maliciously put him down just to spoil his record, knowing that the defeat will be a permanent blot in the press and breed records, and that the elated winner will publish his victory to the four corners of the earth. It is impossible for an expert not to feel a passing irritation at the silliness or spite of Jacks-in-office, but generally it is a case of 'I pities their ignorance and despises 'em.'

Whenever a judge has made more than the usual hash of his classes and the exhibitors are angry enough to lynch him, it may be reported that 'the awards gave general satisfaction'. Novices should never judge at championship shows, as they are bound to make mistakes, and good exhibits may suffer most undeserved reverses at their hands. This is all the more unfair, because these reverses are published forever unexplained in the show records, and challenge certificates should never be granted to classes judged by novices unless these happen to be breeders themselves of high class stock which forms a reliable ground for knowing that though they have not been show judges before, they do know a good horse or dog.

In the days of ignorance, I used to imagine that a specialist judge was an individual with a special knowledge of his subject. I was, however, soon disillusioned. People get on to a specialist panel for many reasons totally unconnected with competency, including the old school tie or official

A Borzoi line-up.

rank as a gilded presidential pill. 'Specialisation is vexation', and its practice is certainly enough to drive one mad when a man has no knowledge of his subject.

Judges are unfortunately often chosen simply and solely for diplomatic reasons. A club president may be an admirable business asset of uncompromising rectitude but an execrable judge and incapable of either judging himself or of selecting judges, yet he often does both with unblushing self-confidence. The first rule in selecting judges should be to remember that a man who keeps and breeds inferior and ugly specimens himself is not suitable as a judge, because he is accustomed to bad points and his eye gets spoilt. In order to be a good judge it is necessary to have a good eye and a decided character.

Judging requires a clear head and firmness of mind. Decision can only be attained by knowing one's mind. It is no use judging if you have no mind to know. A good judge must have natural aptitude as well as experience. No amount of training can replace it and a lot of nonsense is talked about training young judges. Nothing is worse than training in a bad school and a lot of old judges would have to go to an elementary school themselves before they would be able to teach. Yet the worst judges are often the hottest advocates of leading the Young Idea, and it becomes a case of the incurably blind leading the short sighted.

Novices can learn more from old stud grooms, old handlers, friendly vets and successful breeders than from 'shamateur' judges. Let the horse novice pick the brains of breeders who have produced the goods and study the goods produced and preferably talk with men who have worked their way up in the stables themselves. The sergeant-major knows a lot more about men than the brass hat. A judge without natural aptitude will always judge laboriously and slowly. A natural eye for a horse is like the natural eye for a ball or an ear for music. It cannot be taught.

A natural judge knows in a flash what he likes; the best exhibits stand out like moons among stars, and his rapidity of decision infuriates novice exhibitors, who imagine he cannot have looked at the exhibits properly. The natural genius for sorting and valuing is a gift.

The first look round his class shows him the best exhibits. He looks them over carefully, in order to discover faults or to compare two that are very close in points, but, unless there is something very unusual about them, his first glance round is really the deciding one as far as the first prize is concerned, unless the quality of the exhibits is far more level than is usual at shows. A very good way for a judge to make up his mind, if he is hesitating between two animals, is to ask himself which he would choose if each were offered to him at the same price and he could only buy one of them.

Although written nearly 50 years ago, these words are as true today as they were then, though few would write in such an open and honest way. But do not despair: the new exhibitor with an outstanding dog and perseverance will eventually get the credit he or she deserves.

True breed specialist judges own or have owned Borzois of the highest quality. They know the special breed points and are so immersed in the breed that they can tell the breeding of a Borzoi just by looking at it. If two dogs are in competition, one with a beautiful head but a little lacking in angulation and the other with a plain head but perfect angulation, the breed specialist will usually give the prize to the beautiful head. The true breed specialist will have seen many Borzoi puppies grow, and will know which ugly ducklings are likely to turn into swans. Borzoi puppies have so much growing to do that they are ugly ducklings for a long time.

All-rounder judges started as breed specialists in other breeds, usually breeds of 'normal' construction. They should have learned the specialist points of the Borzoi before being passed by The Kennel Club to give CCs in the breed. Their emphasis will be on those points of the Borzoi that overlap with their own breeds, with a greater emphasis on correct movement. Faced with the same two hounds, the all-rounder would give the prize to the one with perfect angulation.

In a perfect world, the balance between these two types of judge keeps the breed functional and with good breed points.

One of the principal functions of a breed club should be to keep the standard of judging high. The lack of formal judging training in Britain leads to a variable standard of judges. The clubs produce lists of approved judges, but it seems that the associations running all-breed shows pay no attention to these lists when choosing their judges.

People start to judge when asked if they will. Before the war there was a long apprenticeship – the best judges were often the kennel managers of huge establishments, and had examined a large number of dogs, among them some that were very good indeed. Today people are asked to judge far too soon, when they have gone over far too few dogs and often have never been over a top quality dog until they award CCs for the first time. They may attend seminars on judging, but there is no substitute for going over many dogs of varying degrees of correctness, including some of the best.

Many people are 'kennel blind', thinking that the dogs they own or breed are the best. There is nothing more likely to make me disregard everything someone says than the claim that such-and-such a dog of his or her breeding was the best Borzoi ever but did not gain its title because of some unfairness.

Some people are asked to judge because they consistently support local shows with their one or two Borzois. The show committee is unlikely to have anyone on it who can tell a good Borzoi from a bad one, so ends up asking someone with experience only of his or her own dogs, which are quite possibly of doubtful quality. In this case the prizes will go to dogs resembling the judge's own, thus promoting dubious quality and doing the breed a great disservice.

Those professional terrier handlers of the 1930s who became the best of the judges of the 1970s had their informal judging seminars on the trains that carried them and their exhibits to the shows. There, in the guard's van, they went over each other's charges, often the cream of a number of breeds. None of today's seminars can provide the number of quality dogs that were available then.

Judging usually starts at open show level and the prospective judge is asked to do more breeds than just the Borzoi. Even if the judge is fully conversant with the Borzoi structure, there can be problems. Borzoi structure is unique – a Beagle with fall-away is a very bad specimen of its breed. Those who start with a gundog have an advantage over a Borzoi person, as almost all gundogs share a large amount of their 'normal dog' structure. The Labrador judge transferring to the Golden Retriever experiences much less of a culture shock than the Borzoi judge transferring to Afghans. Before Borzoi specialists can judge other breeds they must understand 'normal dog' construction.

Critiques and non-British titles

Critiques are the reports that judges write on the winning dogs. These are published in the weekly dog papers, *Dog World* and *Our Dogs*. They represent one of the greatest differences in practice between Great Britain, the United States of America and continental Europe.

I have already described the system in Great Britain. In the United States, no critiques are written; American show results simply give the names of the winners and the number of exhibits they have beaten. All American shows are 'championship', even if only a handful of Borzois are exhibited. A Borzoi can win Best of Breed just by being the only one there, and can win points towards its title by being placed in the group. There are no CCs: American titles are gained by winning points for first places, the number of points increasing with the number of dogs defeated. The American system is one of many small shows, as opposed to the British one of a few huge ones. Once a dog has its American title it moves to a champion class so that it will not prevent other dogs from winning their titles. This means that, for a breed with comparable registrations in Great Britain and the United States, ten times as many champions will be made up in the United States.

In mainland Europe, South America, Israel, Australia and Eire the ultimate governing body at dog shows is the Fédération Cynologique Internationale (FCI). All entries at FCI shows have critiques written about them for the exhibitors to take away with them. The entries are much smaller than at British shows. All breeds have breed classes at the shows, the shows being of two types: national and international. At national shows the certificate on offer is the Certificat d'Aptitude au Championnat (CAC), which ultimately leads to the national title (French Champion, Swiss Champion, etc). At international shows the certificate is the Certificat d'Aptitude au Championnat International de Beauté (CACIB). To maintain the high standard of champions the judge has to withhold the certificate if the quality is not high, and this happens far more frequently than for the British CCs, a reflection of the much lower number of entries at the FCI shows. In some breeds there is frequently only one exhibit.

Critiques written by FCI judges are usually better quality than those written by British judges. FCI judges have had formal teaching in judging and critique writing, and it shows. Russ Albert, a British Dobermann exhibitor, summed up the worst of British critiques when he wrote:

The majority of judges presently giving out CCs appear to know little or nothing about construction and soundness and the critiques which follow their appointments are either figments of their imagination, or plain and simple nonsense. Phrases such as 'two plane head' (every Dobermann has a two plane head but that does not make them parallel) or 'good/nice straight front' (if every individual piece of a dog's front was straight, ie perpendicular, they would look very peculiar indeed) prove that they do not deserve to have the dogs entered under them in the first place.

How would these judges manage to bluff their way through if words such as good, nice and okay were disallowed in critiques? The term 'front' is used so vaguely by many judges now that one can only assume that they do not have sufficient knowledge to be more specific.

The best critiques written by European judges are of far more value; they tend to be more outspoken, actually mentioning faults of specific dogs ('angulation should be a little more pronounced', 'body should be a little shorter' and 'elbows turn out a little') as well good points ('good angulation front and rear giving free and even movement').

Photographs

Your dog will be remembered from written descriptions and by photographs. Many people publish terrible photographs of quality dogs. Those who never see the dog in the flesh, seeing that picture, will think the dog really looked like that so, instead of incorporating the dog into their breeding programme, they will do everything in their power to avoid it.

All you need is one quality photograph that can be reproduced again and again. Professional show photographers take the best photographs and it is a good investment to pay for a professional photography session. Most of my drawings of faulty Borzois in chapter 2 come from photographs in old year books which were intended to promote the dog in question.

Borzoi Breeding

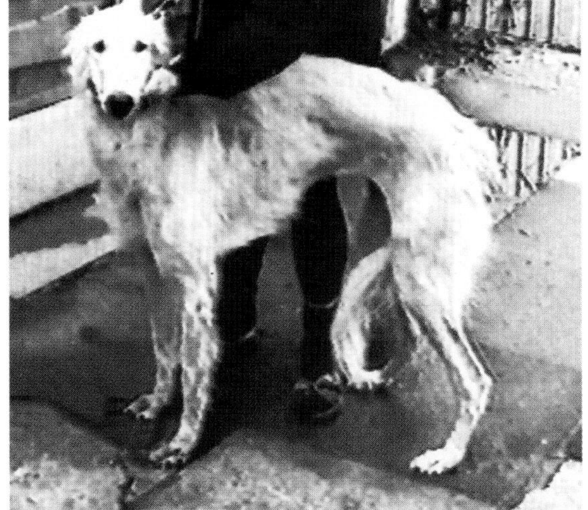

Attitudes towards breeding dogs have changed during the last 40 years. Previously, there were many fewer pedigree dogs than there are today and their relative purchase price was much higher. A large proportion of people owning pedigree bitches would have had litters from them; indeed, veterinary opinion at that time supported the theory that to have puppies was beneficial to a bitch's health. Breed clubs gave awards to breeders who produced the largest number of registered puppies each year, and rescue was not discussed. There were huge kennels owned by very wealthy people. During the 'golden era' for Great Danes the millionaires Arthur Rank and Gordon Stewart vied with each other to produce champions. Photographs of Mr Stewart's kennel show 100 Great Danes together, all obedience trained and with one member of kennel staff for every three or four dogs.

Top: A Borzoi that had gone to the wrong home.
Above: The same Borzoi after tender, loving care.
Photos by courtesy of Northern Borzoi Rescue.

None of the Borzoi kennels of that time was quite that large, but they were still sufficiently big for a real breeding plan to be thought out; a plan that looked forward several generations, so that the odd disappointing litter did not matter so much. It is only by breeding more than the occasional litter that a breeder can produce a recognisable strain, so that a new dog entering the ring is instantly known to be bred by So-and-so. According to such a plan, inferior quality dogs and bitches would never be mated and there would be more flexibility. For instance, with more than one stud dog on offer, if a bitch owner arrived wanting to use the champion, the stud dog owner could suggest that the stud dog's brother had slightly better angulation if this happened to be the bitch's weakness. The brother would then be the better choice as sire of the prospective litter. Few Borzoi kennels keep more than one stud today.

In those days the breeder was rarely the one who cleaned the puppy excreta from the floor; kennel staff carried out the mundane and unpleasant tasks. Today breeders generally have to do these things themselves, and the person contemplating a litter of puppies must be aware of the mess, smell, lack of sleep and worry that this enterprise entails. They must also be aware that they need to find suitable lifetime homes for the eight or so little beings they have caused to be born.

The first question to ask yourself, then, is whether it is a good idea to breed from your bitch. Is she of good enough quality? This is a hard one to answer, as most people look at their own bitches, particularly the first or second ones, through rose-coloured spectacles. Very often the breeders go to the same optician as the owners, and impartial observers are very reluctant to tell fresh-faced enthusiasts that their bitches are just terrible.

Next question: can you cope with all the fuss? Apart from actually going through the experience, the best way to get an idea of what actually happens when puppies are born is to watch the whelping video produced by Guide Dogs for the Blind. While not faithfully reproducing the sleeplessness, smell and messy fluids that are an integral part of the process, this is a very informative and well-made production.

Can you find homes for all the puppies? There is not a big demand for Borzois. Whereas a pet quality Golden Retriever litter will sell, similar litters of Borzois have ended up with every pup in rescue. Look at the photographs on page 187, reproduced by courtesy of Northern Borzoi Rescue. This is what can happen to a Borzoi that goes to the wrong home. Is this the life you want for the puppies you have bred?

It follows from all this that, unless you have a quality bitch who has been chosen carefully with the future of the breed in mind, she is not worth breeding from.

Choice of stud dog

Once you have decided to go ahead with a litter, the stud dog has to be chosen. Provided that care has been exercised in buying your bitch, this is easy: do exactly as her breeder advises. In 1997, the Polish Lowland Sheepdog was awarded Challenge Certificates (CCs) for the first time and I spent an enjoyable couple of hours at Crufts watching the judging. The judge was the original importer of the breed but she was no longer a regular competitor in the show ring. The mother and daughter who sat next to me had bought a bitch puppy of the breed after six interviews with her breeder. They had signed forms that gave the choice of sire to the breeder and just about anything they did with the puppy had to be approved. The line-up for the very first Polish Lowland Sheepdog Bitch CC comprised sisters, half-sisters and cousins of that puppy. They were as alike as peas in a pod, and I had not seen the challenge for CC in any breed comprise such similar exhibits for a long time. The pleasure the owners of the bitch puppy derived from seeing their pet's relations winning was heartening. They were interested in having a litter, and it was obvious that, even if they had not signed breeding forms, their best move would have been to do exactly what the breeder advised. The chances were that they would breed a litter of which they could be proud.

It is important to choose the stud dog and ask his owner whether he or she would agree to this well in advance. There are various reasons why the owner may refuse:

- The owner does not want the dog to be used at stud – it changes a dog's attitude to life.
- Some domestic crisis may render it impossible for a bitch to visit.
- The owner may think that the bloodlines do not mix.

If the answer is 'No' it is as well to know this well in advance, and if it is 'Yes' there is still a great deal to discuss. For instance, the stud owner will be grateful for some idea of when the bitch will be in season. You will also need to discuss the stud fee, which you must expect to pay in full at the time of service. Discuss what happens if your bitch does not become pregnant, remembering that you are actually paying for use of the stud dog, not a pregnancy. Most stud owners give another service free of charge if there are no puppies, but this is a courtesy, not a legal requirement. Perhaps the stud fee is a puppy, or a puppy and some money. Which puppy? The pick of the litter? Get all this in writing well before the mating. You may miss all the Puppy classes if there is a prolonged legal wrangle about who owns which puppy, as The Kennel Club suspends the registration of dogs that are the subject of such legal cases.

Reproductive cycle of the bitch

The reproductive cycle of the bitch is quite different from that of the female human. The bitch has only two very, very fertile days a year. These are the days when she ovulates, that is, produces eggs that can be fertilised by the spermatozoa (sperm) produced by the male (see fig 1 overleaf). In humans there are twelve cycles a year, each of which leads to the production of an egg and, if the egg is not fertilised, the lining of the uterus (womb) breaks down two weeks later as a menstrual period. The bitch has two cycles a year and there is a blood-stained discharge about two weeks before she ovulates. Therefore, in the canine species, bleeding from the vagina indicates that the most fertile time is about to occur.

The reproductive cycle of the bitch is in four stages:

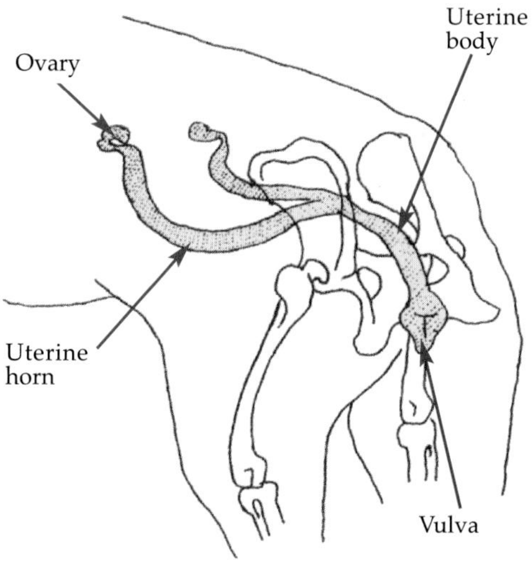

Pro-oestrus: When the bloody discharge starts. This usually lasts about 9 days, but can be 2–27 days. The bitch is attractive to dogs but will not let them mate her.

Oestrus: The stage when the bitch will allow the dog to mate her. This usually lasts about 9 days, but can be 3–21 days. Ovulation usually occurs 2 days into this stage. The bloody discharge turns less bloody and yellower. The vulva is very enlarged.

Met-oestrus: Occurs only if the bitch is not pregnant. Average 90 days. High hormone levels, the time when false pregnancies occur.

Anoestrus: Low hormone levels, the reproductive system is in a 'resting' phase. Average 75 days.

Fig 1: The female reproductive tract.

Primitive breeds like the Basenji and the Anatolian Shepherd Dog tend to have one cycle a year, like the wolf. One of the greatest Basenji breeders was Miss Veronica Tudor Williams and, during the 1940s, her bitches were so regular in their seasons (late summer – early autumn) that one year they produced five litters in one week, three being born on the same night. 'The sort of thing to give one a headache,' was her comment. The production of this number of litters a year, with each available puppy snapped up by eager buyers, allowed her to breed 12 of the first 15 champions in the breed. Not until champion number 18 was there a Basenji champion with neither parent bred in her kennel.

Mating

As soon as the bloody discharge is seen, telephone the stud dog owner to ascertain whether it is still possible to carry out the mating. It is not a good idea to use a dog at stud for your maiden bitch if he has not been used at stud before, especially if it is the first mating you have been concerned with. It is better if at least the dog and his owner know the ropes. Your puppy's breeder is unlikely to have advised you to use an untried dog. Another benefit of using a proven dog is that you know he is fertile.

The mating plan most often used is that a first mating takes place 12–14 days after the start of the bloody discharge and another 48 hours later. It is more comfortable for the bitch if she passes urine before the mating and if it takes place some time after her last meal. Ideally, there should be the least possible interference, but remember that two dogs who do not know each other are being put together in an emotionally charged state. The bitch should be on a lead for greater control. If the timing is wrong she may not want to mate the dog, and his unwelcome advances could precipitate a fight. The bitch could also take an instant dislike to the dog and may never be persuaded to mate him. Some Borzois are colour prejudiced; there are black bitches who would never stand for a red and white dog, and vice versa.

There should be two people present, one to hold the bitch's lead and the other to control the dog if necessary. Borzois are very sensitive and the whole atmosphere should be one of calm and reassurance. In a successful mating the experienced stud carries out his job with the minimum of interference. There will be a courtship, during which the dog and bitch dance around and play, finishing when the bitch stands to the dog, putting her tail to the side and exposing her swollen vulva. The dog then mounts, placing his penis in the vagina, and the penis swells so that is impossible for the dog to withdraw it. Next, the dog carefully dismounts the bitch and, in most breeds, turns so that he is at 180° to the bitch with his penis still inside her. This is known as the tie. Borzois stand side by side for the tie.

There does not have to be a tie for a successful mating. The tie needs to be carefully supervised as the dog is very vulnerable at this stage. If the bitch tries to get away before the penis shrinks and the dog can remove it, he may be badly injured. Once the tie has finished and the dog and bitch separate, both should be checked for injury. If the stud owner is an experienced breeder he or she will have seen many matings and should be able to resolve any problem that arises. With the health of two valuable animals at stake, there is no substitute for a quick decision made on the basis of past experience.

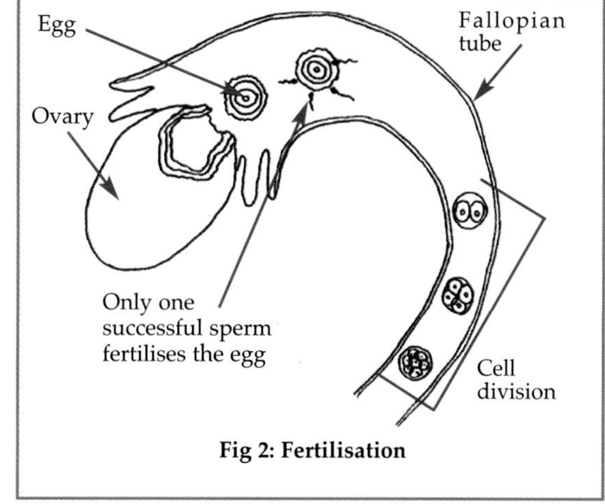

Fig 2: Fertilisation

The timing of the pregnancy

Pregnancy is usually timed from the date the bitch was mated, which is often the date of ovulation and conception. The length of pregnancy is 63 days from the time of ovulation. However, a bitch may stand for a dog several days before ovulation, and the sperm survive in her reproductive tract for a few days. When she ovulates, the egg can then be fertilised (see fig 2 on previous page). This will make the pregnancy seem to have lasted longer than the 63 days, perhaps up to 72 days, although it would still be 63 days from the date of ovulation. It could also happen that the bitch will allow the dog to mate her a few days after ovulation. If the egg has survived that long, a pregnancy will start. In this case the pregnancy will seem short, perhaps down to 58 days, but it would still be 63 days from the real time of ovulation.

It is possible to discover the exact time of ovulation by taking swab tests from the bitch, but this is far from common practice except in large breeding establishments such as those run by the Guide Dogs for the Blind Association.

Confirmation of pregnancy

Until recently, the only way to confirm early pregnancy in the bitch was by X-rays, although this was not the safest of practices. For the first 35 days X-rays can have a very harmful effect on embryonic puppies. There is no chemical urine pregnancy test like that for humans, so the safest and most reliable method of confirmation is by ultra-sound scans. These are completely harmless and painless and are widely used in human obstetrics. The scan is carried out with the bitch in a relaxed standing position, and the only preparation necessary is the clipping of some of the coat on the tummy and the application of gel that helps the sound waves pass into the bitch's abdomen.

Ultrasound can detect a pregnancy 15 days after ovulation, but it is not until the 22nd day that the heartbeat can be detected and we can say that the pregnancy is viable. The creation of a new life is an amazing phenomenon, but sometimes an embryo has a faulty set of genes. In the dog, this embryo dies and is reabsorbed by the bitch; in contrast, the human mother has a miscarriage and expels the dead embryo from the body with some bleeding. Unviable embryos are common in both species. Thus a very early positive scan does not mean there will be a successful pregnancy although, given the bitch's usual multiple pregnancy, litter-mates often survive.

Borzois are very sensitive dogs, so the best plan is often to leave the bitch well alone and assume that she is in whelp. Any disturbance may cause her to reabsorb the embryos.

Abdominal palpation can be helpful at certain times in the pregnancy, but is only really helpful when conducted by an experienced person. At 21–28 days the embryonic puppies are in sacs of fluid that are tense enough to feel like golf balls 1–2cm (1/2–3/4in) in diameter. From 42 days onwards the individual foetuses may be felt and their movement detected. What you feel needs to be related to puppy development. Look at the various stages of development of the puppy (fig 3) and the alterations in the bitch (fig 4).

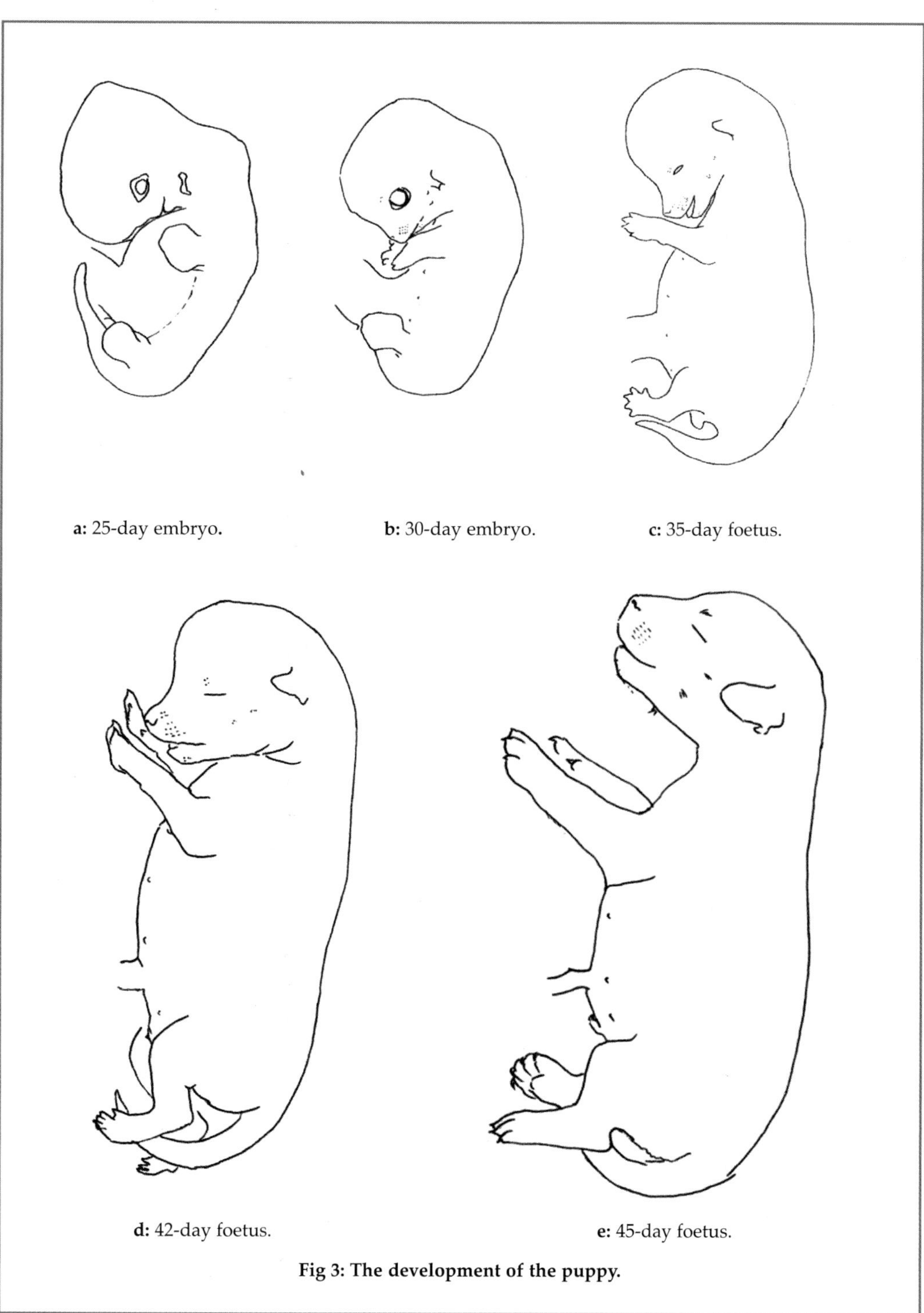

a: 25-day embryo.

b: 30-day embryo.

c: 35-day foetus.

d: 42-day foetus.

e: 45-day foetus.

Fig 3: The development of the puppy.

How the puppy develops

In the very early weeks of the developing puppies are called embryos. From 35 days onwards they are called foetuses, meaning young ones.

Day 17–18

The egg now settles into the womb lining. The outer cells reach out like roots to link with the mother's blood supply. The inner cells divide into two, and later three, layers. Each layer grows into different parts of the puppy's body. One becomes the brain, nervous system, skin, eyes and ears. The second becomes the lungs, stomach and gut. The third becomes the heart, blood, muscles and bones.

A groove forms in the top layer of cells. The cells fold up and round to make a hollow tube, which will become the puppy's brain and spinal cord, so the tube has a 'head end' and 'tail end'. At the same time the heart is forming, and the puppy already has some of its own blood vessels. A string of these connect puppy and mother and will become the umbilical cord.

Day 21–22

There is now a huge bulge where the heart is, and a bump for the head where the brain is developing. The heart begins to beat and can be seen beating on a ultrasound scan. Dimples on the side of the head will become ears and there are thickenings where the eyes will be. On the body are emerging bumps that will become muscles and bones, and small swellings ('limb buds') show where the front and back legs are growing (see figs 3a and 4a).

Day 30–31

A face is forming slowly. The eyes are more obvious and have some colour in them. There is a mouth with a tongue. Front and rear paws are developing, with ridges where the individual toes will be. Major interior organs are all developing: heart, brain, lungs, kidneys, liver and gut (see figs 3b and 4b).

Day 35

Just 35 days after conception the foetus is fully formed. It has all its organs, muscles, limbs and bones. From now on it has to grow and mature (see figs 3c and 4c).

Day 40

The puppy is now growing quickly. The body grows bigger, so the head and body are more in proportion and the puppy does not look so top-heavy. The head begins to look much more like that of a dog, and the hair is beginning to grow, together with eye-brows and eye-lashes. The eyelids stay closed over the eyes. The sexual organs are well developed.

Day 45–55

Continuing rapid foetal growth. If there are several puppies this is the stage where folding of the uterine horns occurs because of the size of the foetuses. This causes a dramatic change in the shape of the bitch (see fig 4d). The bones of the foetus are changing from cartilage to bone (see fig 3d).

From day 57

Live full-term puppies can be born (see fig 3e).

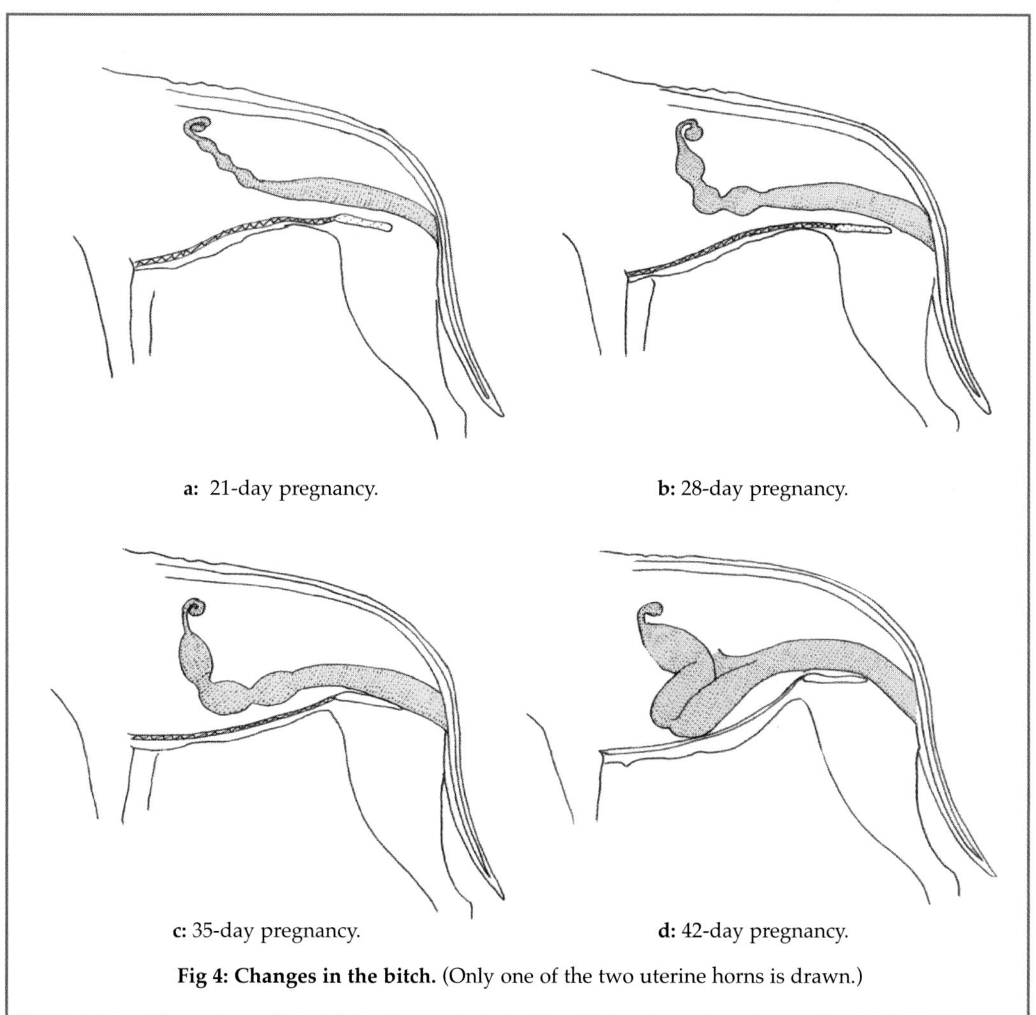

a: 21-day pregnancy.

b: 28-day pregnancy.

c: 35-day pregnancy.

d: 42-day pregnancy.

Fig 4: Changes in the bitch. (Only one of the two uterine horns is drawn.)

Inside the bitch

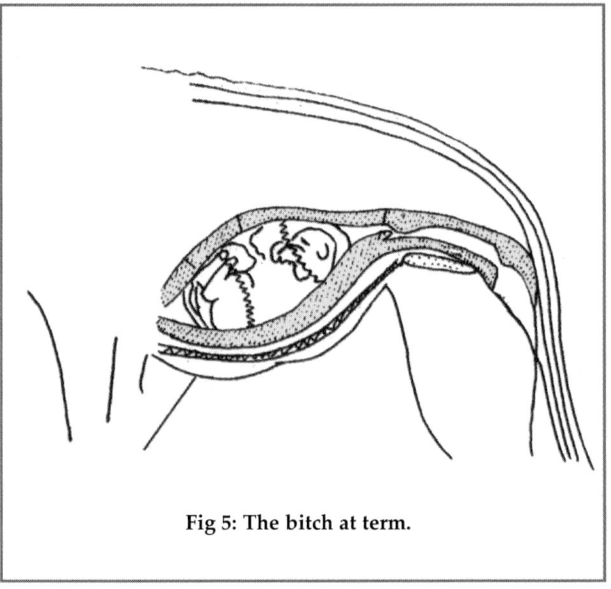

Fig 5: The bitch at term.

The foetus and the membranes and fluids surrounding it are known as the foetal unit. Fig 5 shows the foetal unit at the end of the pregnancy, that is at term. Each puppy is encased in its own individual bag of fluid and has its own placenta. The placenta is discharged from the body as the afterbirth, and its function during foetal development is to give nourishment to the puppy via the umbilical cord. The placenta is a mixing of maternal and foetal blood vessels, enabling food and oxygen to be brought to the puppy and waste products to be taken away.

Since in humans there is usually only one foetus, the whole uterus is filled with a single bag of fluid: just one foetal unit. The placenta is attached to the uterine wall like a pizza stuck to a wall by its topping, and from this 'pizza' comes the umbilicus to connect it to the foetus. Each canine foetal unit has its own placenta wrapped around it like napkin ring that sticks to the uterine wall by its external surface.

Care of the pregnant bitch

The Borzoi is a slow-maturing breed, not reaching maturity until at least two years. A pregnancy takes a lot out of a bitch, so she should not be mated before she is two; an early pregnancy will prevent her from reaching her full growth potential. The very first season is probably not a good time to have her mated; her reproductive cycle is just getting started and she may not actually produce an egg this time. Teenage girls often do not ovulate during their first few menstrual cycles.

Fortunately, the incidence of problem birth among Borzois is low, but it does occur. Unfortunately, the vet is often treated like the fire-brigade – called in an emergency, never having seen the bitch before. Human beings have organised ante-natal care throughout the pregnancy to try to anticipate problems and the veterinary profession is keen to have a similar (though simpler) version of such care.

At a pre-mating consultation the bitch has a general health check and, if she has suffered from infertility in the past, she should have a bacteriological swab taken to make sure she does not have an infection of her reproductive tract.

Your vet would like to see your bitch at least once during her pregnancy. He or she will carry out another health check and discuss any problems that may have arisen. The Borzoi is an ideal shape for giving birth, having wide hips because of the capacious pelvis, and the puppies have small heads. The vet's heart sinks when a Bulldog breeder walks into the surgery because the Bulldog breed standard requires a small pelvis and big head. The Caesarean rate in that breed is so high that the vet often plans a section rather than letting the bitch go through a traumatic labour that ends with a stuck puppy, necessitating an emergency section. The mother takes much longer to recover from an unplanned Caesarean section. Caesarean sections are uncommon in Borzois. Those that do occur may be due to a large, single puppy or a constricted pelvis resulting from a road accident.

Some bitches experience a period of mild illness at about the third week or occasionally the fifth week of pregnancy. Miss Collett, the successful breeder of the Barwich Chow Chows, noted: *When my own bitches have had previous litters, it is nearly always possible for me to tell by their manner if they are in whelp or not as early as the third or fourth week. They are quiet and contented, and extra demonstrative, and often just slightly off their food and perhaps have a little sickness, especially first thing in the morning.*

Feeding in pregnancy

If you feed your bitch on a good quality, balanced diet, there is no need to alter it at first. Since 70% of the puppies' growth takes place in the last three to four weeks of pregnancy, you should continue at the usual maintenance level for the first five to six weeks. During the last three weeks of pregnancy the food requirement rises 25% above the maintenance level.

It is unusual for it to be so obvious that a bitch is expecting.
It would be prudent to cut the long coat to prevent the puppies from being strangled.

Once the puppies have been born the energy demands to supply them with milk mean that the bitch needs two-and-a-half times her maintenance requirements.

Exercise

The desire for and ability to take exercise decrease during pregnancy. Some active exercise should be maintained throughout but excessive exertion, such as jumping and climbing stairs, should be discouraged.

Drugs in pregnancy

Drugs should be avoided as much as possible, especially during the first 35 days when the puppies' body systems are developing. In cases of infection certain antibiotics are safe, and antibiotic treatment is safer for the bitch and puppies than the alternative of letting the infection run riot.

The hormones of pregnancy activate any toxocara worm larvae lying dormant in the bitch's tissues. These activate and cross the placenta to infect the puppies before they are born. The best way to break this chain is regular worming when the bitch herself is a puppy and throughout the period before pregnancy. Modern worming agents are safer than the older ones. You should discuss the problem of worming with your vet before conception to get the most up-to-date information.

Cut the hair prior to birth.
(left) before and (right) after.

Coat preparation

The hormones that help the puppies grow also stimulate the growth of the bitch's coat. The picture on page 197 shows a heavily pregnant Borzoi – in fact it is not usually so obvious that a bitch is expecting. As you see, she has a very luxuriant coat. To prevent the puppies from being strangled by those long hairs, it is prudent to cut some of the coat away, as shown in the two pictures opposite.

Whelping accommodation

The bitch should be introduced to the place where you want her to give birth three weeks before the event, but preferably this should be in her own kennel or area of the house. Many different kinds of structure can be used for whelping, but whichever you choose should have the following characteristics:

- Be isolated from other dogs, noise and bustle and unauthorised visitors of any species.
- Have some form of heating (infra-red lights above are popular).
- Be large enough for a Borzoi bitch and about eight puppies.
- Have three full sides and one lower side, so that the puppies cannot fall out but the bitch can get in and out without banging her pendulous mammary glands and teats on the side of the box.
- Ideally, it should have anti-crush barriers around the edge so that, when the bitch is as far over to the side of the box as possible, there is still space for a puppy so that it does not get crushed.

The whelping box can be specially made of wood or it can be constructed from a couple of refrigerator crates. The best flooring for the box during whelping is newspaper, as this can be changed often. Whelping is a very messy procedure. Once the worst of the mess is over, the box can be lined with a polyester fur rug. This is soft and warm and made of one of the few fabrics from which the tenacious green discharge that is one of the normal products of birth can be removed by washing.

For the luxury whelping we have:

- A bed for the breeder next to the whelping bed.
- A cordless telephone to speak to the vet while actually looking at the bitch.
- A sink in the whelping room.
- A door in the whelping room leading to a part of the garden set aside for the bitch's exclusive toilet use.

The whelping tool kit should include:

- A small box to put the puppies in if they have to be removed from the bitch.
- A hot water bottle to put in that small box to keep the puppies warm. When you fill the hot water bottle, make sure there is not an air bubble in it; if there is it will rise to the top and, since air bubbles don't heat up, puppies carefully placed on the bottle will not keep warm.

- Many towels, preferably old ones that can be thrown away if beyond washing.
- Plastic bin bags to fill with discarded paper, towels, etc.
- A clock.
- A piece of paper and pencil to note down:
  a) The time the bitch starts straining; that is, the beginning of the second stage of labour.
  b) The time each puppy is born.
  c) Whether a placenta has been delivered.

  With a big litter you will forget these things if they are not written down, and this information could be vital to the vet, whose telephone number should be written clearly at the top of the paper.
- Antiseptic fluid.
- Sterile cotton wool balls.

Normal whelping

During the last week of pregnancy, the ligaments of the pelvis relax, causing the bony ring of the pelvis to have some 'give' to ease the passage of the puppies.

The most reliable indicator of imminent labour is a drop in the bitch's temperature of up to 1°C, the average normal temperature for a dog being 38.6°C (101.5°F). This drop occurs within 24 hours of whelping. It is a good idea to take the bitch's temperature twice a day during the week before the puppies are due. Use a special clinical thermometer with a thin covering of lubricant such as vaseline. Be gentle: remember that a thermometer is made of glass and has the poisonous metal mercury inside it. Ask your vet to teach you how to insert the thermometer into her back passage through the anus. Never insert anything into her vagina, specially if she is starting to whelp, as this could be a focus for infection.

First stage of labour

The stages of canine labour take their names from the similar stages in human birth, but they are not so obvious as in human birth.

The first stage is the period of time the cervix or neck of the uterus takes to become fully dilated. Cervical dilation is easily assessed in humans as the cervix is near enough to be felt during a vaginal examination. The cervix of the dog is much more than a finger's length from the outside, so it is not possible to tell that the cervix is opening up by a series of examinations. The first stage therefore has to be assessed by the behaviour of the bitch. Human behaviour is no guide at all to cervical dilation, but fortunately this is not true of the bitch. During the first stage she is restless, often shivering and panting, and occasionally vomits. Usually she does not want to eat, and it is important that she does not have solid food, just in case something goes wrong and she needs a general

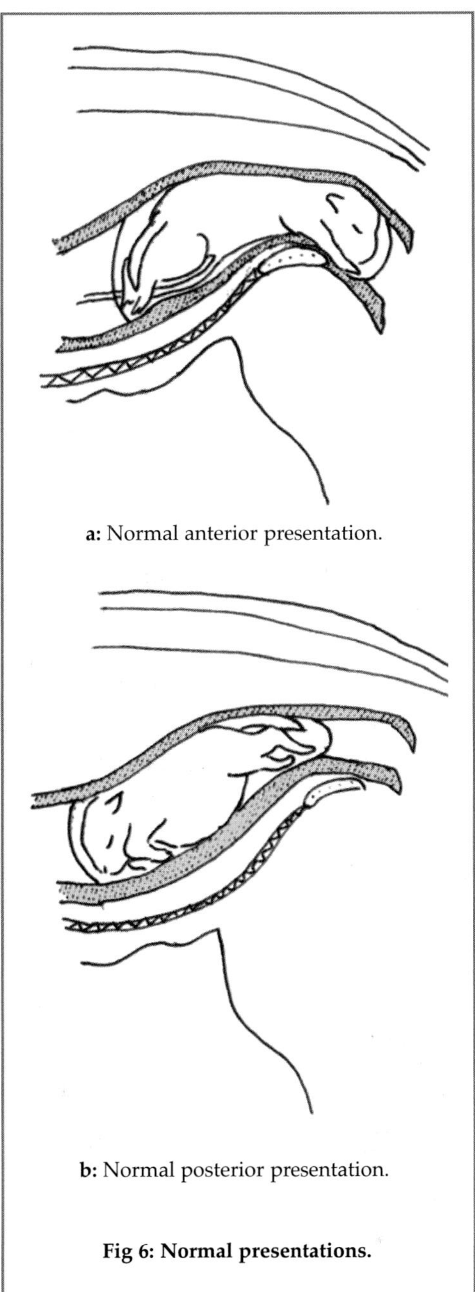

a: Normal anterior presentation.

b: Normal posterior presentation.

Fig 6: Normal presentations.

anaesthetic for surgery. Anaesthesia with a full stomach is very dangerous; if the bitch vomits while she is asleep she cannot prevent it from going down her airways and will drown in it.

Labour uses up a lot of energy, so water or milk with glucose dissolved in it can help. Fluids also prevent dehydration.

Second stage of labour

This stage lasts from full cervical dilatation until the birth of the puppy. The bitch usually lies on her side during delivery but occasionally walks around, pausing to strain in a squatting position. The sac containing the puppy and the fluid surrounding it enters the pelvic canal. It does not matter which direction the puppy's head is pointing as long as the limbs are outstretched (see fig 6).

Once the presenting part of the foetus has engaged in the pelvis, reflex abdominal straining commences and the puppy is usually delivered after two or three expulsive efforts. The first puppy should be born within two hours of the commencement of the second stage of labour. The interval between puppies is 5–60 minutes (average 30 minutes), tending to be longer near the end of the delivery of the litter. During the delivery a dark green discharge accompanies the puppies. This arises from a region called the marginal haematoma, which is the edge of the placental ring.

As each puppy is delivered, the bitch normally licks its head and opens the membranes. She severs the umbilical cord with her teeth about 2cm (an inch) from the puppy. If she does not, help to tear the membranes and carefully tear through the umbilical cord 2cm from the puppy's tummy. Above all, don't panic!

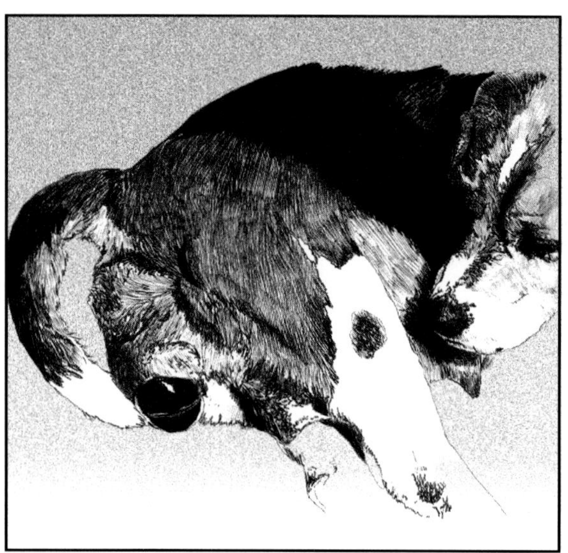

A Beagle bitch at the moment of birth...

The pictures on this page show the birth of a Beagle puppy with its membranes still intact.

Third stage of labour

This is the delivery of the placenta and membranes. The bitch will often eat these, making careful counting of them difficult. It is very important that the whole placenta and membranes are discharged; if they are retained they are a focus for lethal infection.

In human multiple pregnancies the labour progresses through first, second and third stage. All the babies are born, then all the placentas are discharged. Identical twins share a placenta. However, in canine birth the progression is first, second, third, and then a new puppy is born so we have, second, then third again, and so on.

Abnormal labour

There are no prizes for realising that things are not going well and trying to 'muddle through'. If this is your first experience of whelping it is best to have an experienced breeder with you as 'midwife', who will have the experience to deal with minor problems and know when professional help is needed. Vets are experts at abnormal deliveries, but few will have seen as many normal deliveries as a dog breeder of many years' standing. Unfortunately, it is all too common in all aspects of dog management for problems to arise if the vet and the experienced dog breeder do not respect each other's knowledge. Both are experts in their own fields.

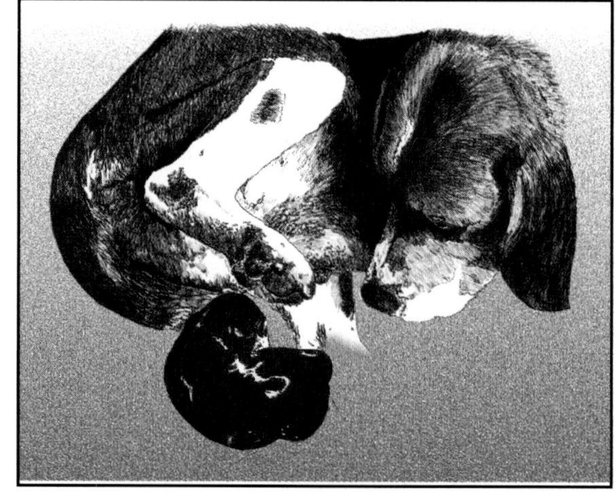

... with the membranes of the puppy still intact.

If you have any worries about a whelping, especially if you do not have expert help, then telephone your vet at any time of the day or night. It may be that simple advice is all that is needed. However, if the vet is unhappy about things, he or she will want to see the bitch and will usually ask you to take your bitch into the surgery. This is because, if things go badly wrong, the puppies will have to be born by Caesarean section, which is only possible in the vet's operating theatre.

Mother and children doing well – a Borzoi litter just a few minutes old.

The most highly skilled part of the whelping process is deciding whether the length of time between puppies is normal or too long. It is generally agreed that about two-and-a-half hours between puppies is a reasonable interval. However, if the bitch is spending this time straining ineffectively and not resting contentedly with the puppies already born, do not delay in summoning professional help.

If it is two or three hours since the last puppy has been born and the bitch is happily and contentedly feeding the puppies, it is probable that they have all been born. If her temperature drops prior to labour and there are no puppies within 24 hours, contact your vet. In fact, if you are unsure about anything, contact your vet. Better a question that subsequently makes you think 'How silly of me!' than a dead bitch and dead puppies.

Care of the newborn puppies

The greatest danger faced by newborn puppies is loss of heat. The whelping room needs to be kept at 25–30°C (77–86°F) for the first few days to try to reduce puppy hypothermia. This can be reduced gradually after the first few days, as the bitch will find it too warm. Don't guess – use a thermometer.

It is kinder to ask your vet to put to sleep puppies with obvious birth defects such as cleft palates. It is difficult enough to find homes for healthy puppies, without passing on a puppy that will incur large veterinary bills and much heartache.

It is customary to remove dew claws from Borzoi puppies if they have these. Dew claws are the extra toes on the side of the leg that are never in contact with the ground, so will need constant attention throughout the dog's life if they are left. The vet or an experienced breeder can remove them.

Puppies need to take in food regularly. If they go too long without a feed they become dehydrated. The very first fluid produced by a bitch's teat is a straw-coloured substance called colostrum. This does not contain much nourishment but it is filled with antibodies to protect the puppies from disease. If things go dreadfully wrong and the puppies have to be hand reared on artificial milk, every effort must be made to get at least a small amount of colostrum into the puppies.

Contented puppies sleep when they are not suckling. It may be that a smaller puppy needs to be put on a teat to start feeding, and it is best to express some milk gently from the teat to encourage the puppy to hang on and suck. A healthy puppy is a warm, plump, firm little thing that sleeps and sleeps. It makes few noises apart from a low murmur or the odd squeak of rage when a litter-mate squashes it or knocks it off the teat.

Puppies knead with their front feet as they suckle. Make sure their nails are kept short; the dam's teats are sensitive and could do without being punctured with little needles.

Bottle feeding

This is not as good a start to life as mother's milk for dogs, any more than it is for humans. If natural feeding is not possible and no foster mother is available, you are in for a time of sleep deprivation. If you leave too long an interval between feeds the puppies will die of dehydration. The best feeding bottles can be obtained from your vet, whose help and support you will need through this difficult time. To prevent infection it would be a good idea to obtain a bottle sterilising system of the kind used for human babies.

The milk you use needs to be designed for puppies, as milk differs considerably between species. If you don't believe me, try goat's milk on your cornflakes – it takes a bit

At least one of these puppies grew up to be a show dog (see page 149).

of getting used to. Start by feeding the puppies every four hours, including during the night. When the puppies are 10 days old, one of the nightly feeds can be cut out.

Bottle-fed puppies can become constipated, because artificial formula is not as good as the real thing. A little vaseline or olive oil on the back passage may help. If it does not, ask the vet for advice. The bowels of a young puppy are small and delicate.

If the dam is not there to clean and stimulate the puppies you will need to keep them clean with a slightly moistened towel. Never leave them wet, as this would chill them. After feeding, a dam encourages her puppies to pass faeces and urine by licking their back ends. Simulate this by rubbing the puppies' abdomens with warm, damp cotton wool until both are produced.

Becoming independent

Bottle-fed puppies can be weaned at just over two weeks. The top-of-the-range dog food manufacturers produce very good weaning foods. Most naturally-fed puppies can start on these solids, made up and weighed out according to the manufacturers' instructions, at three weeks.

By now the puppies need a much larger run, and their dam will value time away from them, most especially because their front teeth are through, and these are very sharp. They also need a sleeping area, and polyester fur fabric makes good bedding. Their play area should be covered in newspaper, as it will be constantly messed upon so will need to be changed regularly.

Play helps their development, and many show dogs learned to 'stand' when only a few weeks old, but take care not to upset the puppy by trying to push it too far too quickly.

Selling your puppies

You are now in the reverse situation to when you bought your first puppy, and must yourself ask all the same questions with a view to finding suitable homes for your puppies. However, we now live in a world of litigation, and I give the following as a cautionary tale, which I think supports Charles Dickens' view that 'the law is an ass'.

There is a high incidence of hip dysplasia in Labradors. It cannot be diagnosed at birth but appears later in life. Generally, the more serious it is, the earlier the symptoms appear. I discuss it, together with the British Veterinary Association/Kennel Club scheme to reduce its occurrence, in chapter 6.

A responsible Labrador breeder had her breeding stock screened but, unfortunately, a puppy she bred from parents with average hip scores had bad hip dysplasia and needed surgery at eight months of age. She had explained to the puppy owners about hip dysplasia, done all that was possible to avoid breeding a puppy with this disease and, when the problem arose, offered to take back the puppy and refund the purchase price. Despite this, the owners took her to court, with claims for the cost of medical treatment, the distress caused to them and the legal fees.

Alarmingly, they won the case. The breeder's efforts to produce sound puppies by having the parents screened were considered irrelevant, as was the evidence of the geneticist on the inheritance of the disease. The breeder's solicitor said: *The verdict was that the purchasers had known nothing about the breed, that in consequence they should have been told about hip dysplasia, and that their evidence that they had not been told about hip dysplasia was more convincing than that of the breeder.*

Fortunately, hip dysplasia is not a problem in Borzois, but this case must be taken into consideration for its wider implications. If you sell a puppy then, in the eyes of the law, you are a trader, and must adhere to the Sale of Goods Act 1979 and its amendments. The safest way to sell puppies is through a contract, and the solicitor for the defendant in this case made the following suggestions:

1 Put everything in writing. Keep a diary by the telephone and, after every call, note the time, the person to whom you have spoken and as much of what was said as possible. Do it immediately, not later that night. Do not think that anything might be unimportant; write it down. If a purchaser calls to see a puppy, note in the diary what was said at the time. Do not alter or delete anything; the diary may be needed in evidence. Take your time and get it right first time.

2 Have two copies of a written contract at the time of sale, signed by both you and the purchaser. This should include wording to the following effect:

a) The breed, date of birth, sex, colour, name and Kennel Club registration number of the puppy.

b) This puppy is believed to be in good health, but you are strongly advised to take it to your veterinary surgeon to be given a general health check within four days of purchase. This check, and any examinations associated with it, must be at your own expense.

c) If your veterinary surgeon finds any problem which, in his opinion, renders the puppy unfit for sale, I will take the puppy back and refund the purchase price in full on condition that the puppy is returned within seven days of the date of purchase and is in the same state of health as when it was sold. Before purchase, you should consider that a puppy is a living thing which may become a well loved member of the family in a short time and this may affect what you wish to do if return of the puppy becomes necessary. I cannot be held responsible for distress or upset caused by the return of a puppy after drawing your attention to this possibility.

d) You must confirm before purchase that you have consulted your veterinary surgeon about this breed and any possible diseases, genetic or otherwise, to which it is prone, and you accept that, if such a disease develops later in life after a satisfactory preliminary examination by your veterinary surgeon, I cannot be held responsible.

Appendix A British Show Champions

Champion	Sex	DOB	Sire	Dam	Breeder	Owner	CCs
1892							
Ch Krilutt	d	27.04.1886	Dorogai	Nagla	Mr Knotneff	Hon Mrs Wellesley	4
1893							
Ch Milka	b	N/K	Propodai	Milka	Col Tschesbishoff	Duchess of Newcastle	3
1895							
Ch Windle Courtier	d	25.09.1893	Korotai	Windle Snow	R Coup	R Coup	12
1896							
Ch Vikhra	b	02.04.1894	Golub	Vedma	Duchess of Newcastle	Duchess of Newcastle	4
1897							
Ch Tsaretsa	b	01.02.1895	Pilai Podar	Kolpitsa	Gen Boldariff	Duchess of Newcastle	17
1898							
Ch Velsk	d	26.12.1895	Korotai	Ch Vikhra	Duchess of Newcastle	Duchess of Newcastle	9
Ch Alex	d	11.05.1894	Ataman The Great	Outcheschka	A J Rousseau	HRH Princess of Wales	7
1900							
Ch Statesman	d	22.11.1896	Windle Earl	Windle Princess	H S Howell	Capt S P Borman	5
Ch Tatiana	b	15.03.1898	Ch Velsk	Ch Tsaretsa	Duchess of Newcastle	Duchess of Newcastle	7
Ch Velsk Votrio	d	15.03.1898	Ch Velsk	Ch Tsaretsa	Duchess of Newcastle	Duchess of Newcastle	4
1901							
Ch Caspian	d	23.06.1899	Fedia	Ina	Mrs P Farrer Baynes	P F Baynes	3
Ch Velasquez	d	26.12.1895	Korotai	Ch Vikhra	Duchess of Newcastle	Duchess of Newcastle	4
Ch Theodora	b	15.03.1898	Ch Velsk	Ch Tsaretsa	Duchess of Newcastle	Duchess of Newcastle	6
1902							
Ch Knoeas	b	09.09.1897	Ch Velsk	Grand Duchess Alma	N Kilvert	N Kilvert	5
Ch Vassal	d	23.06.1899	Fedia	Ina	Mrs P Farrer Baynes	Duchess of Newcastle	7
Ch Showman	d	22.11.1896	Windle Earl	Windle Princess	H G Powell	H G Powell	4
1903							
Ch Votrio Vikhra	b	05.02.01	Ch Velsk Votrio	Ch Vikhra	Duchess of Newcastle	Duchess of Newcastle	3
Ch Selwood Olga	b	17.01.1898	Ch Windle Courtier	Selwood Stelka	Mrs R Hood Wright	Mrs R Hood Wright	3
Ch Kieff	d	23.03.01	Fedia	Ina	Mrs P Farrer Baynes	Mrs L Kilvert	6
1904							
Ch Sunbeam	b	26.02.1899	Windle Earl	Windle Princess	H G Powell	H G Powell	16
Ch Ivan Turgeneff	d	08.06.02	White Tzar	Ch Sunbeam	Duchess of Newcastle	Duchess of Newcastle	9

1905							
Ch Berris	d	25.05.01	Ch Caspian	Selwood Stelka	Dr L Phillips	Mrs G May	5
Ch Mythe Czar	d	18.02.03	Ch Kieff	Salaba	J B Brooks	Mrs E L Borman	3
Ch Miss Piostri	b	24.02.03	Piostri	Princess Ruby Koff	Mrs E L Borman	Mrs E L Borman	20
Ch Strawberry King	d	10.08.03	Ch Kieff	Maid of Honour	Mrs Aitchison	Mrs Aitchison	17
1906							
Ch Padiham Nordia	d	15.04.01	Fedia	Norah	H Murphy	H Murphy	3
Ch Ramsden Ranger	d	21.04.05	Ch Padiham Nordia	Dainty	C M Trappes-Lomax	Mrs E L Borman	3
1907							
Ch Ramsden Radient	b	21.04.05	Ch Padiham Nordia	Dainty	C M Trappes-Lomax	Mrs E L Borman	4
1908							
Ch Elena	b	23.02.05	Ch Ivan Turgeneff	Marie	Mrs Aitchison	Mrs Aitchison	3
Ch Vassilka	d	18.05.02	Ch Velsk	Gatchina	HRH Queen Alexandra	HRH Queen Alexandra	3
1909							
Ch Ramsden Rajah	d	04.05.07	Ch Ramsden Ranger	Ch Miss Piostri	Mrs E L Borman	Mrs E L Borman	20
Ch Mythe Mischa	d	15.07.05	Ch Ivan Turgeneff	Petrovna	Miss E M Robinson	Miss E M Robinson	13
Ch Livonia	b	18.03.07	Ch Strawberry King	Azima	F Gardner	Mrs Aitchison	3
1910							
Ch Mythe Vanita	b	17.04.08	Clayton Snatcher	Mythe Vanda	Miss E M Robinson	Miss E M Robinson	8
1911							
Ch Catherina	b	09.08.08	Ch Strawberry King	Kalka	Mrs J Aitchinson	J W Dore	5
Ch Kielse	d	10.05.08	Ch Strawberry King	Athara	Mrs J Aitchinson	Mrs J Aitchinson	4
Ch Ramsden Radium	d	26.04.09	Ch Ramsden Ranger	Ch Miss Piostri	Mrs E L Borman	Mrs E L Borman	12
1912							
Ch Ramsden Rosemary	b	26.04.09	Ch Ramsden Ranger	Ch Miss Piostri	Mrs E L Borman	Mrs E L Borman	3
Ch Queen of Hearts of Addlestone	b	28.04.10	Ch Ramsden Rajah	Yenia	Mrs A A Vlasto	Mrs A A Vlasto	6
1913							
Ch Ramsden Refrain	b	16.06.10	Ch Ramsden Ranger	Ch Miss Piostri	Mrs E L Borman	Mrs E L Borman	4
Ch Pavlova of Addlestone	b	27.04.11	Ch Ramsden Rajah	Yenia	Mrs A A Vlasto	Mrs A A Vlasto	11
Ch Trumps of Addlestone	d	28.05.10	Ch Ramsden Rajah	Yenia	Mrs A A Vlasto	Mrs A A Vlasto	3
1914							
Ch Grand Duke of Addlestone	d	21.04.11	Michael of Addlestone	Dounia of Addlestone	Mrs A A Vlasto	Mrs A A Vlasto	3
Ch Nizam of Addlestone	d	28.05.12	Ch Trumps of Addlestone	Czarina of Addlestone	Mrs A A Vlasto	Mrs A A Vlasto	7

Champion	Sex	DOB	Sire	Dam	Breeder	Owner	CCs
1915							
Ch Grand Duchess of Addlestone	b	21.04.11	Michael of Addlestone	Dounia of Addlestone	Mrs A A Vlasto	Mrs A A Vlasto	3
Ch Lotka of Addlestone	b	03.04.12	Michael of Addlestone	Yenia	Mrs A A Vlasto	Miss T Parry	3
1916							
Ch Petrovski	d	26.02.12	Ch Mythe Mischa	Ch Mythe Vanita	Miss E M Robinson	Miss T Parry	3
1920							
Ch Suzanne of Addlestone	b	21.07.13	Ace of Addlestone	Ch Ramsden Rosemary	Mrs E L Borman	Mrs A A Vlasto	3
Ch Village Wonder	d	02.01.16	Mischa of Addlestone	Vara	M Long	Mrs D Lillis	5
1921							
Ch Shower of Addlestone	b	24.09.16	Rainbow of Addlestone	Ch Suzanne of Addlestone	Mrs A A Vlasto	Mrs A A Vlasto	4
1922							
Ch Marquis of Addlestone	d	09.11.19	White Prince of Addlestone	Joybells of Addlestone	Mrs A A Vlasto	Mrs A A Vlasto	3
Ch The Gift	b	11.11.15	Ch Grand Duke of Addlestone	Aida of Addlestone	Mrs A A Vlasto	Mrs Shepherd-Turneham	3
Ch Pobedim of Notts	d	24.10.20	Dainty Anna's Fame	Vicky-Van	Mrs C Kennett	Duchess of Newcastle	3
Ch Earlestown Exortive	b	21.03.21	Ripley Perfection	Earlestown Exordial	H T Brown	H Thompson	3
1923							
Ch Mythe Maslova	b	15.12.20	Muscovy's Rhapsody	Nevarc Valda	Miss E M Robinson	Miss E M Robinson	14
Ch Grosni of Addlestone	d	15.08.22	Sparrowhawk of Addlestone	Ch Marie of Addlestone	Mrs A A Vlasto	Mrs A A Vlasto	3
Ch Nevarc Bubbles	b	19.05.21	Ripley Perfection	Vaynor Gift	Mrs A Craven	Mrs A Craven	4
Ch Ripley White Marquis	d	10.05.20	Vaynor Dimitri	Ch The Gift	Mrs H Ingham	Mrs H Ingham	4
1924							
Ch Otlai of Addlestone	d	15.08.22	Sparrowhawk of Addlestone	Ch Marie of Addlestone	Mrs A A Vlasto	Mrs A A Vlasto	3
Ch Mythe Valdina	b	15.10.22	Sparrowhawk of Addlestone	Mythe Volga	Miss E M Robinson	T R Mills	3
Ch Novikoff of Haywra	d	18.08.22	Sparrowhawk of Addlestone	Ch Marie of Addlestone	Mrs A A Vlasto	B Timberlake	4
Ch Prospek of Addlestone	d	15.08.22	Sparrowhawk of Addlestone	Ch Marie of Addlestone	Mrs A A Vlasto	Mrs V Stringer	3

1925							
Ch Krassie of Addlestone	d	29.11.22	Sparrowhawk of Addlestone	Colchan of Addlestone	Mrs A A Vlasto	Mrs A A Vlasto	3
Ch Marie of Addlestone	b	24.10.20	Dainty Anna's Fame	Vicky-Van	Mrs C Kennett	Mrs A A Vlasto	3
1926							
Ch Zigani of Vedma	b	24.03.23	Bedin Achotnik	Marie of Haywra	Maj Borman	S H Fox	5
Ch Buchanan	d	03.09.21	Muscovy's Rhapsody	Kestor Nina	Mrs P Huth	Mrs P Huth	5
Ch Mythe Maxim	d	12.12.24	White Elegance	Mythe Volga	Miss E M Robinson	Miss E M Robinson	21
1927							
Ch Aureola of Llanfair	b	07.06.26	Max	Zara of Haywra	J Cramb	J Cramb	4
1928							
Ch Lovkaya of Addlestone	b	15.04.25	Chack Kozak of Shay	Achotnik of Shay	H Thompson	Mrs A A Vlasto	3
Ch Podar of Notts	d	15.04.25	Chack Kozak of Shay	Achotnik of Shay	H Thompson	Duchess of Newcastle	6
Ch Ripley Prima Donna	b	30.09.24	Ripley Perfection	Charlotte of Notts	Mrs H Ingham	Mrs H Ingham	4
1929							
Ch Dozar of Addlestone	d	11.11.25	Ch Otlai of Addlestone	Achotnik of Shay	Mrs A A Vlasto	Mrs A A Vlasto	3
Ch Bistraya of Addlestone	b	11.11.25	Sparrowhawk of Addlestone	Talmina of L'Ermitage	Mrs A A Vlasto	Mrs A A Vlasto	4
Ch Zavist of Addlestone	b	12.12.26	Tzigan Tiran	Ch Marie of Addlestone	Mrs A A Vlasto	Mrs A A Vlasto	4
1930							
Ch Mythe Voronoff	d	01.01.28	Ch Podar of Notts	Mythe Volia	Mrs F W Moor	Miss E M Robinson	3
Ch Princess Katinka of Vladimar	b	06.01.29	Ch Ripley White Marquis	Komley Katinka	D McKerlie	Mrs B E Seymour Stonely	4
1931							
Ch Zanoza Zia	b	22.08.27	Zanoza Zorronick	Zanoza Zoe	Miss D W Parry	Mrs F W Howden	3
Ch Kestor Maxim	d	16.03.28	Ch Mythe Maxim	Ruth Ellen of Haywra	B Timberlake	Mrs P Huth	3
Ch Sandra of Addlestone	b	06.06.29	Ch Podar of Notts	Lilya of Haywra	Mrs Staples Smith	Mrs A A Vlasto	3
Ch Lady Luck of Barnaigh	b	20.12.26	White Hawk	Arncliffe Taritzia	J Richardson	Mrs K McNeil	4
Ch Boris of Hawkdale	d	29.04.29	Ch Podar of Notts	Ch Lady Luck of Barnaigh	Mrs K McNeil	Mrs J G Dugdale	3
1932							
Ch Siegerin of Addlestone	b	03.10.30	Gordey of Addlestone	Ch Zavist of Addlestone	Mrs A A Vlasto	Mrs A A Vlasto	4
Ch Felstead	d	24.04.27	Mythe Novikoff	Topsetta	E H Guy	E H Guy	3
Ch Mythe Ivanoff	d	24.03.30	Ivan of Rebma	Mythe Vaga	Miss E M Robinson	Miss E M Robinson	9
Ch Gromkaya of Addlestone	b	03.10.30	Gordey of Addlestone	Ch Zavist of Addlestone	Mrs A A Vlasto	Mrs A A Vlasto	3

Champion	Sex	DOB	Sire	Dam	Breeder	Owner	CCs
1933							
Ch Patricia of Ashburn	b	14.10.28	St George of Manderlea	Arncliffe Taritzia	J Richardson	J Richardson	3
Ch Mythe Petroushka	b	03.06.30	Gordey of Addlestone	Mythe Petrovna	Miss E M Robinson	Miss E M Robinson	3
Ch Mythe Mazeppa	d	23.08.31	Gornostay of Addlestone	Mythe Moya	Miss E M Robinson	Miss E M Robinson	8
Ch Mara of Addlestone	b	03.10.30	Gordey of Addlestone	Ch Zavist of Addlestone	Mrs A A Vlasto	Mrs A A Vlasto	3
Ch Zikovitch of Brunton	d	17.12.28	Call Boy	Lady Jean of Neidpath	Mrs J K Dryden	Mrs A Forsyth-Caddell	3
Ch Sladkaya of Addlestone	b	18.03.31	Hrabriy of Addlestone	Sablia of Addlestone	Mrs A A Vlasto	Mrs A A Vlasto	7
1934							
Ch Ivarin of Addlestone	b	04.07.31	Ivan of Rebma	Xenia of Addlestone	Mrs A A Vlasto	Mrs A A Vlasto	3
Ch Mythe Mauris	d	05.06.32	Ivan of Rebma	Mythe Moya	Miss E M Robinson	Miss E M Robinson	6
Ch Achilles of Tangmere	d	03.03.32	Gordey of Addlestone	Golden Girl of Barnaigh	F W George	F Emm	4
Ch Ballerina of Bransgore	b	05.06.32	Gordey of Addlestone	Ch Sandra of Addlestone	Mrs E L Gingold	Mrs E L Gingold	3
1935							
Ch Porosha of Addlestone	b	04.07.31	Ivan of Rebma	Xenia of Addlestone	Mrs A A Vlasto	Mrs A A Vlasto	3
Ch Yaroslav of Addlestone	d	09.06.32	Gornostay of Addlestone	Xenia of Addlestone	Mrs A A Vlasto	Mrs A A Vlasto	4
Ch Brazhnik of Bransgore	d	06.04.33	Gornostay of Addlestone	Ch Siegerin of Addlestone	Mrs E L Gingold	Mrs E L Gingold	6
Ch Gromada of Addlestone	b	20.06.32	Gornostay of Addlestone	Ariane O'Valley Farm	Mrs E Laurie	Mrs A A Vlasto	3
Ch Dido of Tangmere	b	25.10.32	Menelaus of Tangmere	Otlika of Notts	F W George	F W George	3
1936							
Ch Mythe Mitya	d	17.06.34	Ch Zikovitch of Brunton	Mythe Ivanka	Miss E M Robinson	Miss E M Robinson	4
Ch Miss Mazeppa of Barnaigh	b	01.08.33	Ch Mythe Mazeppa	Ch Lady Luck of Barnaigh	Mrs K McNeil	Mrs K McNeil	3
Ch Mazourka of Addlestone	b	16.02.33	Gornostay of Addlestone	Grischa Frisia Pascholl	Mrs A A Vlasto	Mrs A A Vlasto	3
1937							
Ch Nadejda of Addlestone	b	05.03.34	Lubimetz of Addlestone	Ch Mara of Addlestone	Mrs A A Vlasto	Mrs A A Vlasto	4
Ch Peroun of Addlestone	d	30.09.34	Lubimetz of Addlestone	Zvezda of Addlestone	Mrs A A Vlasto	Mrs A A Vlasto	3
Ch Vanda of Nostell	b	14.05.34	Snejok of Addlestone	Princess Sonia of Rosamond	Mrs H Broughton	Mrs J G Scoular	3
Ch Brussilofkin of Bransgore	d	25.01.35	Brussiloff of Bransgore	Zagavor of Bransgore	Mrs E L Gingold	Mrs E L Gingold	3
Ch Mythe Petchora	b	11.08.33	Ch Mythe Mazeppa	Ch Mythe Petroushka	Miss E M Robinson	Miss E M Robinson	3
1938							
Ch Panther of Barnaigh	d	12.34	Templewood Atman	Mythe Malodka	Mrs Martin	Mrs K McNeil	3
Ch Mythe Molva	b	12.05.36	Ch Mythe Mazeppa	Mythe Marika	Miss E M Robinson	Miss E M Robinson	4
Ch Mythe Marinsky	d	12.05.36	Ch Mythe Mazeppa	Mythe Marika	Miss E M Robinson	Miss E M Robinson	4

Ch Alesha of Addlestone	d	04.06.35	Lubimetz of Addlestone	Ch Ivarin of Addlestone	Mrs A A Vlasto	Mrs A A Vlasto	4
Ch Zakar of Carradale	d	11.11.35	Lubimetz of Addlestone	Verona Valdina	H A Hawkin	H A & Miss S A Hawkin	3
Ch Brussilovna of Bransgore	b	25.01.35	Brussiloff of Bransgore	Zagavor of Bransgore	Mrs E L Gingold	Mrs E L Gingold	3
Ch Fet	b	12.05.36	Ch Mythe Mazeppa	Mythe Marika	Miss E M Robinson	E H Guy	3
1939							
Ch Ceres of Tangmere	b	28.07.36	Ch Achilles of Tangmere	Ch Dido of Tangmere	F W George & Miss D Atkinson	F W George & Miss D Atkinson	3
Ch Kouldon of Addlestone	d	21.02.38	Pernatch of Addlestone	Ch Mazourka of Addlestone	Mrs A A Vlasto	Mrs A A Vlasto	3
Ch Nigerette	b	01.07.37	Ch Achilles of Tangmere	Marienne of Tangmere	F Emm	J Richardson	3
Ch Mythe Morozov	d	13.04.35	Ch Mythe Mazeppa	Mythe Vanni	C Hutchings	Miss E M Robinson	3
Ch Baraban of Bransgore	d	12.05.36	Ch Brazhnik of Bransgore	Brodovka of Bransgore	Mrs E L Gingold	Mrs E L Gingold	3
Ch Mythe Marousia	b	30.01.36	Ch Mythe Mazeppa	Mythe Felia	Miss E M Robinson	E H Guy	3
1947							
Ch Moryak of Moskowa	d	29.12.42	Ch Mythe Marinsky	Moskowa Borzaya of Bransgore	Mrs M E Bates	Miss B Murray	3
Ch Ladoga Nalivka	b	24.10.45	Kuban's Almaz	Kuban Nadeja	C J Graham	E H Guy	4
1948							
Ch Zavan of Carradale	d	01.11.38	Ch Zakar of Carradale	Yonita of Carradale	H A & Miss S A Hawkin	Miss S A Hawkin	3
Ch Dante	d	07.07.46	Challenge	Ladoga Varya	E H Guy	E H Guy	3
Ch Fearless Lass	b	22.04.46	Challenge	Faith of Lenoken	E H Guy	E H Guy	3
Ch Delightful of Rydens	b	20.07.46	Rimski of Rydens	Jane O'Precious	F E Ellery	Miss J Cherry	4
Ch Winjones Ataman	d	03.05.46	Kuban's Almaz	Astrakan of Barnaigh	Mrs W E Chadwick	Mrs K McNeil	4
Ch Blue Train	d	27.10.46	Challenge	Godiva	E H Guy	E H Guy	6
1949							
Ch Winjones Balvoniza	b	24.04.47	Balalaika of Rydens	Winjones Bistri	Mrs W E Chadwick	Mrs W E Chadwick	6
Ch Snitterfield Cossack	d	10.10.46	Barinsky of Barinoff	Snitterfield Zena	Mrs E M Wingate	Mrs E M Wingate	3
Ch Denes Zarina	b	05.04.45	Kuban's Almaz	Tasha	L Lloyd Jones	Mrs D H Norton	4
Ch Antoinette of Rydens	b	05.08.44	Rimski of Rydens	Olga of Lenoken	Mrs W S Young	Mrs W S Young	3
Ch Folly of Fortrouge	b	01.07.45	St Arvans Moscow Moonlight	Krown Kassia	Miss A Howarth	Miss B Murray	3
Ch Netheroyd Zomahli Alexey	d	18.07.48	Ch Moryak of Moscowa	Zomahli Natasha	Mrs L Pearson	Mrs I M Abson	11
Ch Eglon of Rydens	d	14.12.46	Rimski of Rydens	Olga of Lenoken	Mrs W S Young	Mrs W S Young	4
Ch Elegance of Rydens	b	14.12.46	Rimski of Rydens	Olga of Lenoken	Mrs W S Young	Mrs W S Young	3

Champion	Sex	DOB	Sire	Dam	Breeder	Owner	CCs
1950							
Ch Winjones Bolshaia	b	24.04.47	Balalaika of Rydens	Winjones Bistri	Mrs W E Chadwick	Mrs G Beresford	3
Ch Onyx of Barnaigh	b	14.07.48	Ch Winjones Ataman	Natasha of Barnaigh	Mrs K McNeil	Mrs K McNeil	4
Ch Lady Luck of Rydens	b	16.04.49	Balalaika of Rydens	Jane O'Precious	Mrs L Hulbert	Mrs W S Young	4
1951							
Ch Normans of Rydens	d	27.07.49	Ch Eglon of Rydens	Nasha Neva of Woodcourt	Mrs W S Young	Mrs W S Young	3
Ch Zilda of Carradale	b	22.09.49	Ch Eglon of Rydens	Zola of Carradale	H A & Miss S A Hawkin	H A & Miss S A Hawkin	6
Ch Winjones Ermolai	d	09.10.48	Ch Winjones Ataman	Winjones Jiffy of Nenefen	Mrs W E Chadwick	Mrs W E Chadwick	5
Ch Ivanoff of Rydens	d	10.07.48	Rimski of Rydens	Posa	Mrs W S Young	Mrs W S Young	5
Ch Nicolai of Swalescar	d	03.07.48	Ch Moryak of Moskowa	Marion of Lenoken	Mrs M A Brown	Mrs M A & Misses M & J Brown	3
1952							
Ch Apex of Woodcourt	d	15.03.50	Ch Eglon of Rydens	Carissima of Woodcourt	Mrs J Curnow	Mrs J Curnow	6
Ch Aureola of Woodcourt	b	15.03.50	Ch Eglon of Rydens	Carissima of Woodcourt	Mrs J Curnow	Mrs J Curnow	4
Ch Petroff of Norvell	d	24.07.49	Ch Eglon of Rydens	Ch Denes Zarina	Mrs D H Norton	Mrs D H Norton	3
Ch Tessina of Yadasar	b	13.05.49	Zikovitch of Mantavani	Sorokina of Mantavani	Mr & Mrs H Clayton	Mrs G Beresford	5
Ch Melody of Yvill	b	21.02.50	Merryboy of Lenoken	Harmony of Rydens	Mrs C H Hill	Mrs N G Anstey	14
Ch Zardin of Carradale	d	30.09.50	Ch Eglon of Rydens	Zola of Carradale	H A & Miss S A Hawkin	H A & Miss S A Hawkin	10
1953							
Ch Loretta of Norvel	b	24.07.49	Ch Eglon of Rydens	Ch Denes Zarina	Mrs D H Norton	Mrs D H Norton	3
Ch Ulick of Rydens	d	20.03.51	Ch Norman of Rydens	Ch Lady Luck of Rydens	Mrs W S Young	Mrs F Forsyth-Caddell	6
Ch Bronzmaun Juliette	b	21.02.50	Merry Boy of Lenoken	Harmony of Rydens	Mrs C H Hill	Mrs N G Anstey	4
Ch Rydens Destiny of Astonoff	b	18.03.51	Ch Eglon of Rydens	Bertramilva of Astonoff	Mrs M Etherington	Mrs W S Young	3
1954							
Ch Winjones Naljot	d	01.03.52	Ch Winjones Ermolai	Winjones Dunyashya	Mrs W E Chadwick	Mrs W E Chadwick	11
1955							
Ch Melba of Quernmore	b	10.09.52	Ch Apex of Woodcourt	Kismet v Bergland	Mrs J Curnow	S W Milston	3
Ch Tzar of Astonoff	d	16.11.52	Ch Eglon of Rydens	Ch Rydens Destiny of Astonoff	Mrs M Etherington	Mrs M Etherington	3
Ch Winjones Lebediska	b	09.01.51	Ch Winjones Ermolai	Winjones Bistri	Mrs W E Chadwick	Mrs W E Chadwick	10
Ch Zadiah of Carradale	b	02.10.52	Ch Winjones Ermolai	Zola of Carradale	H A & Miss S A Hawkin	H A & Miss S A Hawkin	8
1956							
Ch Reyas Romancer	d	14.05.51	Reyas Mende	Winjones Akulina	E Sayer	E Sayer	3
Ch Winjones Razluka	d	24.08.54	Valdaihills Jock Jinks	Winjones Dunyashka	Mrs W E Chadwick	Mrs W E Chadwick	11

1957							
Ch Emperor of Woodcourt	d	28.02.54	Ch Apex of Woodcourt	Kismet v Bergland	Mrs J Curnow	Mrs J Curnow	3
Ch Zomahli Nadia	b	26.05.54	Gay Cavalier of Yadasar	Lady Nadia of Aberwynd	Mrs D Pugsley	Mrs L Pearson & K L Prior	4
Ch Winjones Ritzar	d	24.08.54	Valdaihills Jock Jinks	Winjones Dunyashka	Mrs W E Chadwick	J R Steele	3
Ch Zerlina of Carradale	b	15.09.54	Netheroyd Zamba of Carradale	Ch Zadiah of Carradale	H A & Miss S A Hawkin	H A & Miss S A Hawkin	10
1958							
Ch Reyas Rubato	d	29.07.54	Dimski of Rydens	Reyas Rosalia	E Sayer	E Sayer	3
Ch Zia of Carradale	b	24.10.56	Horst of Woodcourt	Ch Zadiah of Carradale	H A & Miss S A Hawkin	Mrs J Curnow	19
Ch Reyas Sandra	b	02.12.55	Jonathan of Yadasar	Reyas Rosalia	E Sayer	E Sayer	3
1959							
Ch Nice Fella	d	26.05.54	Gay Cavalier of Yadasar	Lady Nadia of Aberwynd	Mrs D Pugsley	Mrs D Pugsley	5
Ch Ebony of Woodcourt	b	28.02.54	Ch Apex of Woodcourt	Kismet v Bergland	Mrs J Curnow	Mrs J Curnow	3
Ch Reyas Joad of Fortrouge	d	19.08.55	Rydens Rhythm of Yvill	Fleet of Fortrouge	Miss B Murray	E Sayer	3
1960							
Ch Arnorinski of Greenhaven	d	14.09.57	Marcellus of Fortrouge	Winjones Radonga	Mrs G Harrison	Mrs G Harrison	4
Ch Reyas Mischa	d	02.12.55	Jonathan of Yadasar	Reyas Rosalia	E Sayer	E Sayer	3
Ch Zavist of Carradale	b	24.10.56	Horst of Woodcourt	Ch Zadiah of Carradale	H A & Miss S A Hawkin	Mrs L Pearson & K L Prior	3
1961							
Ch Zomahli Chernila	d	17.11.58	Zeraph of Carradale	Ch Zavist of Carradale	Mrs L Pearson & K L Prior	Mrs L Pearson & K L Prior	21
Ch Zastro of Carradale	d	21.07.58	Horst of Woodcourt	Ch Zerlina of Carradale	H A & Miss S A Hawkin	Mrs D O'Hare	4
1962							
Ch Zarah of Carradale	b	21.07.58	Horst of Woodcourt	Ch Zerlina of Carradale	H A & Miss S A Hawkin	H A & Miss S A Hawkin	4
Ch Barnaigh Barthill Red Rose	b	28.08.58	Aksakoff Marcovitch	Lustre of Yadasar	Mrs E F Harpur	Mrs K McNeil	4
Ch Ruth of Fortrouge	b	31.03.59	Ch Reyas Rubato	Francesca of Hindham	Miss B Murray	K B Wallis	4
Ch Barnaigh Barthill Marcovitch	d	04.11.59	Aksakoff Marcovitch	Lustre of Yadasar	Mrs E F Harpur	Mrs K McNeil	4
1963							
Ch Angelola of Enolam	b	14.02.62	Reyas Ringer	Ch Reyas Black Magic	Mrs M Malone	Mrs J Bennett Heard	9
1964							
Ch Reyas Roberto	d	21.04.60	Ch Reyas Rubato	Reyas Zoraya of Carradale	E Sayer	E Sayer	4
Ch Falconcrag Zsa Zsa	b	28.03.62	Barthill Fedorovitch	Lataband Anita	Mrs E F Harpur	Mrs S M Marston	5
Ch Reyas Black Magic	b	10.10.58	Aksakoff Markovitch	Reyas Russalka	E Sayer	Mrs M Malone	4
Ch Springbank Barthill Marcus	d	28.03.62	Barthill Fedorovitch	Lataband Anita	Mrs E F Harpur	Mrs V Sayer	5
Ch Black Tarquin of Enolam	d	14.02.62	Reyas Ringer	Ch Reyas Black Magic	Mrs M Malone	Mrs M Malone	3
Ch Barthill Duskie Rose	b	04.11.59	Aksakoff Marcovitch	Lustre of Yadasar	Mrs E F Harpur	Mrs E F Harpur	3

Champion	Sex	DOB	Sire	Dam	Breeder	Owner	CCs
1965							
Ch Iliad of Woodcourt	b	02.09.60	Ch Emperor of Woodcourt	Ch Zia of Carradale	Mrs J Curnow	Mrs G Beresford	3
Ch Shelbor's Apollo	d	17.12.61	Ch Arnorinski of Greenhaven	Reyas Sapphire of Bobrowska	Mrs B Hargrave	Mrs B Hargrave	3
Ch Reyas Ravenna	b	16.04.62	Reyas Marquis	Reyas Royalise	E Sayer	E Sayer	3
1966							
Ch Black Diamond of Enolam	d	14.02.62	Reyas Ringer	Ch Reyas Black Magic	Mrs M Malone	Mrs M Malone	3
Ch Reyas Rainmaker	d	21.01.62	Reyas Rainbow	Ledvedka Perchino	E Sayer	E Sayer	4
Ch Zomahli Evolgo	d	21.03.63	Zomahli Dyasha	Ch Zavist of Carradale	Mrs L Pearson & K L Prior	Mrs L Pearson & K L Prior	3
Ch Gay Navarree of Matalona	d	20.03.62	Matalona Babur of Rydens	Ruth of Matalona	Mrs E E Ruggles	Mrs A Thornwell	4
Ch Springbank Reyas Raincloud	b	21.01.62	Reyas Rainbow	Ledvedka Perchino	E Sayer	Mrs V Sayer	4
Ch Zomahli Keepers Douteuse	d	02.05.64	Ch Zomahli Chernila	Ch Angelola of Enolam	Mrs J Bennett Heard	Mrs L Pearson & K L Prior	4
Ch Matalona Sudorka of Fortrouge	b	01.03.65	Boran	Carlotta of Fortrouge	Miss B Murray	Miss E E Ruggles	4
Ch Barnaigh Vorenoff Bielko	d	18.12.63	Runskoff Ivanovitch	Ch Ruth of Fortrouge	Mr & Mrs Heller	Mrs K McNeil	4
1967							
Ch Reyas Moyana	b	10.02.63	Reyas Rijeka	Ledvedka Perchino	E Sayer	E Sayer	3
Ch Grand Manner of Colhugh	d	02.01.62	Lataband Alexi	Reyas Red Plume	K Berney	R A Bassett	5
1968							
Ch Zomahli Feleekan	d	05.09.65	Ch Zomahli Evolgo	Zomahli Nayada	Mrs L Pearson & K L Prior	Mrs L Pearson & K L Prior	6
Ch Yana of Yadasar	b	20.03.66	Barthill Fedorovitch	Ch Iliad of Woodcourt	Mrs G Beresford & Mrs A Tomlinson	Mrs G Beresford & Mrs A Tomlinson	6
Ch Zest of Fortrouge	b	21.06.66	Boran	Carlotta of Fortrouge	Miss B Murray	Miss B Murray	3
Ch Petroff of Enolam	d	27.04.66	Jobi Reyas Rohan	Ch Reyas Black Magic	Mrs M Malone	Mrs M Malone	6
Ch Black Limelight of Enolam	b	27.07.65	Ch Keepers Michael Angelo	Ch Reyas Black Magic	Mrs M Malone	Mrs M Malone	4
1969							
Ch Wellthornes Kalinka	b	05.08.64	Ch Arnorinski of Greenhaven	Galina of Matalona	Mrs A Thornewell	Mrs A Thornewell	4
Ch Francehill Fairybridge Balinka	b	29.04.66	Francehill Russian Cocktail	Fairybridge Ballerina	Mmes Bailey & Anthony	Mr & Mrs Searle	3

Ch Zomahli Fororna	b	05.08.64	Ch Zomahli Evolgo	Zomahli Nayada	Mrs L Pearson & K L Prior	Mrs L Pearson & K L Prior	3
Ch Keepers Michael Angelo	d	02.05.64	Ch Zomahli Chernila	Ch Angelola of Enolam	Mrs J Bennett Heard	Mrs J Bennett Heard	3
Ch Magic Dust of Enolam	b	23.04.67	Ch Black Diamond of Enolam	Francehill Martini of Enolam	Mrs M Malone	Mrs M Malone	4
Ch Keepers The Baron	d	27.05.66	Boran	Ch Angelola of Enolam	Mrs J Bennett Heard	Mrs J Bennett Heard	3
1970							
Ch Tina of Colhugh	b	13.01.67	Ch Grand Manner of Colhugh	Annikka of Greenhaven	R A Bassett	R A Bassett	7
Ch Zomahli Gueroy	d	23.11.67	Ch Black Diamond of Enolam	Zomahli Nayada	Mrs L Pearson & K L Prior	Mrs L Pearson & K L Prior	5
Ch Keepers Angeline Les Angels	b	26.08.65	Keepers Johnny Angel	Ch Angelola of Enolam	Mrs J Bennett Heard	R Duckworth	3
Ch Wellthornes Kitov	b	05.04.67	Ch Gay Navarree of Matalona	Ch Wellthornes Kalinka	Mrs A Thornewell	Mrs A Thornewell	3
Ch Zircon of Fortrouge	d	21.06.66	Boran	Carlotta of Fortrouge	Miss B Murray	Miss B Murray	3
Ch Swallowcroft Reyas Ivanovitch	d	09.06.68	Reyas Falconcrag Zenith	Reyas Rodana	Mrs V Sayer	G Bower	5
Ch Reyas Keepers Kwango	d	27.05.66	Boran	Ch Angelola of Enolam	Mrs J Bennett Heard	E Sayer	3
Ch Alexi of Colhugh	d	13.01.67	Ch Grand Manner of Colhugh	Annikka of Greenhaven	R A Bassett	R A Bassett	3
Ch Zomahli Gratseeya	b	23.11.67	Ch Black Diamond of Enolam	Zomahli Nayada	Mrs L Pearson & K L Prior	Mrs L Pearson & K L Prior	5
1971							
Ch Domino of Enolam	b	23.04.67	Ch Black Diamond of Enolam	Francehill Martini of Enolam	Mrs M Malone	Mrs M Malone	3
Ch Francehill Diamond Lil	b	06.07.69	Ch Black Diamond of Enolam	Springbank Lili	Miss B Murray & Mr & Mrs Searle	Mr & Mrs Searle	7
Ch Zomahli Harorshyi	d	13.01.69	Zomahli Gordey	Zomahli Narida	Mrs L Pearson & K L Prior	Mrs E Barratt	9
Ch Keepers Baroness	b	14.05.68	Ch Keepers The Baron	Keepers Sardi	Mrs J Bennett Heard	Mrs J Bennett Heard	9
Ch Francehill Joker	d	05.04.67	Reyas Rodin	Francehill Sweet Sherry	Mr & Mrs Searle	Mr & Mrs Searle	3
1972							
Ch Galina of Colhugh	b	13.01.67	Ch Grand Manner of Colhugh	Annikka of Greenhaven	R A Bassett	Mrs J L Gibb	3
Ch Zomahli Igrok	d	28.07.70	Ch Zomahli Gueroy	Zomahli Narida	Mrs L Pearson & K L Prior	Mrs L Pearson & K L Prior	3
Ch Wellthornes Tilosky	d	09.09.69	Ch Keepers Michael Angelo	Ch Wellthornes Kalinka	Mrs A Thornewell	R A Bassett	12

Champion	Sex	DOB	Sire	Dam	Breeder	Owner	CCs
Ch Deanlands Boris	d	15.07.69	Ch Keepers The Baron	Wellthornes Landa of Matalona	S J Protheroe	Mrs & Miss Marston	3
Ch Sarclash of Colhugh	b	01.08.69	Ch Grand Manner of Colhugh	Annikka of Greenhaven	R A Bassett	R A Bassett	4
Ch Francehill Pantaloons	b	26.06.70	Ch Alexi of Colhugh	Francehill Mary Poppins	Mr & Mrs Searle	Mr & Mrs Searle	6
Ch Wellthornes Bronsky	d	09.09.69	Ch Keepers Michael Angelo	Ch Wellthornes Kalinka	Mrs A Thornewell	Mrs A Thornewell	3
Ch Petronella of Yadasar	b	28.03.70	Barthill Nero	Barthill Amber Rose	Mrs E Harpur	Mmes G Beresford & A Tomlinson	4
1973							
Ch Patroonia Keepers Bolshoi	d	14.04.68	Ch Keepers The Baron	Keepers Sardi	Mrs J Bennett Heard	Miss A Blair	7
Ch Falconcrag Esmerarna	b	08.11.70	Ch Grand Manner of Colhugh	Ch Falconcrag Zsa Zsa	Mrs Marston	Mrs & Miss Marston	4
Ch Rodgivad Brigand	d	29.04.69	Ch Keepers The Baron	Rodgivad Virago	Mrs Etheridge	Mrs Etheridge	5
Ch Shelbor Desirable	b	24.03.70	Sunbarr Invader of Fortrouge	Shelbor Natasha	Mrs B Hargrave	Mrs B Hargrave	4
Ch Black Jack of Fortrouge	d	18.10.68	Ch Gay Navarree of Matalona	Vorenoff Diane of Fortrouge	Miss B Murray	Miss B Murray	4
1974							
Ch Francehill Pimlico	d	16.12.71	Ch Zomahli Harorshyi	Springbank Lili	Mr & Mrs Searle & Miss B Murray	Mr & Mrs Searle	3
Ch Colhugh Mia	b	09.09.71	Ch Grand Manner of Colhugh	Annikka of Greenhaven	R A Bassett	C A Lange	3
Ch Zomahli Nadesda	b	07.01.73	Ch Zomahli Harorshyi	Zomahli Iskra of Racingold	M & Miss C Dean	Mrs L Pearson & K L Prior	16
Ch Sadko of Colhugh	d	01.08.69	Ch Grand Manner of Colhugh	Annikka of Greenhaven	R A Bassett	R A Bassett	3
Ch Bacaret Copper Queen	b	10.11.69	Ch Keepers Michael Angelo	Busa of Matalona	Mrs B Long	Mrs B Long	3
1975							
Ch Colhugh Valla	b	09.09.71	Ch Grand Manner of Colhugh	Annikka of Greenhaven	R A Bassett	R A Bassett	7
Ch Waycross Roksana	b	13.02.72	Ch Wellthornes Tilosky	Lisa of Waycross	Mmes Barclay & Anderson	Mmes Barclay & Anderson	7

Ch Dark Enchantress of Enolam	b	30.11.69	Ch Petroff of Enolam	Francehill Martini of Enolam	Mrs Malone	Mrs Malone	3
Ch Sholwood Seraph	d	12.12.70	Ch Keepers Michael Angelo	Ch Keepers Angeline Les Angels	R Duckworth	R Duckworth	6
Ch Lubimoff Galinka of Shelbor	b	25.04.71	Ch Francehill Joker	Racingold Polka	Mrs Fisher	Mrs B Hargrave	3
Ch Waycross Alexander	d	01.03.71	Ch Alexi of Colhugh	Anastasia of Waycross	Mmes Barclay & Anderson	Mmes Barclay & Anderson	3
1976							
Ch Colhugh Crystal	b	06.12.73	Ch Wellthornes Tilosky	Ch Sarclash of Colhugh	R A Bassett	R A Bassett	8
Ch Dimland Kohoutek of Colhugh	d	5.12.73	Ch Wellthornes Tilosky	Dimland Zerlina of Colhugh	G Hill	R A Bassett	3
Ch Francehill Diamond Ring	b	22.11.72	Ch Sadko of Colhugh	Ch Francehill Diamond Lil	Mr & Mrs Searle	Mr & Mrs Searle	3
Ch Zomahli Nachal	d	07.01.73	Ch Zomahli Harorshyi	Zomahli Iskra of Racingold	Mrs & Miss Dean	Mrs L Pearson & K L Prior	4
Ch Nakora Aludka	b	18.05.73	Ch Sholwood Seraph	Zomahli Hazyaika	M P Real	M P Real	8
Ch Colhugh Oriole of Dimland	b	20.04.73	Ch Wellthornes Tilosky	Ch Tina of Colhugh	R A Bassett	G Hill	8
Ch Bacaret Summer Storm	d	09.06.73	Ch Sholwood Seraph	Plurenden Zoe	Mrs B Long	Mrs B Long	3
Ch Keepers Black Hawk	d	02.05.73	Ch Keepers The Baron	Rodgivad Moonflower	Mrs E Etheridge	Mrs J Bennett Heard	3
Ch Lanclare Count Nikolai	d	15.09.73	Ch Zomahli Harorshyi	Index Anastasia of Lanclare	Lt Col & Mrs Lange	Lt Col & Mrs Lange	5
1977							
Ch Stonebar Nikolenka	d	14.02.73	Ch Wellthornes Tilosky	Lisa of Waycross	Mrs G Rose	Mrs G Rose	4
Ch Yadasar Robin Hood of Boranya	d	03.08.73	Ch Wellthornes Bronsky	Ch Petronella of Yadasar	Mmes G Beresford & A Tomlinson	Mrs S Woollands	4
Ch Colhugh Clangers	d	22.05.76	Ch Dimland Kohoutek of Colhugh	Keepers Falling Leaves	R A Bassett	R A Bassett	32
Ch Lanclare Sir Nigel	d	15.09.73	Ch Zomahli Harorshyi	Index Anastasia of Lanclare	Lt Col & Mrs Lange	Lt Col & Mrs Lange	3
Ch Racingold Yasha of Lanclare	d	07.01.73	Ch Zomahli Harorshyi	Zomahli Iskra of Racingold	Mrs & Miss Dean	Lt Col & Mrs Lange	5
Ch Yadasar Red Riding Hood of Boranya	b	03.08.73	Ch Wellthornes Bronsky	Ch Petronella of Yadasar	Mmes G Beresford & A Tomlinson	Mrs S Woollands	3
1978							
Ch Lanclare Tcherkisa	b	30.09.75	Ch Sholwood Seraph	Ch Colhugh Mia	Lt Col & Mrs Lange	Lt Col & Mrs Lange	7
Ch Greenhaven Barrie	d	23.12.72	Ch Keepers The Baron	Anastacia of Greenhaven	Mrs G Harrison	Mrs G Harrison	3
Ch Dimland Petya	d	21.04.75	Ch Sadko of Colhugh	Ch Colhugh Oriole of Dimland	G Hill	G Hill	11
Ch Manitia Count Hugo	d	08.01.75	Manitia Total Eclipse	Manitia Yakutia	Miss M Manning	Mrs A Randall	7

Champion	Sex	DOB	Sire	Dam	Breeder	Owner	CCs
1979							
Ch Shelbor Red Velvet	b	23.03.75	Ch Wellthornes Tilosky	Swissroyal Anoushka	Mrs B Hargrave	Mrs B Hargrave	4
Ch Bacaret Zebe of Zoribo	d	14.03.75	Ch Sholwood Seraph	Plurenden Zoe	Mrs B Long	P H Langley	6
Ch Zomahli Ozopnik	b	01.09.76	Falconcrag Khristov	Ch Zomahli Nadesda	Mrs L Pearson & K L Prior	Mrs L Pearson & K L Prior	6
Ch Stonebar Sovereign	b	24.05.75	Ch Stonebar Nikolenka	Francehill Full Hand	Mrs G Rose	Mrs G Rose	4
Ch Annaleen of Wellthornes	b	20.03.73	Ch Wellthornes Tilosky	Ch Tina of Colhugh	R A Bassett	Mrs A Thornwell	3
Ch Keepers Elsa	b	26.12.74	Keepers Vaguely Noble	Keepers Selphides	Mrs J Bennett Heard	Mrs J Bennett Heard	3
Ch Francehill Nancy	b	20.10.76	Francehill Pickwick	Ch Francehill Pantaloons	Mr & Mrs Searle	Mr & Mrs Searle	4
Ch Azka Gregori	d	8.12.73	Ch Wellthornes Tilosky	Trisha of Glynde	Mrs C A Hill	A W Hill	3
Ch Dimland Kommissar	d	21.04.75	Ch Sadko of Colhugh	Ch Colhugh Oriole of Dimland	G Hill	Mrs D Martin	5
Ch Enolam Black Prinz	d	17.11.75	Ch Sholwood Seraph	Ch Dark Enchantress of Enolam	Mrs M Malone	Mr & Mrs Tyerman	3
Ch Francehill Petunia	b	27.04.74	Ch Francehill Pimlico	Ch Francehill Pantaloons	Mr & Mrs Searle	Mr & Mrs Searle	3
Ch Netheroyd Miss Elegance	b	19.11.73	Ch Petroff of Enolam	Tajmirs Miss Freedom	Mrs Morton	Miss M Malone	4
1980							
Ch Bacaret Lord Supertramp	d	15.08.76	Ch Patrioona Keepers Bolshoi	Ch Bacaret Copper Queen	Mrs B Long	Mrs B Long	8
Ch Zomahli Molba	b	16.08.76	Falconcrag Khristov	Racingold Yelena	Mrs L Pearson & K L Prior	Mrs L Pearson & K L Prior	4
Ch Colhugh Cara	b	16.05.75	Ch Wellthornes Tilosky	Shelbor Belle Bodel	R A Bassett	R A Bassett	6
Ch Keepers Enchantress of Livny	b	26.12.74	Keepers Vaguely Noble	Keepers Selphides	Mrs J Bennett Heard	Mrs Stears	3
Ch Colhugh Collette of Olias	b	16.04.76	Colhugh Buttons	Ch Colhugh Valla	R A Bassett	Mrs J Mabey	4
Ch Olias Tangerine Dream	d	13.07.78	Ch Dimland Petya	Ch Colhugh Collette of Olias	Mrs J Mabey	Mrs J Mabey	5
Ch Tayu Casmilla of Yadasar	b	27.12.77	Yadasar Rider of the Night	Falconcrag Ebony	Mr & Mrs Hough	Mrs A Tomlinson	3
1981							
Ch Yadasar Midnight Rider	d	14.03.78	Yadasar Rider of the Night	Yadasar Greta	Mrs A Tomlinson	Mrs A Tomlinson	9
Ch Olias Crimson Queen	b	13.07.78	Ch Dimland Petya	Ch Colhugh Collette of Olias	Mrs J Mabey	Mrs J Mabey	3
Ch Stonebar Reflection of Ryazan	b	20.07.77	Ch Stonebar Nikolenka	Francehill Full Hand	Mrs G Rose	Miss J Clare	5

Ch Zomahli Radooga	b	10.09.78	Falconcrag Khristov	Racingold Yelena	Mrs L Pearson & K L Prior	Mrs L Pearson & K L Prior	5
Ch Stonebar Portrait	b	20.06.79	Ch Stonebar Nikolenka	Portia of Fortrouge	Mrs G Rose	Mr & Mrs Rowell	4
Ch Strelkos Stormy Morn	d	03.06.76	Francehill Golden Eagle	Sissinheimon Strelka	Mrs C Spencer	Mrs C Spencer	4
Ch Dimland Balalaika	b	26.03.77	Ch Dimland Kohoutek of Colhugh	Ch Colhugh Oriole of Dimland	G Hill	G Hill	3
Ch Colhugh Chaos	d	01.12.77	Ch Colhugh Clangers	Ch Colhugh Crystal	R A Bassett	Mrs D Martin	6
Ch Strelkos Dawn Horizon	b	21.10.80	Ch Strelkos Stormy Morn	Stonebar National Velvet	Mrs C Spencer	Mr & Mrs Marcus	4
Ch Yaltika Victoria	b	21.05.79	Ch Dimland Kohoutek of Colhugh	Colhugh Catasha of Yaltika	Mrs A Webb	Mrs A Webb	12
1982							
Ch Yadasar Black Orchid	b	09.12.79	Francehill Pickwick	Ch Tayu Casmilla of Yadasar	Mrs A Tomlinson	Mrs A Tomlinson	20
Ch Colhugh Crumpet	b	13.03.77	Ch Dimland Kohoutek of Colhugh	Waycross Katerina	R A Bassett	R A Bassett	4
Ch Waycross Rosana	b	12.02.78	Ch Dimland Kohoutek of Colhugh	Ch Waycross Roksana	Mrs C Simmonds	Mrs C Simmonds	3
Ch Zomahli Udachnik of Colhugh	d	17.06.80	Ch Yadasar Midnight Rider	Ch Zomahli Molba	Mrs L Pearson & K L Prior	R A Bassett	21
Ch Undomiel Arrathorn Imper	d	04.04.78	Bacaret Milord of Matalona	Anastasi Petite Lady of Undomiel	D E Bell	D E Bell	3
Ch Nakora Boyarina	b	07.10.76	Falconcrag Khristov	Ch Nakora Aludka	M P Real	Mrs S Marston	4
Ch Shelbor Petranova	b	20.03.78	Ch Dimland Petya	Shelbor Black Minx	Mrs B Hargrave	Mrs B Hargrave	3
Ch Dimland Balanchine	d	20.05.79	Ch Dimland Petya	Greenhaven Circle of Colhugh	G Hill	Mr & Mrs Downes	5
Ch Fortrouge Moses of Stonebar	d	24.03.78	Ch Stonebar Nikolenka	Portia of Fortrouge	Miss B Murray	Mrs G Rose	3
1983							
Ch Veedeques Maricopa	b	18.11.78	Ch Dimland Kohoutek of Colhugh	Veedeques Haidi	Miss V D Quincey	Ms J Mahoney	4
Ch Swiftcroft Pretty Woman	b	29.05.77	Francehill Pickwick	Swiftcroft Aires'n'Graces	Mrs J Rampley	Mrs J Rampley	3
Ch Livny Whispering Windrush	d	07.02.80	Bacaret Milord of Matalona	Livny Autumn Sorrel	Mr & Mrs Stears	Mr & Mrs Stears	8
Ch Hammonds Roana	b	08.01.80	Ch Manitia Count Hugo	Manitia Karelia	Mrs A Randall	Mrs A Randall	5
Ch Colhugh Chanel	b	18.04.80	Ch Colhugh Clangers	Ch Colhugh Valla	R A Bassett	G Hill	3
Ch Colhugh Caminickers	b	02.03.81	Ch Olias Tangerine Dream	Ch Colhugh Crumpet	R A Bassett	R A Bassett	40

Champion	Sex	DOB	Sire	Dam	Breeder	Owner	CCs
1984							
Ch Olias Oberon	d	06.04.81	Ch Colhugh Clangers	Ch Colhugh Collette of Olias	Mrs J Mabey	Mr & Mrs Mabey	15
Ch Colhugh Cameron of Dekaos	b	08.05.79	Ch Dimland Petya	Ch Colhugh Crystal	R A Bassett	Mr & Mrs Clark	5
Ch Swiftcroft Fleeting Spirit	d	02.08.78	Bacaret Prince Noir	Swiftcroft Elusive Spirit	Mrs J Rampley	Mmes J Rampley & Ridge Reeves	7
Ch Colhugh Capucine	b	18.04.80	Ch Colhugh Clangers	Ch Colhugh Valla	R A Bassett	Mr & Mrs Downes	3
Ch Waycross Rockafella of Zackaville	d	12.12.78	Ch Dimland Kohoutek of Colhugh	Ch Waycross Roksana	Mrs C Anderson	Mr & Mrs Blake	3
Ch Chasefield Gold Dust	d	14.01.82	Ch Dimland Kommissar	Dimland Jezabel of Chasefield	Mrs D Martin	Mrs D Martin	4
Ch Baroncroft Custard of Colhugh	b	09.05.82	Ch Zomahli Udachnik of Colhugh	Dimland Kalista	Miss P Morgan	R A Bassett	17
Ch Colhugh Calpernia	b	27.01.83	Ch Zomahli Udachnik of Colhugh	Fortrouge Circe	R A Bassett	R A Bassett	5
Ch Dimland Katusov	d	18.06.79	Ch Colhugh Clangers	Ch Colhugh Oriole of Dimland	G Hill	Mr & Mrs Downes	5
Ch Zomahli Ushmeka of Nakora	b	17.06.80	Ch Yadasar Midnight Rider	Ch Zomahli Molba	Mrs L Pearson & K L Prior	M R Real	10
Ch Pasquinel Picador	d	30.01.81	Ch Zomahli Ozopnik	Ninotchka of Kenstaff at Pasquinel	Messrs Reilley & T Jepson	Mrs J van Schaick	4
Ch Fortrouge Floby	b	04.05.81	Ch Bacaret Zebe of Zoribo	Fortrouge Nicholette	Miss B Murray	Miss B Murray	3
1985							
Ch Yanjoy Eliza Doolittle	b	19.06.81	Ch Dimland Petya	Ch Veedeques Maricopa	Ms J Mahoney	Ms J Mahoney	5
Ch Cohugh Clever Dick	d	20.05.81	Colhugh Cobnut	Dimland Catina of Colhugh	R A Bassett	R A Bassett	4
Ch Livny Black Eagle	d	09.05.83	Bacaret Milord of Matalona	Livney Autumn Sorrel	Mr & Mrs Stears	Mr & Mrs Stears	14
Ch Fortrouge Martha	b	24.03.78	Ch Stonebar Nikolenka	Portia of Fortrouge	Miss B Murray	Mrs Y F Monteith	3
Ch Wellthornes Kalinda	b	04.07.78	Bacaret Milord of Matalona	Ch Annaleen of Wellthornes	Mrs A Thornewell	Mrs A Thornewell	3
1986							
Ch Stonebar Sebastian	d	31.01.83	Ch Strelkos Stormy Morn	Ch Stonebar Sovereign	Mrs G Rose	Mrs G Rose	17

Ch Livny Tamarind	d	13.10.81	Ch Livny Whispering Windrush	Ch Keepers Enchantress of Livny	Mr & Mrs Stears	Mr & Mrs Robinson	4
Ch Yanjoy Artful Dodger	b	19.06.81	Ch Dimland Petya	Ch Veedeques Maricopa	Ms J Mahoney	Miss J Dove	3
Ch Bondi Beach Boy of Skyrose	d	21.12.82	Ch Pasquinel Picador	Tinryland Hi There	B Johnson	Mrs M Gooder	3
Ch Stonebar Soloman of Strelkos	d	10.09.80	Ch Strelkos Stormy Morn	Ch Stonebar Sovereign	Mrs G Rose	Mrs C Spencer	3
Ch Czarina Gemstone	b	17.04.81	Ch Dimland Kommissar	Penclaire Tatiana	Miss C Lewthwaite	Mr & Mrs Morgan	5
Ch Vimern Black Destiny	b	16.12.81	Ch Zomahli Ozopnik	Planxty Prima Donna	Mr, Mrs & Miss Paton	Mrs S Marston	5
Ch Rodgivad Morwenna	b	27.05.80	Ch Fortrouge Moses of Stonebar	Fortrouge Silver Jubilee of Rodgivad	Mrs E Etheridge	Mrs E Etheridge	5
Ch Dekaos Appianni	b	30.05.82	Ch Colhugh Clangers	Ch Colhugh Cameron of Dekaos	Mr & Mrs Clark	Mr & Mrs Clark	6
Ch Colhugh Claude of Longuin	d	02.03.81	Ch Olias Tangerine Dream	Ch Colhugh Crumpet	R A Bassett	Miss C Broxup	4
Ch Colhugh Cyngle	b	27.06.82	Ch Zomahli Udachnik of Colhugh	Fortrouge Circe	R A Bassett	Mrs M Broxup	3
1987							
Ch Waycross Rokamber	b	18.02.82	Colhugh Cobnut	Waycross Carisma of Colhugh	Mrs C Simmonds	Mr & Mrs Simmonds	3
Ch Colhugh Crimebuster	d	02.03.81	Ch Olias Tangerine Dream	Ch Colhugh Crumpet	R A Bassett	R A Bassett	3
Ch Zoribo Oscarvitch	d	21.07.82	Zoribo Dshomini	Bacaret Easter Gift	Mr & Mrs Langley	Mr & Mrs Langley	5
Ch Stillwater Virginia Reel	b	05.04.81	Stillwater The Tennessean	Stillwater Hoedown	Mr & Mrs Tyson	R Duckworth	5
Ch Fortrouge Ben of Longuin	d	24.12.84	Ch Zomahli Udachnik of Colhugh	Fortrouge Circe	Miss B Murray	R A Bassett	15
Ch Vronsky Zapata	d	05.10.84	Ch Dimland Katusov	Ch Colhugh Capucine	Mr & Mrs Downes	Mr & Mrs Downes	12
Ch Stonebar Orient of Minchikov	b	03.05.84	Ch Olias Oberon	Ch Stonebar Sovereign	Mrs G Rose	Mr & Mrs Marcus	4
1988							
Ch Colhugh Cuddles	b	27.01.83	Ch Zomahli Udachnik of Colhugh	Fortrouge Circe	R A Bassett	R A Bassett	4
Ch Baroncroft Cinnamon	b	29.09.85	Ch Colhugh Clever Dick	Tanygroes Sonia	Miss P Morgan	Miss P Morgan & Mrs A Tomlinson	3
Ch Moscow Red Banner	d	23.08.83	Ch Olias Oberon	Ch Czarina Gemstone	Mr & Mrs Morgan	Miss J Smith	4
Ch Zomahli Xaveetoi	d	09.02.84	Zomahli Vesseloy	Ch Zomahli Radooga	Messrs Prior & Keys	Messrs Prior & Keys & Mrs Randall	3
Ch Creusa Prince of Darkness	d	10.03.85	Ch Colhugh Clangers	Colhugh Cornish of Creusa	Mrs B Phillips	Mrs B Phillips	4

Champion	Sex	DOB	Sire	Dam	Breeder	Owner	CCs
Ch Waycross Melody	b	10.08.84	Ch Zomahli Udachnik of Colhugh	Waycross Carisma of Colhugh	Mr & Mrs Simmonds	Mr & Mrs Simmonds	4
Ch Diamond Edge of Enolam	d	09.01.84	Ch Yadasar Midnight Rider	Enolam Christaiana	Mr & Mrs Watson	B Johnston & N Laycock	3
1989							
Ch Matalona Cordelia of Creusa	b	17.10.82	Matalona Orestes	Matalona Pride	Mrs E Ruggles	Mrs B Phillips	3
Ch Starborough Shere Khan	d	28.01.85	Ch Swiftcroft Fleeting Spirit	Zoribo Otrima of Starborough	Mrs L Marchant	Mrs S Ridge-Reeves	3
Ch Zoribo Petronella	b	19.09.85	Ch Zoribo Oscarvitch	Bacaret Katya of Zoribo	Mr & Mrs Langley	Mr & Mrs Langley	3
Ch Colhugh Cartier	d	04.08.86	Ch Colhugh Claude of Longuin	Ch Colhugh Calpernia	R A Bassett	R A Bassett	6
Ch Top Secret of Chasefield	b	11.02.84	Zomahli Ukraser of Yadasar	Zomahli Teesheena of Hammonds	Mrs R A Randall	Mrs D Martin	3
Ch Livny Winston	d	18.07.86	Ch Livny Black Eagle	Livny Autumn Sorrel	Mr & Mrs Stears	Mr & Mrs Stears	3
1990							
Ch Tamaroff Tribal Prince	d	27.10.85	Ch Stonebar Sebastian	Ferngore Firedance	Mrs P Barham	Mr P Barham	27
Ch Rae Ravell	b	18.03.87	Ch Stonebar Sebastian	Ch Colhugh Chanel	Mr & Mrs Heap	Mr & Mrs Heap	6
Ch Tarsa Dancer	b	23.08.83	Ch Olias Oberon	Ch Czarina Gemstone	Mr & Mrs Morgan	Mr & Mrs Pye	3
Ch Longuin Lord Rowley	d	14.07.83	Ch Colhugh Clever Dick	Colhugh Caltriche of Longuin	Miss C Broxup	Mr & Mrs Spencer	3
Ch Colhugh Cwite Preti	b	12.01.87	Ch Zomahli Udachnik of Colhugh	Colhugh Cinders	R A Bassett	R A Bassett	7
Ch Merrie Monarch of Enolam	d	09.01.84	Ch Yadasar Midnight Rider	Enolam Christaiana	Mr & Mrs Watson	Mr & Mrs Tyreman	3
Ch Ninoushka of Santerman	b	23.08.83	Ch Olias Oberon	Ch Czarina Gemstone	Mr & Mrs Morgan	Mrs Masterman	3
Ch Colhugh Czara of Longuin	b	04.08.86	Ch Colhugh Claude of Longuin	Ch Colhugh Calpernia	R A Bassett	R A Bassett	6
Ch Namdac Touch of Fire	d	25.11.85	Namdac Red Nightlinger	Planxty Goltrai	Miss R Cadman	Miss R Cadman	3
Ch Sholwood Sonnet	b	23.02.88	Ch Livny Black Eagle	Ch Stillwater Virginia Reel	R Duckworth	R Duckworth	8
Ch Call Me Madam at Enolam	b	23.03.87	Kalominsky of Enolam	Kenour Ana	Mrs J van Schaick	Mrs M Malone	6
Ch Dekaos Chantilly	b	21.03.88	Ch Olias Oberon	Ch Colhugh Cameron of Dekaos	Mr & Mrs Clark	Mr & Mrs Clark	4

1991							
Ch Olias Dancing Brave	d	06.06.88	Ch Vronsky Zapata	Olias Ivory Queen	Mrs J Mabey	Mr & Mrs Mabey	4
Ch Dimland Brunel	d	23.10.85	Colhugh Cavalier of Dimland	Dimland Mazurka	Mr & Mrs Hill	Mr & Mrs Hill	5
Ch Cranog Tsarella of Tazeb	b	24.02.87	Ch Diamond Edge of Enolam	Zoribo Olivia	B Johnston & N Laycock	Mrs E Whitehead	3
Ch Rae Rembrandt	d	18.03.87	Ch Stonebar Sebastian	Ch Colhugh Chanel	Mr & Mrs Heap	Mr & Mrs Heap	3
Ch Sophia of Rothesby	b	13.03.86	Hissing Sid of Baroncroft	Colhugh Clementina of Olias	Messrs Wilson & Ainsworth	Mrs S Carter	5
Ch Dimland Dream Maker	b	13.04.89	Ch Vronsky Zapata	Yanjoy My Fair Lady of Remargae	Mr & Mrs Hill	Mr & Mrs Hill	15
Ch Waycross Scheherazade	b	29.08.89	Olias King Crimson at Stonebar	Trefaldu Serenade of Waycross	Mr & Mrs Simmonds	Mr & Mrs Simmonds	3
Ch Sholwood Striking Midnight at Datcha	d	06.10.89	Sholwood Stars'n'Stripes	Ch Sholwood Sprig Muslin	R Duckworth	Mrs I Knieschke	8
Ch Fortrouge Maria	b	28.07.85	Fortrouge Ulrice	Rodgivad Magnolia	Miss B Murray	Miss B Murray	3
Ch Colhugh Capercali	b	17.01.87	Ch Zomahli Udachnik of Colhugh	Colhugh Cinders	R A Bassett	R A Bassett	3
1992							
Ch Colhugh Clarice Cliff	b	14.03.89	Ch Colhugh Cartier	Colhugh Cinders	R A Bassett	R A Bassett	26
Ch Ryazan Czardas	d	24.12.88	Ch Rae Rembrandt	Ryazan Tosca of Stonebar	Miss J Clare	Miss J Clare	4
Ch Princess Precious Stone	b	05.09.88	Ch Vronsky Zapata	Ch Czarina Gemstone	Mr & Mrs Morgan	Mr & Mrs Morgan	3
Ch Colhugh Cwincey of Longuin	d	04.08.86	Ch Colhugh Claude of Longuin	Ch Colhugh Calpernia	R A Bassett	Miss C Broxup	3
Ch Yadasar Orlando of Labinska	d	13.01.90	Olias King Crimson of Yadasar	Ch Ryazan Laura of Yadasar	Mrs A Tomlinson	Mr & MrsPeskett	3
Ch Talgavar The Entertainer	d	14.08.87	Ch Longuin Lord Rowleigh	Yadasar Evening Mist of Talgavar	Mr & Mrs Spencer	Mr & Mrs Spencer	4
Ch Sholwood Sprig Muslin	b	13.06.86	Ch Livny Black Eagle	Velvet of Fortrouge	R Duckworth	R Duckworth	3
Ch Colhugh Cachet	b	02.04.89	Ch Colhugh Claude of Longuin	Ch Colhugh Cwite Preti	R A Bassett	E Minns	4
Ch Falconcrag Krassai	d	05.11.89	Ch Livny Black Eagle	Vimern Sweet Enchantment of Falconcrag	Mrs S Marston	Miss P Marston	3

Champion	Sex	DOB	Sire	Dam	Breeder	Owner	CCs
1993							
Ch Maia Keyhole Kate	b	29.11.87	Swiftcroft Superstar	Hammonds Ariadne of Maia	Mr & Mrs D'Wit	Mrs Rampley	3
Ch Yadasar Huckleberry Horace	d	23.08.88	Ch Olias Oberon	Yadasar Black Angel	Mrs A Tomlinson	Mrs A Tomlinson & Miss P Morgan	3
Ch Tatiana Chaumiere	d	23.04.88	Ch Vronsky Zapata	Olias Opal Rae of Tatiana	Mr & Mrs Leyland Quarmby	Miss J Grey	5
Ch Olias Noblesse of Vronsky	b	06.06.88	Ch Vronsky Zapata	Olias Ivory Queen	Mrs J Mabey	Mr & Mrs Downes	5
Ch Yadasar Huckleberry Friend	d	23.08.88	Ch Olias Oberon	Yadasar Black Angel	Mrs A Tomlinson	Miss P Harris	10
Ch Olias Miesque at Starborough	b	06.06.88	Ch Vronsky Zapata	Olias Ivory Queen	Mrs J Mabey	Mrs L Marchant	4
Ch Sholwood Seed Pearl of Creusa	b	28.10.89	Sholwood Stars'n'Stripes	Sholwood Shadowlight	R Duckworth	Mrs B Phillips	3
1994							
Ch Rae Belle Epoque	b	20.03.91	Ch Colhugh Cwincey of Longuin	Ch Rae Ravell	Mr & Mrs Heap	Mr & Mrs Heap	3
Ch Colhugh Celinor of Malbrin	d	04.08.86	Ch Colhugh Claude of Longuin	Ch Colhugh Calpernia	R A Bassett	Miss M Ursell	3
Ch Ryazan Laura of Yadasar	b	23.10.87	Ryazan Byron	Ryazan Tosca of Stonebar	Miss J Clare	Miss J Clare	3
Ch Nosirrah Sea Lavender	b	03.10.90	Gismonda Chip Off The Rok	Camero Flambere	Mrs D Harrison	Mrs A Brown	4
Ch Rothesby Saker	d	14.03.92	Sholwood Stars'n'Stripes	Ch Sophia of Rothesby	Ms S Carter	Ms S Carter	8
Ch Falconcrag Othello	d	01.10.91	Ch Falconcrag Krassai	Falconcrag Krilatka	Mrs S Marston	Mrs S Marston	3
Ch Dashava Vishinka	d	20.08.91	Ch Livny Black Eagle	Nakora Honorzova	Ms S Graham	Ms S Graham	6
Ch Vashla Votan	d	11.08.84	Ch Olias Oberon	Vashla Voorget-me-not	Mr & Mrs Tuton	Mr & Mrs Tuton	4
Ch Randas Sylvester of Baroncroft	d	03.11.90	Ch Livny Black Eagle	Ch Baroncroft Cinnamon	Mr & Mrs Binnington	Mrs A Randall	7
Ch Desaev Baby Clair	b	11.07.87	Ch Vronsky Zapata	Namdac Red Roxanne	Mr & Mrs Coles	Mr & Mrs Sharp	3
Ch Mariinsky Andrei	d	08.10.87	Mariinsky Nicolai	Vimern Sweet Enchantment of Falconcrag	D Drum	D Drum	3
1995							
Ch Rae The Revolution of Santerman	d	18.03.87	Ch Stonebar Sebastian	Ch Colhugh Chanel	Mr & Mrs Heap	Mrs M Masterman	5
Ch Vronsky Careless Whisper	b	29.09.90	Olias King Crimson of Stonebar	Vronsky Sweet Charity	Mr & Mrs Downes	Mrs A Webb	3
Ch Shelbor Gold Charm at Matford	b	19.04.89	Ch Colhugh Cartier	Olias Queen Bee of Shelbor	Mrs B Hargrave	Messrs Maryan & O'Callaghan	3

Ch Starborough Sharmanka	b	14.03.90	Gismonda Chip Off The Rok	Ch Olias Miesque at Starborough	Mrs L Marchant	Mrs L Marchant	9
Ch Starborough Gorse at Redbanner	d	17.08.92	Ch Yadasar Orlando of Labinska	Ch Olias Miesque at Starborough	Mrs L Marchant	Mrs J Stevens-Smith	30
Ch Vanathan Emma	b	25.07.87	Ch Diamond Edge of Enolam	Vanathan Alanya	Mrs J van Schaick	T Jepson	3
Ch Sholwood Striking Rubies	b	18.08.91	Sholwood Stars'n'Stripes	Ch Sholwood Sprig Muslin	R Duckworth	R Duckworth	7
Ch Vronsky Kindred Spirit of Tatiana	d	29.09.90	Olias King Crimson of Stonebar	Vronsky Sweet Charity	Mr & Mrs Downes	Mr & Mrs J Leyland Quarmby	3
Ch Rothesby Serin of Sholwood	b	14.03.92	Sholwood Stars'n'Stripes	Ch Sophia of Rothesby	Ms S Carter	Ms S Carter	13
Ch Solaise Indian Summer	b	14.04.91	Ch Vronsky Zapata	Baroncroft Nutty Nutmeg of Solaise	Mrs M James	Mrs M James	3
1996							
Ch Saringa's Angostura	d	20.08.90	Ch Livny Black Eagle	Tovarisjtj's Takhomova	Miss J Dove & V Harrison	Miss J Dove & V Harrison	4
Ch Lelant Galena	b	28.01.89	Ch Livny Black Eagle	Matalona Cressida	Mrs B Blyth	Miss B Blyth	4
Ch Stubbylee Shades of Night	d	08.04.89	Ch Diamond Edge of Enolam	Manitias Lacovia at Stubbylee	Mr & Mrs Dawson	Mrs P Heys	3
Ch Yadasar Oprah	b	13.01.90	Olias King Crimson of Stonebar	Ch Ryazan Laura of Yadasar	Mrs A Tomlinson	Mrs G Macrae	3
Ch Waycross Shadayid	b	09.09.93	Ch Ryazan Czardas	Ch Waycross Scheherazade	Mr & Mrs Simmons	Mr & Mrs Simmons	3
Ch Swiftcroft Hold That Tiger	d	21.09.89	Ch Starborough Shere Khan	Swiftcroft Pretty Flamingo	Mrs J Rampley	Mrs J Edmeades	3
Ch Falconcrag Centime	b	28.12.92	Ch Falconcrag Othello	Yadasar Penny Farthing at Falconcrag	Mrs S & Miss P Marston	Mrs S & Miss P Marston	3
Ch Vronsky Walk on the Wild Side	d	04.02.92	Vronsky Strong Persuader	Leicro's Zilver Spirit of Vronsky	Mr & Mrs A Downes	Miss J Grey	3
Ch Colhugh Conoiseur	d	19.01.92	Ch Colhugh Cartier	Colhugh Cinders	R A Bassett	R A Bassett	3
Ch Colhugh Silk'n'Satin of Chuchin	b	10.10.93	Sholwood Silver Fox	Ch Rothesby Serin of Sholwood	R Duckworth	R Duckworth	3
1997							
Ch Yadasar Odette of Ryazan	b	13.01.90	Olias King Crimson of Stonebar	Ch Ryazan Laura of Yadasar	Mrs A Tomlinson	Miss S Clare	3
Ch Olias Moet of Abamor	b	27.02.90	Ch Vronsky Zapata	Olias Ivory Queen	Mrs J Mabey	Mrs A Gayford	3
Ch Skyrose Nicholai	d	03.09.90	Ch Livny Black Eagle	Laritza of Skyrose	Mrs M Gooder	Mrs M Gooder	4
Ch Rae Paradiso	b	10.10.93	Ch Tatiana Chaumiere	Rae Renaissance	Mr & Mrs Heap	Mr & Mrs Heap	4
Ch Strelkos Summertime	b	05.07.94	Strelkos Wings of Time	Stonebar Sharazari Strelkos	Mrs C Spencer	Mrs C Spencer	4

Appendix B
Show Results
in the United States of America

The United States dog show system is very different from that in Great Britain. Whereas in Great Britain the emphasis is on a small number of very large shows, the American way is to have a much larger number of much smaller shows. In Great Britain, 25 all-breed Championship Shows were held in 1996, with 16,000 entries at the last show of that year (the Ladies Kennel Association), probably slightly larger than the average entry for a British show; in the United States, 1220 all-breed shows were held in 1994, only two of which had 4000 entries, with an average of 1111 per show.

I have described the British system for championship titles in depth already. The American points system that I also touched upon allows a much larger proportion of puppies eventually to become champions. This, coupled with the fact that American Borzoi registrations are much higher than those in Britain, means that a complete list of American Borzoi champions would be very long indeed.

The list of British champions from the restart of shows after the Second World War is roughly a list of the top ten or so Borzois each year. The Phillips Rating System for analysing American show results gives a formal list of the top ten of each breed for each year – a much more managable amount of American data.

The Phillips Rating System was devised by Irene Castle Phillips (later Khatoonian Schlintz) in 1956. Initially, the top 10 dogs in each group were published, and this continued until 1960. In 1961 and 1962 the top dog in each breed was listed, whilst in 1963–1965 this was extended to the top three in each breed. From 1966, the listing was of the top ten in each breed.

Mrs Schlintz (then Mrs Phillips) had started with an Irish Setter, but when she went to her first speciality show in the 1940s, 'one look at these red-coated show dogs and it became evident that the only resemblance they had to our Gypsy was in coat colour'.

Little was published in the dog magazines of the time about the Irish Setter so, in 1945, she started a column in *Western Kennel World*, the editor agreeing as long as the Irish Setter advertising paid for the space. In the early 1950s she received a letter from a lady whose Irish Setter champion had just won a number of Best of Breeds at a series of shows in Texas, and she wished these wins to be publicised. There was no mention of any group placings. Mrs Phillips happened to look over the awards published by the American Kennel Club, and discovered that this dog was the only Irish Setter entered at these shows!

In 1953 she started an analysis of the Irish Setter results. Dogs had to be placed in the group and gained one point for each dog defeated. In 1954 Cocker Spaniels (American) were added, and by 1957 the first set of results for all breeds competing in 1956 were published.

The points for the system were calculated as follows:

Best in Show, one point for every dog defeated; that is, all competitors at the show.
Group First, one point for each dog defeated in that group; that is, all dogs competing in that group.
Group Second, one point for each dog defeated in that group; that is, all the dogs in competition in that group, minus those dogs of the winner's breed.
Group Third, one point for each dog defeated in that group; that is, all the dogs in competition in that group, minus those dogs of the same breed as the winner and the Group Second.
Group Fourth, one point for each dog defeated in that group; that is, all the dogs in competition in that group, minus those dogs of the same breed as the winner of the group, the Group Second and the Group Third dog.

No speciality (breed show) wins were included.

I include the complete Phillips Rating System for Borzois, thanks to the kindness of Mrs Phillips' daughter, Jacqueline Root. She took over the calculations from her mother a number of years ago but, after Mrs Phillips' death in 1991, stopped tabulating the results. Before her death, Mrs Root asked her mother if she should continue the Rating System, but was told to concentrate her efforts on the other data system that Mrs Phillips had devised, the Phillips Top Producer System. The Top Producer System uses the lists of champions published by the American Kennel Club to calculate the top sires and dams in each breed, and the amount of work this involved meant the end of the Rating System. Mrs Phillips felt that the Top Producer data was of greater importance to breeders. Many a top show winner never had any offspring of note. The careful analysis of the breeding of champions revealed those lines that mixed together well, a wonderful help for the serious breeder.

My knowledge of the Borzoi in the United States of America is very patchy. I would love a book that contained photographs and pedigrees of those dogs that are in the Phillips lists, as this would be the greatest key to the breed in the United States. Perhaps one of the American breed clubs would like to pick up this idea?

With the loss of the 'gold standard' method of awarding top dog wins I also need to be advised as to which system of the very many published in the United States is the best in operation. In the meantime, here is the Phillips List of Top Borzois in the United States from 1962 until 1991:

Year	Placing	Name	Points
1962	1	Am Ch Bronze Falcon of Woodhill (Group 6th)	2548
1963	1	Am Ch Bronze Falcon of Woodhill	1042
	2	Am Ch Campaigner's Alix	721
	3	Talix of Twin Elms	693
1964	1	Am Ch Nicolai of Tam-Boer	1124
	2	Am Ch Ducies Wild of Tam-Boer	784
	3	Am Ch Anastasia of Windy Hill	662
1965	1	Am Ch Nicolai of Tam-Boer	1124
	2	Am Ch Ducies Wild of Tam-Boer	784
	3	Am Ch Anastasia of Windy Hill	662
1966	1	Am Ch Makhayl of Tam-Boer	2490
	2	Am Ch Vosmoi of Gwenjon	1945
	3	Am Ch Zomahli Evolgo	1225
	4	Am Ch Vronsky of Volga	649
	5	Am Ch Anastasia of Windy Hill	458
	6	Am Ch Duke Alexander of Twin Elms	394
	7	Am Ch Dons Zephors of Malora	287
	8	Sals Count Bruno	207
	9	Am Ch Trezor Ivan	162
	10	Am Ch Blaise II of Sunbarr	148
1967	1	Am Ch Zomahli Evolgo (Group 2nd)	10147
	2	Am Ch Vronsky of Volga (Group 10th)	4071
	3	Am Ch Makhayl of Tam-Boer	2123
	4	Am Ch Zolotoi Volni of Twin Elms	647
	5	Am Ch Cordova Mishka of Boronoff	511
	6	Am Ch Galands Alexander	373
	7	Am Ch Ranchitos Silversheen	353
	8	Am Ch Duke Alexander of Twin Elms	180
	9	Am Ch Mazeppa of Rancho Gabriel	149
	10	Vanya of Cantante	139

Appendix B

Year	Placing	Name	Points
1968	1	Am Ch Zomahli Evolgo	2981
	2	Am Ch Vronsky of Volga	2001
	3	Am Ch Galands Alexander	1018
	4	Am Ch Makhayl of Tam-Boer	787
	5	Am Ch Llebasi's Prince O'Lutolf	488
	6	Am Ch Zolotoi Volni of Twin Elms	481
	7	Am Ch Adage Duncan	412
	8	Am Ch Gregori of Twin Elms	343
	9	Am Ch Galands Baronoff	319
	10	Am Ch Pegasus of Olympus	292
1969	1	Am Ch Gregori of Twin Elms	2155
	2	Am Ch Zomahli Evolgo	2080
	3	Am Ch Vronsky of Volga	1998
	4	Am Ch Llebas's Prince O'Lutolf	1743
	5	Am Ch Kall of the Wilds Zandor	1239
	6	Am Ch Galands Alexander	1052
	7	Am Ch Lorals Iossif Ivanevitch	850
	8	Am Ch Kostenov Kean	534
	9	Am Ch Flying Dutchman of Tam-Boer	495
	10	Am Ch Balalaika Kry-Lyesa	400
1970	1	Am Ch Kall of the Wilds Zandor	7440
	2	Am Ch Mogadan of Volga	2772
	3	Am Ch Llebasi's Prince O'Lutolf	2671
	4	Am Ch Loral's Iossif Ivanivitch	919
	5	Am Ch Gwejon Kosoi	695
	6	Am Ch Galands Alexander	637
	7	Am Ch Sirhan Poraschai	548
	8	Am Ch Majenkir Sveraki Snow Stag	393
	9	Am Ch Elain Ward's Katawba v Sunbarr	365
	10	Am Ch Marinsky of Volga	337
1971	1	Am Ch Sirhan Poraschai (Group 3rd)	11513
	2	Am Ch Mogadan of Volga	5302
	3	Am Ch Galands Alexander	2450
	4	Am Ch Debonaire Darius O'Night Song	1699
	5	Am Ch Elain Ward's Katawba v Sunbarr	1340
	6	Am Ch Kall of the Wilds Zandor	868
	7	Am Ch Lorals Iossif Ivanivitch	775
	8	Am Ch Trezor Lancer of Buks	729
	9	Am Ch Evoljuov of Krancevich	703
	10	Am Ch Majenkir Sverkai Snow Stag	629

Year	Placing	Name	Points
1972	1	Am Ch Sirhan Poraschai (Group 8th)	7809
	2	Am Ch Mogadan of Volga	4608
	3	Am Ch Great Heart of Fosteria	1105
	4	Am Ch Sihan Pobedim	1087
	5	Am Ch Sunbarr Lancer of Dana Dan	1080
	6	Am Ch Lorals Iossif Ivanivitch	1047
	7	Am Ch Cossacks Aristotle	1025
	8	Am Ch Evoljunov of Kranjcvich	653
	9	Am Ch Bountifuls Erik The Red	589
	10	Am Ch Mendeleev of Cordova	542
1973	1	Am Ch Mogdan of Volga	3556
	2	Am Ch Great Heart of Fosteria	1944
	3	Am Ch Vala Ramanman For All Seasons	1718
	4	Am Ch Lorals Iossif Ivanivitch	1669
	5	Am Ch Ivanov of Volga	1544
	6	Am Ch Sirhan Poraschai	1093
	7	Am Ch Evoljunov of Kranjcevich	936
	8	Am Ch Illyaan of Aristoff	885
	9	Am Ch Cossacks Aristotle	745
	10	Am Ch Aires Bernard Thor	678
1974	1	Am Ch Great Heart of Fosteria	7927
	2	Am Ch Ivanov of Volga	5813
	3	Am Ch Lorals Iossif Ivanivitch	3136
	4	Am Ch Tambura's George v Berghof	1328
	5	Am Ch Eglon of Karistan	1063
	6	Am Ch Cathcade Chico	987
	7	Am Ch Sirhan Poraschai	550
	8	Am Ch Tigw of Tam-Boer	538
	9	Am Ch Lorals Matvey	470
	10	Am Ch Majenkir Sverkai Snow Stag	452
1975	1	Am Ch Tambura's George v Berghof	5839
	2	Am Ch Eglon of Karistan	4038
	3	Am Ch Larissa's Elegant Hijo	3038
	4	Am Ch Labas Arimsky	1958
	5	Am Ch Cathcade Curio	1738
	6	Am Ch Cossack's Echo	1347
	7	Velox Jamis of Ajjarda	1251
	8	Am Ch Rogdai of Volga	1036
	9	Am Ch Garush of Twin Elms	917
	10	Am Ch Del Jers Red Media	851

Year	Placing	Name	Points
1976	1	Am Ch Tambura's George v Berghof	8252
	2	Am Ch Laba's Arinsky	4093
	3	Am Ch Cathcade Curio	3115
	4	Am Ch Larissa's Elegant Hijo	2625
	5	Am Ch Cossack's Echo	2238
	6	Am Ch Lil Tuff Salty Dog	1752
	7	Am Ch Majenkir Gyrfalcon	1039
	8	Am Ch Oxbow's Chateau Le Bleu	917
	9	Am Ch Garush of Twin Elms	680
	10	Am Ch Miro Schka of Markova	631
1977	1	Am Ch Tambura's George v Berghof	6317
	2	Am Ch Cathcade Curio	3749
	3	Am Ch Laba's Arimsky	2362
	4	Am Ch Majenkir Gyrfalcon	1572
	5	Am Ch Kazan of Rising Star	1356
	6	Am Ch Larissa's Elegant Hijo	1299
	7	Am Ch Wildwood's Diva of Phantom Lake	1042
	8	Am Ch Lorals Whistle In The Dark	870
	9	Am Ch Aristoff's Ileahna	731
	10	Am Ch Cossack's Echo	612
1978	1	Am Ch Kashinga's Desert Song (Group 2nd, all breeds 6th)	28820
	2	Am Ch Karinas Arcurov	7382
	3	Am Ch Kashinga's Dalgarth	6537
	4	Am Ch Labas Arimsky	3192
	5	Am Ch Lorals Whistle in the Dark	1933
	6	Am Ch Kazan of Rising Star	1541
	7	Am Ch Taramont Czar of Bardnoff	1325
	8	Am Ch Yasnava's Silva	1195
	9	Am Ch Half Moons Patches	1161
	10	Am Ch Majenkir Gyrfalcon	851
1979	1	Am Ch Kashinga's Dalgarth (Group 8th)	12164
	2	Am Ch Lorals Whistle In The Dark	2184
	3	Am Ch Taramont Czar of Baronoff	1836
	4	Am Ch Kashinga's Desert Song	1704
	5	Am Ch Yasnaya's Silva	1487
	6	Am Ch Karina's Arcurov Yeanovitch	1065
	7	Am Ch Glacier's Go Bananas	857
	8	Am Ch Majenkir Wotan of Foxcroft	619
	9	Am Ch Chataquas Vladimir Bolshoi	500
	10	Am Ch Bkhara's Belladonna	488

Year	Placing	Name	Points
1980	1	Am Ch Kashinga's Dalgarth (Group 2nd, all breeds 9th)	27740
	2	Am Ch Utkinton Ajax of Zencor	3577
	3	Am Ch Taramont Czar of Baronoff	2406
	4	Am Ch Lorals Whistle In The Dark	1762
	5	Am Ch Troykov Moon Hawk	1330
	6	Am Ch Majenkir Wotan of Foxcroft	748
	7	Am Ch Caron's Et Tu Brutus	624
	8	Am Ch Yasnaya's Silva	601
	8	Am Ch Duchenka's Archangel	593
	10	Am Ch Arensky Of The Moorlands	506
1981	1	Am Ch Taramont Czar of Baronoff	2954
	2	Am Ch Lorals Whistle In The Dark	2384
	3	Am Ch Chataguas Vladamir Bolshoi	2119
	4	Am Ch Sartre Osmi of Dilrog	1489
	5	Am Ch Riva Ridge of Rising Star	1412
	6	Am Ch Kashinga's Dalgarth	1192
	7	Am Ch Cossack's Intrepid	895
	8	Am Ch Tuff Cuz Wuz Wrong	828
	9	Am Ch Korsakov's Creator	666
	10	Am Ch Majenkir Wotan of Foxcroft	616
1982	1	Am Ch Riva Ridge of Rising Star	3396
	2	Am Ch Lanel's Lobachevski	2458
	3	Am Ch Tuff Cuz Wuz Wrong	1444
	4	Am Ch Sverkai of Spiritkof	862
	5	Am Ch Tobrien's Ahriman	641
	6	Am Ch Korsakov's Creator	574
	7	Am Ch Oaklara's Hurrah of Lyric	532
	8	Am Ch Cossack's Intrepid	470
	9	Am Ch Tara's La Troika	435
	10	Sundown's Hit Parade	437
1983	1	Am Ch Lanel's Lobachevski	8612
	2	Am Ch Tuff Cuz Wuz Wrong	3417
	3	Am Ch Riva Ridge of Rising Star	3349
	4	Am Ch Tara's La Troika	2169
	5	Am Ch Birchwoods Spell Binder	1314
	6	Am Ch Ajjarda Smoked Sage Okeshari	1020
	7	Am Ch Tremaras Figaro of Goddooga	956
	8	Am Ch Tobriens Ahriman	721
	9	Am Ch Arnolf's Sheik of Araby	709
	10	Am Ch Labas Arinsky	541

Year	Placing	Name	Points
1984	1	Am Ch Lanel's Lobachevski (Group 6th)	14786
	2	Am Ch Seabury's Domino	1976
	3	Am Ch Majenkir Wotan of Foxcroft	1755
	4	Am Ch Tara's La Troika	1223
	5	Am Ch Where Woof of The Borzoi Palace	1024
	6	Am Ch Ajjarda Smoked Sage Okeshari	962
	7	Am Ch Phantom Lake Tadao	668
	8	Am Ch Arneolf's Hot To Trot	537
	9	Am Ch Oakaras Konstantin Hawkeye	530
	10	Not listed	
1985	1	Am Ch Seabury's Damon	3481
	2	Am Ch Sverikai of Spritzkof	1975
	(3	Am Ch Oaklara's Konstantin Hawkeye	1406
	(3	Am Ch P O S H Echovesna's Islaev	1406
	5	Am Ch Lanel's Lobachevski	1276
	6	Am Ch Jaraluv's Amoretto	1024
	7	Am Ch Astarliev Majenkir Mikiev	962
	8	Am Ch Oaklara's Hurrah of Lyric	711
	9	Am Ch Gregoryi of Kalinka	625
	10	Am Ch Gabel's Comrade	565
1986	1	Am Ch Majenkir Orchid of Po Dusham	5775
	2	Am Ch P O S H Echovesna's Islaev	5210
	3	Am Ch Kanel's Kaitan Khanazar	2097
	4	Am Ch Tolstoy of Rising Star	1984
	5	Am Ch Phaedras Aramis Pickfair	1158
	6	Am Ch Foxcroft's Gamil	829
	7	Am Ch Oaklara's Konstantin Hawkeye	760
	8	Am Ch Tobrien's Demon Run	554
	9	Am Ch Cavall D'Eliv	504
	10	Am Ch Venor View Hart to Heart	501
1987	1	Am Ch Lanel's Kaitan Khanazar	8250
	2	Am Ch P O S H Echovesna's Islaev	5412
	3	Am Ch Phaedras Aramis Pickfair	2025
	4	Am Ch Astafiev Proud of Himself	1498
	5	Am Ch Vicson Laser Lorimar	1183
	6	Am Ch Kashinga's Night Rider	1125
	7	Am Ch Seabury's Damon	1021
	8	Am Ch Tolstoi of Rising Star	767
	9	Am Ch Knapovich's Diavolo of Jem	751
	10	Am Ch Oaklara's Konstantin Hawkeye	652

Year	Placing	Name	Points
1988	1	Am Ch Lanel's Kaitan Khanazar	9606
	2	Am Ch Majenkir Jantar Trumpter	4463
	3	Am Ch P O S H Echovesna's Islaev	4187
	4	Am Ch Songmaker's Sotto Voice	2262
	5	Am Ch Foxcroft Coppelia	1710
	6	Am Ch Jett Krustull Oh Calcutta	1376
	7	Am Ch Phaedras Aramis Pickfair	1134
	8	Am Ch Vicson Laser Lorimar	870
	9	Am Ch Knapovich's Diavolo of Jem	527
	10	Am Ch Tobien Electric Horseman	510
1989	1	Am Ch Lanel's Kaitan Khanazar	13978
	2	Am Ch P O S H Echovesna's Islaev	7927
	3	Am Ch Vicson Laser Lorimar	1677
	4	Am Ch Fox Run's Ivy Rose	1419
	5	Am Ch Songmaker's Sotto Voice	1235
	6	Am Ch Astafiev Free Spirit	989
	7	Am Ch Kajai's Caribe	960
	8	Am Ch Sylvan Triton	814
	9	Am Ch Justyl's Starlit Blossom	750
	10	Am Ch Jett Kristull Oh Calcutta	740
1990	1	Am Ch Majenkir Articus	2723
	2	Am Ch Astafiev Free Spirit	1651
	3	Am Ch Vicson Laser Lorimar	1213
	4	Am Ch Fox Run's Ivy Rose	1156
	5	Am Ch Sylvan Thistledown	971
	6	Am Ch Loral Foxcroft Dragonslayer	923
	7	Am Ch Kumsan's State of Tradition	913
	8	Am Ch Kitaro Pickfair	715
	9	Am Ch Steppenwolf King Richard	664
	10	Am Ch Shefard Aquila's Fenix	660
1991	1	Am Ch Majenkir Articus	5845
	2	Am Ch Astafiev Free Spirit	2183
	3	Am Ch Fox Run's Ivy Rose	2034
	4	Am Ch Zenovia High Wind of Falkenar	1925
	5	Am Ch Sky Run Tellstar	1570
	6	Am Ch Rising Star Danilov O'Sunbarr	948
	7	Am Ch Starwinds Lucky Domino	902
	8	Am Ch Nonsuch the Talisman	756
	9	Am Ch Oaklara's Ice Cream	665
	10	Am Ch Majenkir Stepping Stone	532

Videos and Books

This is not a conventional bibliography, for much that I have been taught about Borzois has never appeared in print. Since the Borzoi breed is not blessed with a great number of books and videos, most of this list comprises data about either dogs in general or other breeds. Never close your eye to what is going on in other breeds; the expert in Chihuahuas can make you look at things from a different angle, allowing you to see aspects of the Borzoi that those in the breed cannot see because they are too close to it.

Videos

Elliott, Rachel Page ***Dogsteps*** From the American Kennel Club Video Collection

If you are only allowed one item about dogs in your house, this is easily the one to choose. When I first had this video I watched it every night for two weeks, and was learning something new every time. There is the most wonderful slow-motion film of correct and incorrect canine movement, and the moving X-ray film showing how a dog's bones move is the icing on the cake. The only minus is that breed standards sometimes differ between countries, and the construction of the Borzois depicted in the film is incorrect according to British and proposed International standards, causing them to have good 'normal dog', but incorrect Borzoi, movement.

Guide Dogs for the Blind Three videos: ***Mating, Whelping*** and ***Pregnancy Diagnosis Using Ultrasound*** All available from DBI Communications, 21 Congreve Close, Warwick, CV 34 5RQ

There are eight videos in this series, but these three are of the most interest to those wishing to breed Borzois.

Books

Cole, Robert ***The Basenji Stacked and Moving*** Cole Books

This is a detailed analysis of the Basenji Breed Standard, with top-quality illustrations. This is an important book for the Borzoi enthusiast. The Basenji could be considered a primitive sighthound, and its front construction is very similar to that of the Borzoi. By the end of the book you will be able to tell a quality Basenji from a poor one, and pick out the same good and bad points in a Borzoi.

Elliott, Rachel Page ***The New Dogsteps*** Howell Book House.

The book of the video, and a very good complement to it. If you can only have one, I would suggest that the moving pictures of the video give a better explanation of the dog gait.

British Borzoi Champions: Illustrated Pedigrees Vol One: 1903–1982, Vol Two: 1983–1991 From the Borzoi Club

A superb piece of work, with most of the research by Lesley Wolvey.

Yearbooks From the Borzoi Club and the Northern Borzoi Association

These contain many photographs, and are of great use if you are looking for a puppy, as they give names, addresses and telephone numbers of breeders. Secretaries of breed clubs tend to change, but you can find out the names and addresses of the current holders of the posts from:

The Kennel Club, 1–5 Clarges Street, Piccadilly, London, W1Y 8AB Tel: 0171-493 6651

Index

R

S

T

V

W

Y

Z